Gary Bouton

Adobe

PHOTOSHOP
NOW!

NRP
NEW RIDERS
PUBLISHING

New Riders Publishing, Indianapolis, Indiana

Adobe Photoshop NOW!

By Gary Bouton

Published by:
New Riders Publishing
201 West 103rd Street
Indianapolis, IN 46032 USA

Printed in the United States of America 1 2 3 4 5 6 7 8 9 0

Library of Congress Cataloging-in-Publication Data

Available upon request

Warning and Disclaimer

This book is designed to provide information about the Adobe Photoshop computer program. Every effort has been made to make this book as complete and as accurate as possible, but no warranty or fitness is implied.

The information is provided on an "as is" basis. The author and New Riders Publishing shall have neither liability nor responsibility to any person or entity with respect to any loss or damages arising from the information contained in this book or from the use of the disks or programs that may accompany it.

Publisher	LLOYD J. SHORT
Associate Publisher	TIM HUDDLESTON
Acquisitions Manager	CHERI ROBINSON
Managing Editor	MATTHEW MORRILL
Product Development Manager	ROB TIDROW
Marketing Manager	RAY ROBINSON
Product Director	MATTHEW MORRILL
Senior Editor	TAD RINGO
Production Editor	LISA WILSON
Editor	CLIFF SHUBS
Acquisitions Editor	ALICIA KRAKOVITZ
Technical Editor	SCOTT COOK
Acquisitions Coordinator	STACEY BEHELER
Editorial Assistant	KAREN OPAL
Publisher's Assistant	MELISSA LYNCH
Imprint Manager	JULI COOK
Production Team Leader	KATY BODENMILLER
Cover Design	JEAN BISESI
Book Design	ROGER S. MORGAN

Production Team

NICK ANDERSON KAREN DODSON
RICH EVERS RYAN RADER
MICHELLE M. SELF DENNIS WESNER

Indexers JOHNNA VANHOOSE
SUZANNE SNYDER

Production Analysts MARY BETH WAKEFIELD
DENNIS CLAY HAGER

About the Author

Gary David Bouton is an illustrator and New Riders author whose books address the ever-widening audience of traditional artists who are making the transition to PC-based computer graphics. As Gary puts it, "The MS-Windows environment has attracted a plethora of new, exciting, and sophisticated apps aimed at people who already have their craft refined. The only elements missing here and there are some explanations and examples of how computer graphics software can be adopted by the fine and commercial artist to *integrate* these new tools with the ones already in place."

Gary is owner of Exclamat!ons, a company that "polishes rough ideas." With his wife and partner, Barbara, the two spend as much time training clients in the digital equivalents of traditional media as they do producing electronic presentations, desktop publishing work, logos, graphics, and collateral materials. Gary's background has been in advertising for the past 20 years. He discovered a whole new world of possibilities for the talented designer when he began to use the PC as a supplement to his traditional tools. Gary was a winner in the CorelDRAW! World Design Contest for the past two years, and has received international awards twice for *NewsBytes*, a local Users Group newsletter of which he is editor.

Adobe Photoshop NOW! is Gary's second book on Adobe's imaging program. *Inside Adobe Photoshop for Windows* is a collaboration with Barbara Bouton, and should be considered a companion book to *Adobe Photoshop NOW!*. The assignments in this book are for the more advanced user, and between the two editions, you can find a wide range of practical examples for quick results using Adobe Photoshop.

Gary can be reached at Exclamat!ons, 7300 Cedar Post Road, No. A31, Liverpool, New York 13088-4843.

Acknowledgments

If you read Adobe Photoshop's "splash" screen, you'll notice that the imaging program is a product of a collection of talented individuals. Similarly, *Adobe Photoshop NOW!* wouldn't have been possible without the help and skills of the many fine people whose efforts must be acknowledged here. Thanks to the *Adobe Photoshop NOW!* "core group" and family, who are...

- Matthew Morrill, NRP Managing Editor. Matthew's development of this book helped distill the most essential, high-end Photoshop techniques into the guide you have before you. Matthew, thank you for your Photoshop for Macintosh insights, and for tailoring my observations into a concise "how-to" compendium that I hope anyone who's interested in imaging will appreciate.

- Lisa Wilson, Lead Editor, who kept a sharp vigil on the book to ensure that we actually communicated the information in accessible English. Thanks, Lisa, you were my first editor on the *CorelDRAW! Special Effects* book, and I hope we always keep the magic in these computer graphics books.

- Cheri Robinson, NRP Acquisitions Manager, who shares my conviction that computer graphics on the IBM-PC platform is an undiscovered wilderness that merits exploring through New Riders books. Cheri, thank you for letting me use the "street-wise" approach to explaining some very intricate software applications that I feel readers can tap directly into.

- Stacey Beheler, NRP Acquisitions Coordinator, for her help in providing hardware and software loans and donations without which this book couldn't have been written. Photoshop is not an island, as you'll see throughout this book. It requires many add-ons to create stunning work, and Stacey, I thank you for your gift as a provider of such and many things.

- Scott Cook at Macmillan Computer Publishing, who made sure the information in *Adobe Photoshop NOW!* is accurate and applies to both the IBM-PC and Mac versions of Photoshop.

- Alicia Krakovitz, NRP Aquisitions Editor, who came up with the much-needed SyQuest removable media drive. This is how we compiled, collated, and transported the massive amount of image and program files you'll find on the *Adobe Photoshop NOW! CD-ROM*, with a minimum of headache. Thanks, Alicia!

- Greg Phillips at Diversified Graphics, who compiled the *Adobe Photoshop NOW! CD-ROM* from the sea of image files, shareware, freeware, and other wares included with this book.

- Carol Cornicelli at WexTech Systems, Inc., for providing us with Doc to Help, the program used to compile the *Adobe Photoshop NOW!* OnLine Glossary.

- Spousal Editor Barbara Bouton, who compiled the *Adobe Photoshop NOW!* OnLine Glossary. Barbara and I added numerous entries to the original *Inside Adobe Photoshop for Windows* glossary, and my in-house technical wizard created over 400 hypertext links in this 75 page help line, so our readers can have complete references, terminology, and shortcuts at their fingertips in Photoshop.

- The Proofreaders and Indexers, for whom we rediscovered a revered esteem, after spending several hours compiling the Online Glossary.

- Macmillan Computer Publishing Production Department, for the splendid design and layout of my first four color book. Thanks to all for the hours and patience with the images. Your work makes my work look great.

- Jan Sanford at Pixar for the use of Typestry and RenderMan for Windows. Jan, the images in this book wouldn't have the charm without Pixar software. Thanks for letting me clothe my designs in fantastic virtual apparel.

- Rix Kamlich and Jill Ryan at MacroMedia, for the use of MacroModel. Your modeling program came in handy in situations where actual photography failed, and I hope readers will see the possibilities of using MacroModel in their own imaging work.

- Douglas Richards at Visual Software, for Renderize Live! for Windows. Your product helped create many of the freeware images on the *Adobe Photoshop NOW! CD-ROM*, and was necessary at times to augment this book's assignment images. Thanks, Douglas!

- Corel Corporation's Jeff Johnson, Mike Bellefeuille, Bill Cullen, and Kerry Williams for CorelSCSI! and other support items needed to design this book. You folks were just as gracious and responsive to requests concerning this book as you were when I wrote *CorelDRAW! for Non-Nerds*. I wish every company could get behind a concept with the generosity and enthusiasm you've displayed.

- My brother Dave, aka Reginald Edit, who keeps more convenient hours than a Ford model, and asks a substantially reduced fee for his work. Dave, when you get retouched by all our readers who follow the exercise, I hope it doesn't tickle too much.

- Harry at Pizza Hut, whose Ultimate Pepperoni specials provided sustenance for me many a snowbound winter evening.

- Our good friends at Procomm Technology for the super-extended use of their PhotoCD drive.

- Andy Chang and Yvonne Knott at UMAX, for graciously loaning us their model 840 flatbed color scanner.

- Kristin Keyes at the HSC Corporation for Kai's Power Tools for Windows.

- Daryl Wise at Fractal Design Corporation.

- Greg Morgenson at BioMechanics Corporation of America.

Trademark Acknowledgments

Dedication

This one is for the software developers and authors at Adobe Systems and other companies. They never get thanked enough for giving people like us fine, marvelous virtual tools to create artwork. Artists and art lovers among us, consider for a moment what sort of work would be created if users had to compile the programs in *addition* to painting, drawing, modeling, and writing. You people have made the artist's virtual studio a very rich place, and I'd like us all to acknowledge this truth.

Contents at a Glance

Table of Contents at a Glance

- Quick Mask mode
- Painting/Editing modes
- Type tool
- Paintbrush tool
- Gradient Fill tool
- Paste Behind command

- Levels command
- Hue/Saturation command
- Channels palette
- Define Pattern command
- Paths palette

- Gradient tool
- Channels
- Image modes
- Colorize option
- Levels command
- Magic Wand tool
- Gummi worms

- Duotones
- Custom Index Palette
- Selections based on patterns
- Feather command
- Saturation mode

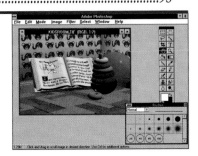

- Paths
- Importing an EPS image
- Channels
- The From Saved option
- Patterns
- Partial masks

- Paths palette
- Magic Wand tool
- Paste Behind command
- Arbitrary Rotate command
- Darken and Multiply modes

Part 3—Image Corrections and Enhancements

- Paths palette
- Painting modes
- Define Pattern command
- Sharpen filter
- Rubber Stamp tool

- Channels
- Distort command
- Paths palette
- Last-Saved Versions
- Levels command

Part 4—Special Effects with Photoshop's Native Tools

- Emboss command
- Channels
- Scale command
- Dissolve mode
- Displace filter
- Paths palette

- Magic Eraser tool
- Rubber Stamp tool
- Lasso tool
- Gaussian Blur filter
- Hue/Saturation command

- Channels
- The Paths palette
- Screen mode
- Dissolve mode
- Border command
- Hue/Saturation command
- Levels command

Table of Contents at a Glance

Table of Contents at a Glance

- Channels
- Patterns
- Gaussian Blur
- Crop tool
- Effects commands

Part 5—Back o' the Book

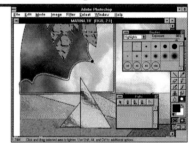

- Magic Eraser tool
- Channels
- Paths palette
- Stroke Paths option
- Fractal Design Painter
- Kai's Power Tools

Table of Contents

PART II   Photoshop and Image Types 55

Chapter 3
Creating a Collage with Scanned Images..57

Chapter 4
The Depths of Digital Color 79

Chapter 5
The EPS Image..95

The Greatest Shop On Earth

I misappropriated the slogan from a traveling carnival for this introduction, but it really *does* apply to *Adobe Photoshop NOW!* On this planet, the only place you will find all the tools and special effects you need to professionally enhance images is under Photoshop's tent. If you have a desire not only to retouch photographs, but to combine all sorts of different electronic media into a visual masterpiece, Adobe Photoshop is your admission ticket. To create the visual "oohs" and "aahs" you've seen in magazines, commercials, and movies, you need to learn the ringmaster's tricks. So step right up and join our backstage tour with *Adobe Photoshop NOW!*

This book was written with one goal in mind—to get you up and running with Photoshop fast. As a Photoshop owner, you know that it's an exceedingly rich and complex program, and it needs to be because that's the nature of computer imaging. But that doesn't mean pulling off a visually sumptuous stunt will take months or years of training to accomplish. Quite the contrary—*Adobe Photoshop NOW!* is a back-to-back series of how-tos that show you the techniques behind the most popular "gee whiz" effects.

Overwhelming is a term that should apply to your finished Photoshop image, but not to the steps required to finish it. This is why the step-by-step instructions on how an effect is created are explained in concise, user-friendly terms throughout this book. If you have a basic working knowledge of the Microsoft Windows operating environment (that is, you know how to copy a file, double-click with a mouse, and get a pretty decent score playing Minesweeper), you're way ahead of the game, and you'll breeze through this book.

How To Get In on the Action

Throughout this book, the key features in the techniques demonstrated are pointed out so that you can separate the feature from the tutorial and use the method in not just one, but many different ways in your work. It's the quickest, most painless way to become a most-revered power user in computer graphics. This book also calls attention to the following:

Notes are little asides that relate to the task at hand. These tiny, seemingly unrelated pearls will help make steps in Photoshop easier down the road.

Tips are provided as suggestions for optimizing your time and efficiency in using Photoshop and your PC. In most cases, these tips will be shortcuts to tasks in Photoshop or tricks for maximizing your time or image manipulation quality.

Stops are signposts along the Adobe Photoshop NOW! *trail indicating that you should proceed with caution before executing an upcoming step. No one likes to make a mistake that costs them time, particularly when it's over a paying assignment.*

Each tutorial is provided in a step-by-step format, and if you follow along, your screen should look like the figures in this book. The underlined letters in Photoshop's menu system that can be used as hot keys appear in this book as bold, underline type. Shortcut key combinations, such as Ctrl+C, also are included and are sometimes referenced parenthetically next to the longer menu commands. Letters or numbers that you must type appear in bold. Messages and dialog box text that appear on-screen are monospace as shown below:

```
Click and drag to paint using foreground color.
```

Most of Photoshop's tools do slightly different things when you hold down the Shift, the Alt, the Ctrl or a combination of these and other keys. These and other multiple key and key-and-mouse combinations appear as Ctrl+Magic Wand, or Ctrl+Alt+F or Alt+Rubber Stamp. Function keys appear as F1, F2, F3, and up.

But before diving into terrific Photoshop effects, we'd like to make a recommendation about what type of PC would be best to run Photoshop. Besides being beige with a lot of knobs and buttons on it, you'll get the most rewarding results from a powerful machine. A PC with a Pentium or a 486-class processor will serve you better in your Photoshop escapades than a 386 machine. It's faster, less tedious to work on, and there may be times when you simply don't have the patience or time to attempt fantastic imagery on a PC that's more suited for word processing than computer graphics. Imaging with a computer is *processor and memory intensive*, which means the faster the machine and the more memory you have installed on it, the happier you'll be working on it.

We recommend at least 16 MB of RAM, although 8 MB will get you where you want to go—just a lot slower. A good rule of thumb is to take the size of the largest image you will be working with and multiply that by three. Most of the images on the *Adobe Photoshop NOW! CD-ROM* "weigh in" at 1 to 2 MB, so this means you need 6 MB of RAM to hold the image in system memory, and then additional RAM for any other image files you have open simultaneously. Also, Windows requires 2 MB of RAM to maintain its environment, and other programs (such as a modem or utilities) that you have running in the background tap into your RAM.

Hard drive space, like RAM, gets especially precious when you start working with photos in Photoshop. You should set aside some serious hard drive space for yourself and the examples you follow using the *Adobe Photoshop NOW! CD-ROM* images (to the tune of at least 40 MB), which you devote solely to your imaging work. Why? Because pictures are big, and really *good* pictures are *really* big. Small, low-resolution pictures typically run 1 to 2 MB each. Large, high-resolution pictures can easily approach 24 MB in size, larger than a lot of software programs. The images you will be working with in this book are byte-sized, but you might want to save variations you've done on a particular image. The cumulative effect of saved multiple copies of small files steals the same from your hard disk as a few saves on a large, hi-res image. Either way, be prepared to use a good deal of hard drive space.

Part I, "The Power User's Basics," sets the tone and the pace of our adventures with Photoshop. Part II, "Photoshop and Image Types," shows you how to work with different types of images—scanned images, grayscale images, EPS files, photos, and material from drawing programs. Part III, "Image Corrections and Enhancements," shows you tricks for correcting and enhancing your images. Part IV, "Special Effects with Photoshop's Native Tools," centers around adding special effects to your work. The tour will conclude with Part V, "Back o' the Book."

The CD-ROM that's in the back of this book includes all the image files, patterns, fonts, and designs needed to create the finished images you see in this book. Throughout the book, we'll refer you to the *Adobe Photoshop NOW! CD-ROM* to retrieve files to use in a chapter assignment. *Adobe Photoshop NOW!* features techniques that you can put to practical use in your own work in every chapter. Also included on the *Adobe Photoshop NOW! CD-ROM* are some handy Windows utilities, freeware, shareware, and charityware fonts, and a lot of royalty-free texture images that you can experiment with.

To make the book as easy-to-use as possible, a CD-ROM disk icon is placed next to every reference to files on the *Adobe Photoshop NOW! CD-ROM*. We provide these icons so that you can quickly see there are supporting files on the CD that relate to specific *Adobe Photoshop NOW!* chapter assignments.

New Riders Publishing

The staff of New Riders Publishing is committed to bringing you the very best in computer reference material. Each New Riders book is the result of months of work by authors and staff, who research and refine the information contained within its covers.

As part of this commitment to you, the NRP reader, New Riders invites your input. Please let us know if you enjoy this book, if you have trouble with the information and examples presented, or if you have a suggestion for the next edition.

Please note, however, that the New Riders staff cannot serve as a technical resource for Adobe Photoshop for Windows or Adobe Photoshop for Windows application-related questions, including hardware-or software-related problems. Refer to the documentation that accompanies your Adobe Photoshop for Windows application package for help with specific problems.

If you have a question or comment about any New Riders book, please write to NRP at the following address. We will respond to as many readers as we can. Your name, address, or phone number will never become part of a mailing list or be used for any other purpose than to help us continue to bring you the best books possible.

New Riders Publishing
Macmillan Computer Publishing
A Division of Paramount Publishing
Attn: Associate Publisher
201 W. 103rd Street
Indianapolis, IN 46290

If you prefer, you can FAX New Riders Publishing at the following number:

(317) 581-4670

We welcome your electronic mail to our CompuServe ID:

74111,664

Thank you for selecting *Adobe Photoshop NOW!*

PART ONE:

The Power User's Basics

Chapter 1

The Big-Time Retouching Sampler

Photoshop's workspace is a happy clutter of integrated tools, each one complementing the other when you sit down to do a specific assignment. You'll probably never encounter a real-life assignment that calls for as many different working examples of Photoshop's integrated feature set as you'll find in this chapter. But then again, this isn't a real-life assignment.

Here begins the fiction part of *Adobe Photoshop NOW!*. Frank, owner of Frank's Franks, has made some unwise business decisions. He speculated foolishly on the Commodity Market Exchange in condiment futures, and mistakenly believed that customers liked to chow down his product with an icy 12 oz. serving of sauerkraut juice.

Frank is now bankrupt. In steps Connie, of Connie's Coneys, who likes his photorealistic logo, but it's got the wrong type of sausage depicted, and Frank's name on the bottom doesn't thrill her either. Your assignment is to revamp Frank's logo into something Connie can identify with.

Using a Mask To Protect Image Areas

Photoshop offers a wide range of tools you can use to define an outline of a specific image area. By encompassing an area with a selection marquee, you can isolate that area of the image, and work within it, applying the changes you make to only that area. Conversely, you can protect the encompassed area from change while you work on the rest of the image. This is the concept behind Photoshop's *selections* and *masks*—one is always the inverse of the other within an active image window.

In the next few steps, you'll see how to use a special selection tool, the Magic Wand tool, to create a selection border, and then refine that border using a variety of Photoshop tools and features.

> *Antialiasing is a computer graphics function that many software manufacturers are building into their programs. Antialiasing ensures that selection areas and areas you apply paint strokes to don't contain those stair-steppy, jagged edges that innately belong to the family of bitmap-type graphics.*
>
> *Antialiasing is the intelligent placement of semitransparent pixels in-between pixels that lie on the edge of a stroke or selection. From a 1:1 viewing resolution of an image, the pixels aren't usually evident in an image, just like film grain in a photograph typically isn't visible to the naked eye.*
>
> *Before you start working with your own images, they must be either RGB type or grayscale type. Photoshop needs a lot of available unique color registers to create antialiasing pixels, and RGB and Grayscale modes fit the bill. Image types like Indexed color (covered in Chapter 4) are limited to 256 colors, an insufficient amount for Photoshop to render soft, multi-tonal edges around areas in images.*

NOTE

Features Covered:

- Quick Mask mode
- Painting/Editing modes
- The Type tool
- The Paintbrush tool
- The Gradient Fill tool
- The Paste Behind command

The Image on the *Adobe Photoshop NOW! CD-ROM*

If you'd like to get hands-on experience with Photoshop selection and retouching techniques as described in the steps to come, this is where the companion CD comes into play. In the Chap01 subdirectory on the companion CD, you'll find FRNXFRNX.TIF, the example image used throughout this chapter. Copy it to a convenient location on your hard disk, and load the image into Photoshop's workspace. Now you'll not only see how the techniques are performed with this sample image, but you'll be able to duplicate them as well.

Selecting the Frankfurter, Masking the Background

You can see the areas Connie the client wants revised in figure 1.1. The first area to address is the frankfurter—it needs to be changed into a coney. The frank is a fairly monotone image area with little color variation. Unlike the Lasso tool or the Rectangular Marquee tool, which uses geometry to determine selection borders, the Magic Wand uses color values to determine which image areas are included in a selection border. This characteristic makes the Magic Wand tool the tool of choice for selecting the frank. In this assignment, you only need to retouch the face of the frankfurter because the dimensional sides of the frank have little color content, and will portray the sides of a blanched coney just fine the way they are.

Figure 1.1

Areas containing few differences in value can be selected with Photoshop's Magic Wand tool.

1. Press Ctrl+ + until you have a 2:1 viewing resolution. Use the Hand tool (click and drag with the cursor on the image) to reposition the image in the active window so that the left side of the frank is centered in your workspace.

2. The Magic Wand tool selects adjacent pixels that have color values that fall within a tolerance setting that you define. To estimate what the most effective tolerance value would be, select only the face of the frankfurter by using the Info palette. The Info palette acts like a virtual densitometer. You'll use it to see how widely the color pixels in the frankfurter part of the FRNXFRNX design differ from each other. Press F8 to display the Info Palette.

3. Choose the Magic Wand tool (actually any tool will do here), and move the cursor around over the face of the frankfurter. The Info palette should tell you that the RGB values don't vary by more than about 20% or so. No hard and fast formula is available for figuring the correlation between RGB value differences and the Magic Wand's tolerance setting. You can get a good idea, though, that out of the 256 possible Magic Wand tolerance values, the number you need to enter next is greater than 10 and less than 50 in this instance.

4. Double-click on the Magic Wand tool's icon. This calls the Magic Wand Options dialog box to the screen.

5. Enter a value of 20 pixels in the Tolerance field, and then click on OK.

6. Click on the left side of the frankfurter, as shown in figure 1.2. The Magic Wand includes all adjacent pixels that bear a color resemblance to the exact pixel you click over within a range of 20 pixels.

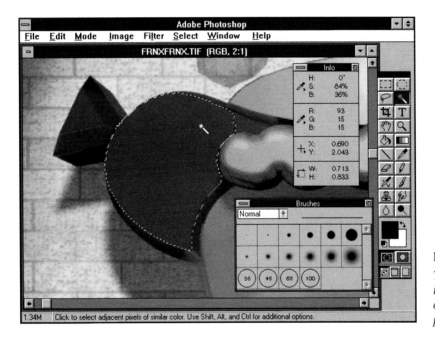

Figure 1.2

The Tolerance option can include a single-color pixel or can include every color pixel in an image.

7. Leave the triangular shape to the left of the frank alone for the moment as it'll serve as an example for a different Photoshop selection technique. But if you don't have a nice marquee outline going around the entire left part of the frank with certain areas left deselected on the frank's face, hold down the Shift key and click in the area you want to add to the selection.

Holding down the Shift key and clicking is the technique for adding to an existing selection area with any one of Photoshop's selection tools.

8. Choose Select, Save Selection. This isn't the same as saving the image. This command saves the selection area you've defined so that you can reuse it at any time without having to redefine the selection.

Customizing Photoshop's Quick Mask

There's something ethereal about the Quick Mask mode in Photoshop. While in this mode, you create and edit a selection area or a masked area. This area is represented on-screen by a tinted overlay. All of Photoshop's selection tools can be used to edit the quick mask overlay. A selection area displayed in Quick Mask mode is for display purposes only, and what appears to be a wash of color on top of your image never actually becomes part of the image.

In the next set of steps, you need to assign a color for this quick mask other than the default red that Photoshop set when it was installed. When the image area you are working on is the same (or nearly the same) color as the color of the quick mask, it becomes hard to distinguish between the two. You'll also change the default setting of an area that is covered by the quick mask color. Photoshop can be set to display either the area you want to work on (the *selection*) or the area you want to protect from changes (the *mask*) with quick mask color.

1. If you've deselected the border you created in the last steps, choose Select, Load Selection so that the marquee border is running around the face of the left half of the frankfurter.

2. Double-click on the Quick Mask mode button, the right-hand one toward the bottom of the toolbox that has a shaded rectangle with an empty circle inside of it.

3. In the Quick Mask Options box, click on the Color Indicates: Selected Areas radio button. You can choose any level of opacity that you desire. The Opacity setting determines how completely this quick mask overlay obscures the underlying image. I usually stick with 65%, which produces an overlay that has a color definition with some heft, but also allows me to see the underlying image without straining my eyes.

4. Click on the color selection box, and Photoshop's Color Picker dialog box appears.

If you've experimented with the dialog boxes found in Photoshop's File, Preferences, General submenus, you might have decided on using Windows Color Picker, a less confusing, serviceable color model, to specify colors to be used in Photoshop. I recommend against using the Windows' Color Picker, especially when designing professional, paying assignments. There's no easy way to pick a neutral gray with the Windows Color Picker. With Photoshop's Color Picker, you can easily define any color or shade of gray by using any of Photoshop's color models. Windows' Color Picker also will not alert you to "illegal" colors you might select.

Photoshop has a lot of user-customizable options, such as the color overlay when in Quick Mask mode. Look for notes throughout this book on occasions when a Photoshop default can or should be changed.

5. In figure 1.3, you see a ghastly green being chosen for the quick mask color. Although it's an unappetizing color for actual sausage, it contrasts quite nicely for our selection purposes. Click and drag the hue slider to the greenish neighborhood, then click and drag the circle in the spectrum box until you have a similar shade.

6. A little exclamation button has appeared to the left of the color picker's OK button. This is an alert that you've selected an "illegal" color. An illegal color is one that a commercial printer cannot reproduce accurately on a print press. If you are selecting a color to use in an image that is to be commercially printed, you'd want to click on the exclamation button to tell Photoshop to select the closest "legal" color. But because you're selecting a color for Quick Mask mode, which is a display color that's never printed along with an image, you can safely ignore this warning, and click on the OK button.

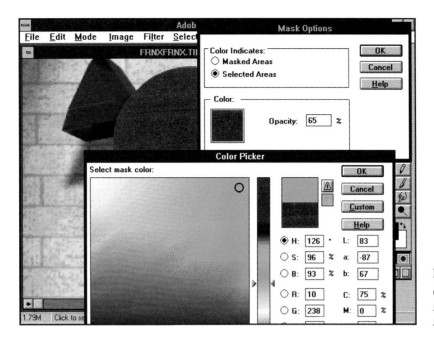

Figure 1.3

Quick Mask mode can be set to display either selection or masked areas.

7. Click on the main dialog box's OK button to confirm all your choices for the quick mask options. You are returned to the workspace, which now features a frankfurter that's green wherever an area was selected with the Magic Wand tool.

    Quick mask overlays are temporary. If you don't save the selection that you've created, the selection disappears forever when you deselect the area. If you've invested a serious amount of time creating the selection and you need to reuse the selection, this can be heartbreaking, and can lead to harsh language.

    Fortunately, you can't accidentally deselect an area while you're in Quick Mask mode; this boo-boo can only occur while in Standard mode. Clicking outside of an active marquee selection border with a selection tool (or by choosing Select, None) when you are in Standard mode deselects the selection area you created within Quick Mask mode.

    Chapter 2, "Channels, Masks, and Selections," has more insights and tips on the selection process and where these saved selection areas are kept. But as you work with Quick Mask mode in this and other chapters, remember that regardless of how solid this area appears in Quick Mask mode, it becomes plastic and quite elusive as an active selection in Standard mode.

Refining a Selection Created in Quick Mask Mode

The left "twist" (triangle) of Frank's frank needs addressing. And this is a perfect place to use the Lasso tool to define a straight-line geometric area.

When you're in Quick Mask mode, defined areas are displayed in color, and this quick mask overlay can be added to or subtracted from with an economy of effort and speed. When the default colors of foreground black and background white are chosen in Photoshop while in Standard mode, you apply color (black) to an image area or remove image color to reveal the image's background (white). But in Quick Mask mode, black represents a quick mask you'll add to an image area, and white removes any quick mask you might have in the image.

This is simpler than it sounds. Use the Lasso tool to add the triangular tip of the frank to the selection area, and follow these steps: *arrows to top right*

1. Click on the Invert colors icon button, the little boxes to the bottom left of the toolbox's color selection boxes. Now your foreground color's white, and the background is black.

2. Select the Lasso tool.

3. Hold down the Alt key, and click on each of the three corners of the triangular twist of the frankfurter. The Alt key constrains the Lasso's normal freehand property to that of creating straight lines only.

4. Press the Del key, or press the Backspace key once or twice. Either action replaces what's inside the selection area with background. As you can see in figure 1.4, you've "revealed" the green overlay in this area. Remember that the actual FRNXFRNX image is untouched; you're only editing a visible selection area in Quick Mask mode. Click outside the marquee border now. The area's been defined.

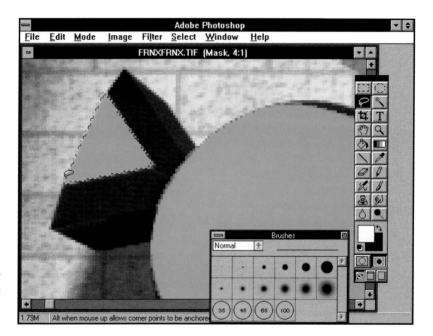

Figure 1.4

Sharp corners and straight geometric shapes are best selected with the Lasso tool.

5. Now that the left side of the frank has been selected, it's time to work on the right side. This frankfurter is pretty symmetrical; therefore, the same basic techniques used to select the right side of the frank will work on the left side of the frank. First, select the Hand tool, place it inside the active image area, and click and drag to the right to move your active view to the right of the image within the active window.

6. Click on the Standard mode button (the one to the left of the Quick Mask mode button). The Magic Wand tool can't be used effectively while you are in Quick Mask mode.

7. Choose the Magic Wand tool. Hold down the ~~Alt~~ *Shift* key, and click inside the right portion of the frankfurter with the Magic Wand. Still holding down the ~~Alt~~ *Shift* key, click once or twice more (move the cursor over a deselected portion of the right side of the frankfurter before you click) if the entire reddish portion of the frank isn't completely encompassed by the marquee border the first time.

8. Click on the Quick Mask mode button again.

9. The color selection boxes on the toolbox should still be set to foreground white and background black. If this isn't the case, click on the Default colors icon button, and then click on the Invert colors icon button to set them this way before moving on.

10. Choose the Lasso tool, and while holding down the Alt key, define the triangular part of the frankfurter to the right of the main part of the frankfurter by clicking on each point of the triangle. Then press the Del key (or the Backspace key). The marqueed area will be filled with quick mask overlay.

11. Click on the Standard mode button, and then choose Select, Save Selection, #4. Do not choose New. The numbers that appear on the Save and Load Selection fly-outs refer to different *image channels*. These are areas (Alpha channels) within an image file where selections are stored. You want the entire active selection area, all the areas you've defined so far, to be saved to the same channel (see fig. 1.5).

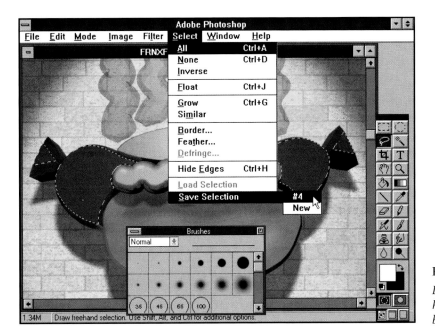

Figure 1.5
Different image areas that have been defined can all be saved as one selection.

If you're going to be working with a selection area consisting of different, noncontiguous image areas, as in this assignment, always save the different areas to the same channel. If you don't, you'll have to load a different selection number for each area you've saved to in order to call it back as an active selection area. This is why Quick Mask mode is used in this assignment; it displays selection areas as color overlays that you can add to or subtract from without the hassle of holding down the Alt key (to add) or the Shift key (to subtract) while selecting.

When you finish editing an area, click on the Standard mode button, and save the sum total of the individual selection areas to the same Save Selection (Channel) number.

Perfecting a Selection Area

You'll often find that areas selected with the Magic Wand tool don't quite define image area borders with the precision and finesse an artist's hand could. Although the Magic Wand is invaluable for selecting vast areas of similarly colored pixels, bitmap-type images don't really have distinct borders where a foreground object ends and the background begins. And this is the case with Frank's Frank here.

1. Zoom into the area where the mustard meets the frank on the right side of the image, load the selection area, and then switch to Quick Mask mode.

You see that the edge of the colored overlay in Quick Mask mode has encroached on the mustard somewhat, and this means that when you change the frankfurter to a coney color shortly, part of the mustard also will be included in the active selection area, and it, too, will be changed.

The purpose of accurately selecting the frankfurter is to ensure that only the frankfurter is altered when you retouch it. You don't want the changes you make to affect any other part of the image area. This calls for some more selection area refinement, as the next step describes.

2. The Quick Mask overlay is a terrific visual guide as to where your selection border ends, but right now, it obscures the area you want to work on. The solution is to remove a small area of the overlay that encompasses this desired image area. First, click on the Default colors icon button to set the background color to white. White removes the overlay color.

3. Choose the Lasso tool, and click and drag a circular shape around the area where the mustard meets the frank on the right side of the image.

4. Press the Del key. This clears the area of color overlay, as shown in figure 1.6. You now can see the edge of the mustard.

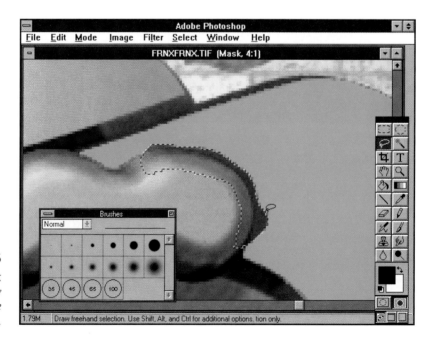

Figure 1.6

You can remove quick mask color overlay by applying white to the overlay.

5. Choose the Paintbrush tool.

6. Choose the second row, smallest tip on the Brushes palette. Make sure the Brushes palette's Opacity is set to 100%, and your painting mode is Normal.

7. Click and drag the Paintbrush tool across the reddish frankfurter area, being careful not to stray into the mustard. You are applying color overlay in Quick Mask mode, and redefining the selection border.

8. If you accidentally wander into the mustard, click on the Invert colors icon button. This sets the foreground color to white (removes quick mask in this editing mode), and clicking and dragging across any green quick mask removes it.

9. When you're happy with your edge work, double-click on the Zoom tool. This returns you to a 1:1 viewing resolution of the active image.

10. Are there other areas of your selection editing work that need refining? Any place you see the Quick Mask overlay outside of the face of the frankfurter, zoom into the area, remove a good portion to expose the image edge like you just did, and then use the Paintbrush tool to manually refine the border of the green tint overlay.

11. When you have an image like the one in figure 1.7 where the entire face of the frankfurter is green, you're done with your selection work. Click back to Standard mode, choose **S**elect, **S**ave Selection, #4 from the fly-out menu.

12. Choose **F**ile, **S**ave (Ctrl+S).

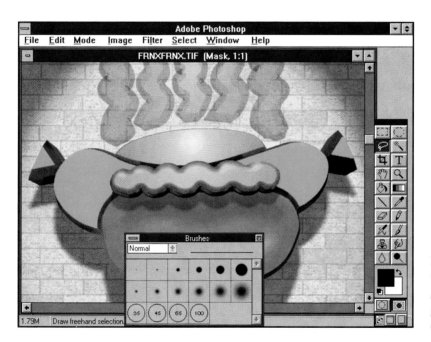

Figure 1.7

The Quick Mask mode displays your selection area far more accurately than active marquee borders.

Changing the Hue of the Frankfurter

The drop-down list on the top left of the Brushes palette's functionality depends on what your activity is in Photoshop. It sets the modes with which you paste a copied selection area into an image, but it also controls how color is painted when a paint tool is active.

The Hue mode is ideal for the first part of recoloring Frank's Frank to suit Connie's advertising needs. When Hue is selected from the drop-down list, areas of an image you paint over retain their saturation and brightness characteristics, but the color of the spectrum, or the *hue*, the color pixels have is modified. This means if you select white as the Photoshop foreground color, you can remove whatever red the frankfurter has in its color characteristic.

The frank won't turn to coney white, though. This is because the frank image area isn't saturated with color. Instead, its color characteristic is mostly derived from its gray content, which accounts for its dark red color. See how the color component can be replaced with white in the next few steps, and then move on to addressing the surplus of gray that results.

1. Choose **S**elect, **L**oad Selection. A marquee selection border appears around the frankfurter face. Everything inside this selection shape is active and can be changed. Areas outside of the marquee border are protected from change.

2. Press Ctrl+H (**S**elect, Hide **E**dges). This doesn't deselect anything; it only makes the active marquee borders invisible. Marquee borders can obscure your view and hinder your retouching work.

3. Choose the Paintbrush tool, and then select the 100 pixel diameter tip on the Brushes palette. Click on the Brushes palette's modes arrow, and choose Hue from the drop-down list.

4. Make sure white is set as your foreground color. Click on the Default colors icon button, and then on the Invert colors icon to quickly set the foreground to white.

5. Click and drag across the frankfurter part of the FRNXFRNX image. You'll see the reddish color replaced with a dull gray. What's actually happening is that the red color component, which there isn't a lot of in the frank, is being shifted to white. The gray component becomes very prominent, as shown in figure 1.8.

6. When the frank has been painted over once or twice, you're done with the Paintbrush and the Hues mode. Notice how precision doesn't matter in these steps. It's because only the frankfurter's face in the image is active.

Figure 1.8

The Hue mode replaces only the color content of pixels you click and drag over with a paint tool.

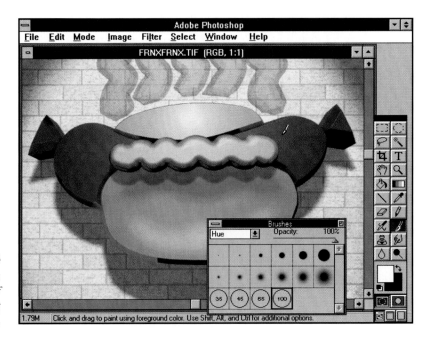

If you'd like to see a more visible example of how the Hue mode replaces color content in an image, try using a digital image with light pastels in it. Pictures that contain light colors typically have little gray component in their color makeup, and therefore display a specific hue more prominently. Experiment with brilliant colors using the Hue mode as well, like those found on a beach ball. Brilliant colors usually are saturated with both a strong hue and gray component.

Bleaching a Digital Image Area

The Screen mode, when used with a painting tool, progressively affects a selected area—a second or third stroke over the same image area continues to intensify the screen effect. The Screen mode bleaches the color found in an image, and simultaneously replaces the color with a tint of the foreground color you select. It's important to give this selected frankfurter area an even shade of off-white by using a single click and drag over the entire selection area. This is why the 100 pixel tip is good for total selection coverage. Here's how to change the virtual sausage to a shade of color more appropriate for Connie's enterprise.

1. Click and drag the Opacity slider on the Brushes palette to about 62%. The Screen mode for painting tools is a very intense effect, and a 100% Opacity would bleach the frankfurter selection to a white color only attainable in laundry commercials. You're aiming for an off-white that highlights can be added to later.

2. Choose the Screen mode from the drop-down list in the upper left of the Brushes palette.

3. Click and drag, but *don't release the mouse button*, even after you've completed a stroke. Figure 1.9 was captured at the beginning of using the Paintbrush tool in Screen mode. As you can see, a nice, even shade is being bleached out of the remaining gray component the image pixels contain.

   A second click and drag in any area that's been gone over once in Screen mode would create a lighter shade of foreground color, and a soft edge would occur between overlapping strokes. These two shades are almost impossible to blend together. Confine your strokes in Screen mode to single click-and-drag moves, unless you're deliberately trying to achieve an overlapping effect.

4. Continue clicking and dragging until the entire selection area displays a flat, even off-white tone. It's only after the area has been completely gone over with one "coat" that you're done and can release the mouse button.

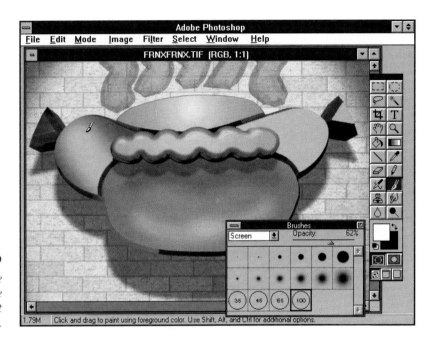

Figure 1.9

The Screen painting mode lightens foreground shade and tints it to the present foreground color.

Creating Virtual Highlights on the Coney

Aside from Photoshop's selection and painting tools, there's a category of tools grouped toward the bottom of the toolbox that modify pixels in an image and don't use foreground or background color attributes. These are called *editing tools*. You'll use the Dodge/Burn tool in the next steps to add some dimension to the newly-transformed coney.

The Dodge/Burn tool performs the digital equivalent of conventional dodging and burning of film emulsion as it's exposed to an image negative through the light source of a condenser head. In its default setting of dodging, you'll use this tool to draw out the highlights in the coney to make it more congruous with its highly stylized and dimensional surroundings.

1. Choose the Dodge/Burn tool. You'll notice that the Opacity slider on the Brushes palette has changed to an Exposure slider, and your selections from the modes drop-down list have changed, also. Not to worry. The Dodge/Burn tool is an editing tool, not a painting tool, so its parameters are a little different.

2. Choose Highlights from the modes drop-down list on the Brushes palette, choose the second row, middle tip, and set the Exposure slider for about 50%.

3. Your selection area should be active, but hidden. If you're uncertain about this, press Ctrl+H. Does the marquee border appear around the frankfurter? If so, you're in good shape, and you can press Ctrl+H again to toggle the border's visibility off again.

4. Stroke the top of the frankfurter where you think a natural highlight would occur given the spotlight shining down on it in this scene. It might take more than one or two strokes to produce a slightly pronounced highlight.

5. Reduce the exposure on the Brushes palette to 30%, and choose the 100 pixel diameter brushes tip.

6. In one stroke, two strokes tops, drag the Dodge/Burn tool across the bottom of the frankfurter. The fact that the bun and surrounding image areas are presently masked gives you the leeway to be painterly with this stroke, as shown in figure 1.10. A broad stroke, weak in intensity, helps add to the mood of the frankfurter's lighting, further suggesting dimension in the image.

7. Congratulations! You've successfully transformed a virtual frank into a virtual coney, and your first round with some of Photoshop's sophisticated painting, selection, and editing tools has concluded. Choose File, Save, and take a break. For some reason, I'm getting a little hungry right now.

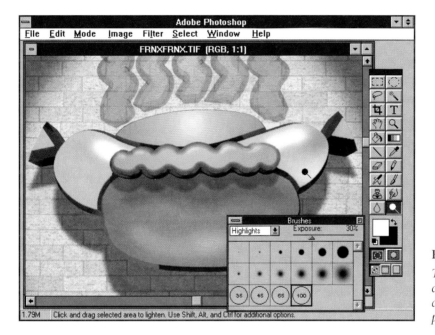

Figure 1.10

The Dodge/Burn tool is customized with the controls on the Brushes palette.

Photoshop users who work with a pressure-sensitive digitizing tablet instead of a mouse can control the amount of opacity, intensity, or pressure a tool is used with by applying varied amounts of force on the stylus. Choose your options for using the digitizing tablet by double-clicking on a tool and making your choice from the dialog box. Mouse-users will get nonfunctional, grayed-out options without the appropriate tablet drivers installed.

This is not really cause for dismay among thousands of Photoshop users who use a mouse as an input device, however. Photoshop effects and features are all accessible with the traditional point-and-click device—they just take a little longer to execute.

Sampling Colors To Use for Type

This assignment calls for changing the name at the bottom of the FRNXFRNX image, and as with the frankfurter part of the assignment, the trick is to leave as much original image area intact as possible. But it's hardly worthwhile to try to select, remove, and then restore each individual character when you have two wonderful Photoshop tools at your disposal to sample, and then faithfully reproduce the background area behind the type. The game plan is to remove the entire bottom gradient fill from FRNXFRNX, replace the fill with an identical gradient, and then add the new typography.

The first step is to sample the original colors that make up the gradient fill area. At the top, just before the brick wall begins, is brown, and at the very bottom is a deep mustard color. "Adopt" these colors using Photoshop's Eyedropper tool so that these same colors will be used to re-create the gradient fill.

1. Double-click on the Hand tool to give a full-frame view of the FRNXFRNX image. Click and drag the image window frame so that you have a clear view of the edges of the entire image. Photoshop provides this border for the express purpose of getting selections and paint strokes clear up to the image edge. Regardless of what desktop colors you might have defined in Windows, Photoshop's image background is always gray.

2. Choose the Rectangular Marquee tool, and then click and diagonally drag the area with the gradient fill and lettering. Choose Select, Save Selection, #4. This overwrites the selection area around the frankfurter you worked on earlier, but that's okay because you're finished with it.

In the next chapter, you'll get an understanding about where saved selections are stored. A quick solution to saved selection management is to overwrite previously saved selections when they are no longer needed. The selection information about the frankfurter's border has been replaced with information about the rectangle you just defined. If you had selected New from the Select, Save Selection submenu, you'd have both a #4 selection and a #5. FRNXFRNX would be a larger image than necessary as stored in RAM or written to disk as the information about the frankfurter's border is no longer useful.

3. Select the Eyedropper tool and click on the top portion of the rectangular selection area, as shown in figure 1.11. The Eyedropper samples a foreground color that's immediately registered in the toolbox's color selection boxes as a new foreground color.

4. Hold down the Alt key, and click on the bottom of the image where the mustard color is. This samples the color you want to use as the background color. The sampled color is immediately displayed as the new background color on the Color selection box on the toolbox.

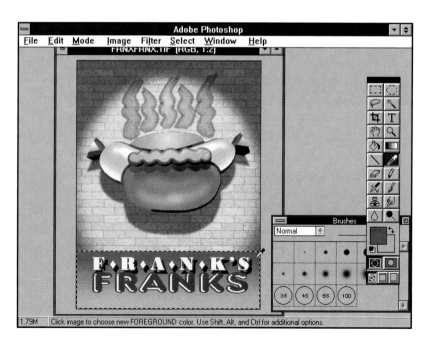

Figure 1.11

The Eyedropper tool samples an image area. You then can paint with that color.

Re-creating the Text's Background with the Gradient Tool

A gradient fill in Photoshop is the transition between foreground and background colors. You might have used this effect in other design programs that referred to the effect as color cycling, a color ramp, or a fountain fill. Before creating the gradient fill in the area you selected and saved, you need to customize the Gradient tool's settings. Photoshop has many exotic ways of applying this gradient color transition, but for this image you want to re-create the rather straightforward fill that currently is the backdrop for Frank's.

1. Double-click on the Gradient tool.

2. Click on the Normal Style radio button, and click on the Linear Type button. Make sure the Midpoint Skew is set to 50%, and then click on OK.

3. Click a point inside the rectangular marquee border near the top, and then drag straight down to a point inside near the bottom of the rectangle, as shown in figure 1.12. Release the mouse button, and the gradient fills the selection area. It's unimportant whether you use the tool in the center, left, or right of the box, but you should make certain that the angle of your drag is parallel to the image's sides. You can determine the angle of a gradient fill by the direction you take when you click and drag.

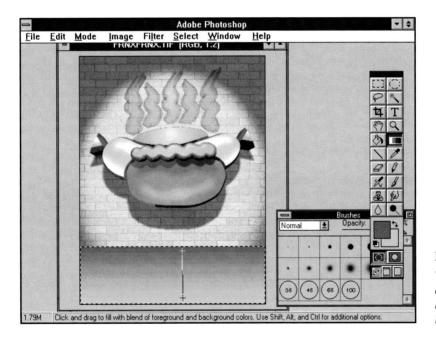

Figure 1.12

The Gradient tool creates a color transition between defined foreground and background colors.

Measuring the Space for the Type

Your newly-retouched image is all primed for some fancy text to announce Connie's name on this logo. You'll use Photoshop's Type tool to create the text, but first you need to measure how much space you have for the text. Type is measured in points, not inches, so a quick detour to customize Photoshop's Rulers is in order.

1. Choose File, Preferences, Units to call the Unit Preferences dialog box to the screen.

2. Choose Points from the Ruler Units drop-down list, and then click on OK.

3. Press Ctrl+R to display rulers around the FRNXFRNX image window.

Like most graphics/DTP software packages, there is a zero origin box where the horizontal and vertical rulers meet. You can click and drag this box into the image area. Wherever the crosshair is when you release the mouse button determines where the zero point on the rulers start. This makes it easier to measure specific areas of the image.

4. As shown in figure 1.13, the zero origin has been dragged to a location near where the type should begin from left to right. The title, Connie's Coneys, can be displayed as large as possible in this gradient filled space if it's set on two centered lines, like Frank's title was. As you can see on the readjusted rulers, 36 points works nicely in terms of type size. And you don't have to worry about the width of the type because you'll see a trick shortly for adjusting the width of anything you can select in Photoshop.

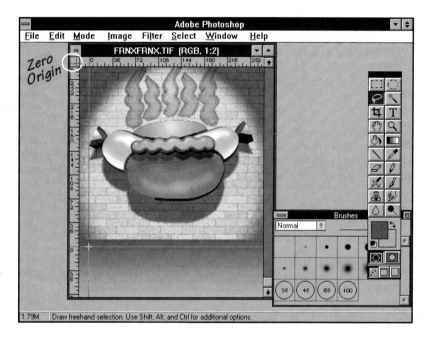

Figure 1.13

Zero origin can be set at any point by dragging the crosshair to a new location on the image.

Inserting the New Logo Text

Photoshop's Type tool produces the lettering you desire from any TrueType or Type 1 font you have installed on your system. Click the Type tool over the point in the image where you want your text to start, and the Type tool's dialog box appears. Text is not created directly within an active image but is entered in a dialog box where you can also set type attributes.

When Photoshop renders text, it initially appears over the active image as a floating selection. This means you're free to reposition it without disturbing the background image until you deselect the type by clicking outside its marquee borders.

The color of type created by the Type tool will be the foreground color on the Color selection box when you click the type insertion point in the image. White seems to be a color that stands off nicely from the gradient fill, so make white the current foreground color before continuing.

The typeface Davida (by Bitstream for ITC) is used in the following figures. If you don't have this typeface, you can use any of your installed TrueType or Adobe Type Manager Type 1s. Try to make it a fun one.

1. Choose the Type tool, and click an insertion point in the center of the gradient fill area.

2. The Type tool dialog box pops up. Select an available typeface in the **F**ont: drop-down list, then enter 36 in **S**ize, choose Points, set Lea**d**ing: 30 points, check the **A**nti-Aliased box, and then choose the **C**entered Alignment radio button, as shown in figure 1.14.

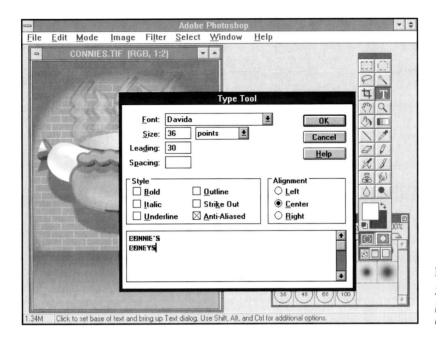

Figure 1.14

Set all the characteristics for type in the Type Tool dialog box.

3. Place your type cursor in the bottom text entry field, and type **CONNIE'S**.

4. Press the Enter key, and type **CONEYS**. Click on OK to return to the workspace.

Proper typesetter's quotes can add a professional touch to the typeset word. If you want an apostrophe instead of a "straight" punctuation, press Alt and then enter 0146 on the key-pad numbers of your 101 extended keyboard (the number keys above the letters don't work).

Similarly, Alt+0147 produces typesetter's open quotation marks, and Alt+0148 produces typesetter's closing quotation marks. All these extended ANSI characters might not be available in every typeface. You might want to check Windows 3.1's CHARMAP.EXE program to find the extended character you need.

Reshaping the Graphical Type To Fit the Design

All the type you create in Photoshop is a graphic—a misspelled word cannot be corrected, and a new font cannot be redefined in a floating selection. But because the title CONNIE'S CONEYS is a graphic, you can stretch and otherwise perform graphical modifications to this area. You can click and drag inside the marquee selection surrounding the type (see fig. 1.15).

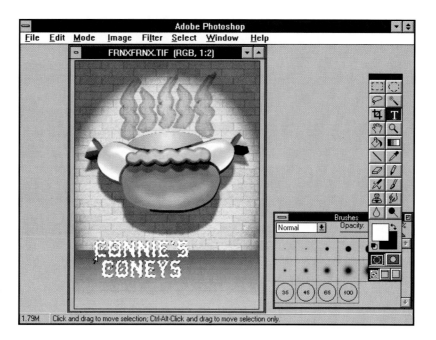

Figure 1.15

Type is repositionable as Photoshop renders it within a floating selection.

1. Position the type so that it's centered in the gradient fill area, like Frank's title used to be.

The title is just fine height-wise, but could stand some widening to become a more predominant element within the image. Here's where a Photoshop Image command comes in handy.

2. Select **I**mage, **E**ffects, and then choose the Scale command.

3. A boundary box with four corner boxes appears around the floating type selection. Place your cursor inside one of these corner boxes, and then push or pull in the direction you want the selection to conform to. As you can see in figure 1.16, by clicking and dragging on the lower right boundary corner, the floating type gets wider.

Holding down the Shift key while dragging on a Scale boundary corner proportionately scales a selection area. Also, if you accidentally click outside any effect submenu boundary box before clicking inside with the gavel cursor, the effect is immediately canceled, and you have to start the command all over again.

4. To finalize the Scale effect, click inside the boundary box when you're happy with your work. The cursor turns into a tiny gavel and "nails" the selected area to the degree of scaling you designed. The selection area is active, as you can still see marquee lines running about its edges. This is good. *Do not* deselect the floating type yet.

5. Choose **E**dit, **C**opy. A copy of this scaled type is now on the Clipboard, and the selection is still floating.

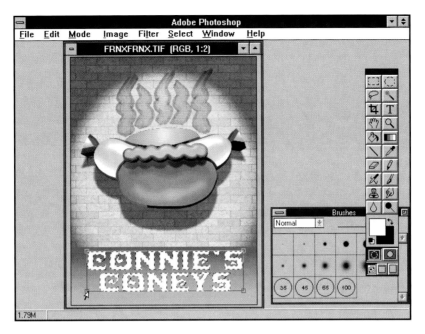

Figure 1.16
The Scale effect can stretch or shrink a selection area vertically or horizontally.

6. Choose <u>S</u>elect, <u>S</u>ave Selection, #4 (not New). This overwrites the rectangular selection area you saved earlier. You now have a centered, scaled type selection saved to a channel you can recall later.

Adding a Drop Shadow to the Text

Now that you have a perfect copy of this scaled type sitting on Windows' Clipboard, kick into ultra high-gear for the finale to this chapter's assignment. Frank obviously commissioned someone who knew typography cold, which is evident with all those fancy diamonds between the characters and the drop-shadowed type. Not to be outdone, you can perform some very realistic, natural-looking shading behind the type with one of Photoshop's filters, the Gaussian Blur.

You will blur the copy of the type in the next few steps. Blurring is sort of messy, so before you blur you need to create a new image window where you can perform the Gaussian Blur.

1. Choose the Eyedropper tool, and click over a dark, shaded area in the FRNXFRNX image. You'll need a color for the shadow you'll create with the blur, and by sampling a color from the original image, you make certain this color won't clash with the overall image color scheme.

2. Choose <u>F</u>ile, <u>N</u>ew. Photoshop is intuitive about the information on Window's Clipboard. Its New dialog box actually contains the image dimensions, resolution, and image type set to accommodate a pasted selection from the Clipboard exactly. But you don't want an exact fit for this copy of the type because the Gaussian Blur will make the type spread out a little. So enter <u>W</u>idth: 4 inches, H<u>e</u>ight: 2 inches, and leave the <u>R</u>esolution and image mode at their default settings.

3. Click on OK. You now have an Untitled-1 active image window in your workspace.

4. Choose **E**dit, **P**aste (Ctrl+V). You now have a marquee border around the floating white type above a white background.

5. Choose the Paint Bucket tool. Like the Gradient tool, the Paint Bucket floods an entire selection area with color, except the Paint Bucket only contains foreground color, not a mix. Also, the Paint Bucket can be set to a specific tolerance of color pixels it floods over in a selection area. But all the pixels in this floating type selection are the same color, so a double-click on the Paint Bucket tool to adjust its tolerance isn't necessary here.

6. Click the Paint Bucket cursor inside the marquee border. It doesn't matter which character you click inside; the selection is contiguous even though the characters are not. As you see in figure 1.17, the floating selection is a nice shadowy color.

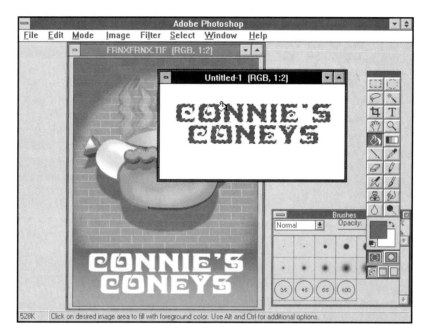

Figure 1.17

The Paint Bucket tool can apply a pattern or a flat foreground color to a selection area.

7. Press Ctrl+D or choose **S**elect, **N**one. You don't need the selection border to define the type any more, and it's time to blur it.

8. Choose Fi**l**ter, Blur, Gaussian Blur. This calls the Gaussian Blur dialog box to the screen. Set the **R**adius (the amount) of the blur to 8 pixels—a pretty strong amount—and then click on OK.

9. Instant fuzzy type that'll give everyone a headache to read is featured in figure 1.18. Refresh your eyes at this point, and prepare to copy this image back into the FRNXFRNX document.

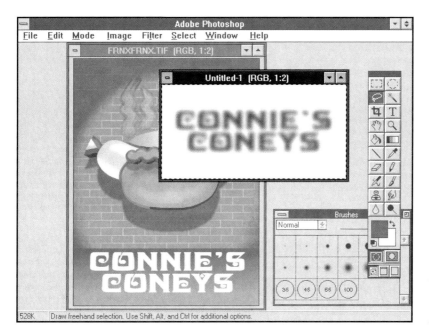

Figure 1.18

Photoshop's Gaussian Blur uses a complicated mapping scheme to simulate a hazy effect.

Adding the Shadow behind the Type

When you deselected the marquee border around the copy of the type in the last few steps, it was to effectively blur the type, which otherwise would've been confined to the selection border and produced a wimpy effect. But because the selection border isn't available for use any more (it wasn't saved), you have no apparent way to copy only the selection of the fuzzy brown type back into the FRNXFRNX image, right?

Fortunately, appearances aside, there is a way to copy the shadow. The trick here is to copy the entire Untitled-1 image area *behind* the white type in FRNXFRNX, and to make the white areas "go away" by using a special mode with the pasted selection. The Multiply mode, found on the drop-down list on the Brushes palette, behaves differently when different toolbox tools are active. With a painting tool, Multiply mode increases the density of paint strokes to achieve an effect similar to progressively stroking a piece of paper with a felt-tip pen—each stroke saturates an area until you get 100% coverage and the ink leaks through.

But when a selection tool is active when you choose Multiply mode, something even weirder and more wonderful happens—all areas of absolute white in the pasted image disappear, leaving only denser areas of color. See this effect in action next.

1. Choose **S**elect, **A**ll (Ctrl+A). This selects the entire image area in the Untitled-1 window.

2. Choose **E**dit, **C**opy, and then double-click on Untitled-1's window command button. This closes the image, and a dialog box pops up that asks whether you want to save changes to the untitled image. Click on No. This was a temporary image, and you want to get back to the FRNXFRNX image with the copy of Untitled-1's blurred type already saved on the Clipboard.

3. Choose **S**elect, **L**oad Selection. This loads the type selection area in the FRNXFRNX image that you saved earlier.

4. Choose **E**dit, Paste **B**ehind. You're achieving sort of a sandwich effect here, in that the pasted copy of the brown, blurry type will now land on top of the frankfurter image, but behind the selection of the white type in the marquee border.

5. Click on the Lasso tool (any selection tool will suffice here, actually). With a selection tool active, the Brushes palette comes to life, and you can select a different mode with which to composite (blend) the two images.

6. Choose Multiply from the mode drop-down list. The white background to the blurry type immediately vanishes.

7. Place your cursor inside the active selection area, and click and drag the brown shadow beneath and to the right of the white lettering. This is the Gaussian Blur filter's finest hour (see fig. 1.19).

Figure 1.19

Different modes affect how a pasted image is composited into a background.

8. When you're happy with the shadow's location, press Ctrl+D (Select, None) to finish the composite.

9. Choose File, Save, and you're done. Connie would be very impressed, and you'd be handsomely rewarded if she weren't a fictitious client.

Chapter 1's Bonus Tip

Photoshop's Filters menu comes with a glorious feature set of dynamic, processor-intensive, and truly bizarre set of effects that third party manufacturers presently are augmenting through plug-ins you can purchase separately. This book covers some of them, plus effects you can create using Photoshop's native effects capabilities. But just to reinforce the thought that the Gaussian Blur is the tamest filter that you can apply to a digital image, let's cap off this chapter with an image enhancement that you'd never want to use on a portrait image or most other realistic pictures.

The fictitious caterer, Connie, would like the world to know that not only is Frank's Franks kaput, but that her coneys are a larger serving of the popular sausage than Frank used to vend. Here's how a Photoshop filter is used to make a plumper coney without adding a drop of virtual corn starch filler.

1. Choose the Rectangular Marquee tool, and click and diagonally drag only the coney and background area. Don't define any of the gradient fill or type in your selection.

2. Choose Filter, Distort, Spherize.

3. Type **45** as the Amount in the Spherize dialog box, click on the Horizontal only radio button, and then click on OK to apply the filter, as shown in figure 1.20.

In figure 1.21, you can see the result of the Spherize command. Connie's fictitious advertising can now claim more coney for the consumer's fictitious dollar.

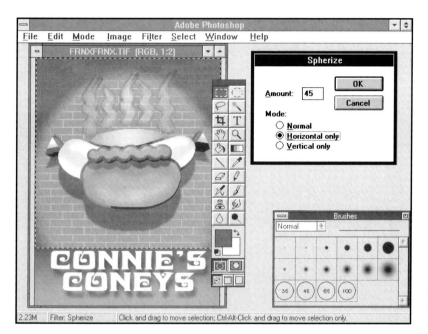

Figure 1.20
The Spherize filter distorts a selection area in one or both planar dimensional directions.

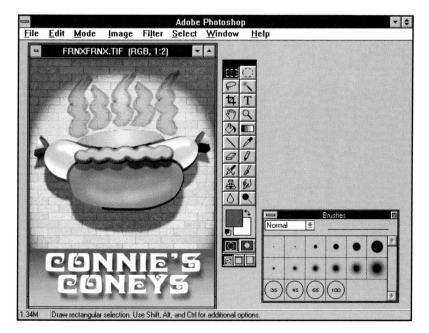

Figure 1.21
Spherizing a selection area can result in subtlety or a crude parody of the original image.

4. Press Ctrl+D (**S**elect, **N**one), and then choose **F**ile, Sa**v**e As and save your finished work under a different name, such as CONNIE.TIF to a location on your hard disk. Do not leave the **S**ave Alpha Channels box checked, as offered in the TIFF Options dialog box. Chapter 2 gets into Alpha channels and the appropriate times you want to save them. Alpha channels contain your saved selections; you don't need to save the selection area of the type any longer (because the piece is now finished), and the saved Alpha channel would needlessly plump up the image file size.

5. Suggest to your fictitious client Connie that she paste a "25% larger" sticker in the upper left side of her new logo to draw attention to your wonderful new graphic image.

The Spherize filter also is great for imitating a photograph taken with a fish-eye camera lens. For this reason, however, it's unflattering to use with people pictures.

Comparing the Before and After

As you can see in figure 1.22, FRNXFRNX.TIF, the original image on the *Adobe Photoshop NOW! CD-ROM*, has been loaded so that you can compare the work done to it in this chapter in a sort of "before and after" comparison. The difference is dramatic, and it's all made possible by understanding that Photoshop's feature set is a far cry from the run-of-the-mill image editing program.

Figure 1.22

Farewell, Frank; congratulations, Connie!

The examples in this book might appear a little far-fetched and larger than life on occasion, but if you can clear the higher hurdles in professional image editing, you'll sail past the lower ones you'll use on a day-to-day basis with ease.

If your appetite has been whetted for more about the way Photoshop treats image pixels like Silly Putty, there's more in store on how to manipulate Alpha channels right around the next page.

Chapter 2

Selections, Masks, and Channels

As you continue to work with Photoshop, you'll probably use the Save Selection command more and more often because it's such a wonderful graphic "bookmark" that you can use to return to an image area you have defined. But the true strength of this Photoshop feature lies in where the saved selections are stored, and how easily you can access this area to edit the selection. A selection area is stored as a grayscale image in an Alpha channel. How bright or dark the pixels are that make up the selection area determines how much of the Alpha channel is selected and how much is masked when you reload the selection by using the Load Selection command.

When you view an Alpha channel produced by saving a selection, you'll see a geometric black area and a white one, indicating totally selected and totally masked areas. They're a result of applying quick mask or using a selection tool while in a channel view of an image to define an image area.

The real fun and power of Photoshop comes into play when you create an Alpha channel by placing different images and portions of images in the channel. Photoshop reads the information and creates very complex and sophisticated selection areas that you can use to make changes in the color composite view of the image. Using Alpha channels makes it easy to create textured images that look photorealistic, as you'll see in this chapter.

Creating an Ancient Tapestry

Suppose that the Nedrow Museum of Art wants a poster advertising that the lost love letters from the Egyptian Pharaoh Tutankhamen to Princess Betty are on display there. No photographs of the relics are allowed, nevertheless your charge is to create a dynamic, realistic image for the occasion. With Photoshop, you can create a simulated piece of papyrus, adorn it with authentic-looking hieroglyphics, and place it on a scanned background image that'll look just as striking as an actual photo.

The Image on the *Adobe Photoshop NOW! CD-ROM*

All the materials used to create this museum poster are located on the *Adobe Photoshop NOW! CD-ROM*. In addition to the image files, you need to load a Type 1 font (TutType) from the CHAP02 subdirectory into Adobe Type Manager for Windows before beginning the assignment. TutType is a symbol font especially designed for the assignment in this chapter. You might even find a use for TutType in your own work if you ever need a quick hieroglyphic or two.

Measuring the Marble for some Papyrus

The papyrus part of the museum poster will have its own space atop a marble background, along with some type. So the first steps are to open the marble image, decide where the papyrus should fit in the composition, and then let Photoshop calculate a new file of proper proportions that will be your canvas for the papyrus.

1. Open the TUTMARBL.TIF image from the CD, and save a copy of it to your hard disk. First a measurement needs to be taken of it to properly size the "papyrus" you'll create.

2. Choose the Rectangular Marquee tool, and select an area similar in size to that shown in figure 2.1. The shape should be about twice as long as it is wide.

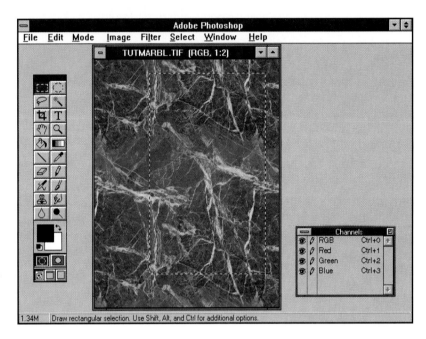

Figure 2.1

Photoshop creates new image files based on whatever the Clipboard is presently holding.

3. Choose Edit, Copy (Ctrl+C). This copies the selected area of marble to the Clipboard, but you're not actually going to use it. Instead, you'll let Photoshop use the information about the selection's size and resolution to calculate a new image canvas that you'll use to design Tut's love letter.

4. Double-click on the command button on TUTMARBL.TIF's image window to close the file. You're done with it for now.

5. Choose File, then New, and accept Photoshop's default suggestions in the New dialog box by clicking on OK. The Height and Width for this New image was about 2" by 4", and yours should be roughly the same.

As soon as Untitled-1 appears on your workspace, select a tiny square using the Rectangular Marquee tool, and press Ctrl+C. This copies a few pixels to the Clipboard for no other reason than to "bump out" the 200 KB or 300 KB of marble that is still stored on the Clipboard. The Clipboard only stores one image at a time, and by replacing the large marble image with a tiny selection area, you free up a sizable hunk of RAM.

Coloring the Virtual Papyrus

Take a good look at this blank canvas because by the time you're through with it, you will have created a photorealistic museum piece out of a minimum of "spare parts"—and unearthed a wealth of newfound Photoshop techniques along the way.

1. Click on the Foreground color selection box on the toolbox to call the Color Picker. You need to select a color for Tut's papyrus. H:37°, S:68%, B:92% is a good, rich color, but feel free to experiment. Just make certain that you select a fairly rich color (high in saturation) because you'll be doing something wonderfully sophisticated and perhaps unexpected soon.

2. Click on OK in the Color Picker dialog box and return to the Untitled-1 image. Then double-click on the Paint Bucket tool. Make sure the setting for Contents is Foreground color, and then click on OK.

3. Click inside the Untitled-1 image window to flood fill the window with the foreground color, as shown in figure 2.2.

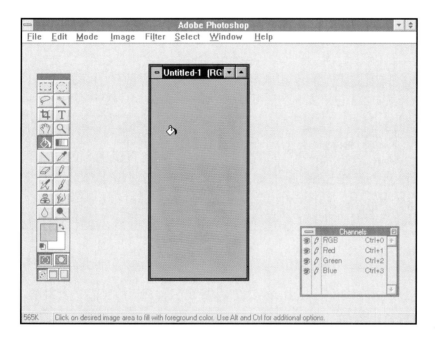

Figure 2.2

The Paint Bucket tool floods an area with foreground color or a predefined pattern.

4. Choose Image, Canvas Size. Increase the Width to 3" and the Height to 5", and then click on OK. The "papyrus" now should have a white border. The white border will make selecting the finished papyrus easier.

5. Save Untitled-1 to your hard disk and name it TUTSCROL.TIF.

6. Load the CLOTH2.TIF image from the *Adobe Photoshop NOW! CD-ROM*. You'll use it to create a design in an Alpha channel.

Adding Hieroglyphics to the Papyrus

The hieroglyphics should be added to the peach-colored area before you add any texture. You want to modify the text as well as the background color so that it appears as though the text is woven into the papyrus, not simply sitting on top of it. Here's how you do it.

1. Click on the Default colors icon button to the bottom left of the color selection boxes.

2. Choose the Type tool, and click an insertion point in the upper left corner of the peach rectangle that will become the papyrus.

3. In the Type tool dialog box, select TutType as the Font.

4. Set the Size at 50 points, and the Leading at 54 points. The leading is not critical, and you might prefer to enter the hieroglyphics characters one-by-one to Untitled-1.

5. Choose the Left Alignment radio button, check the Anti-Aliased checkbox, and place your cursor in the type entry field.

6. Type the character A. If you see an *Ankh*, as shown in figure 2.3, you're in good shape. Click on OK to return to the workspace.

7. The Ankh symbol appears as a floating selection with little marquee lines surrounding it. Place your cursor inside the marquee of the Ankh, and then click and drag it until it's in a good location. Then click outside of the marquee, and the Ankh is composited into the peach background.

Ankh character

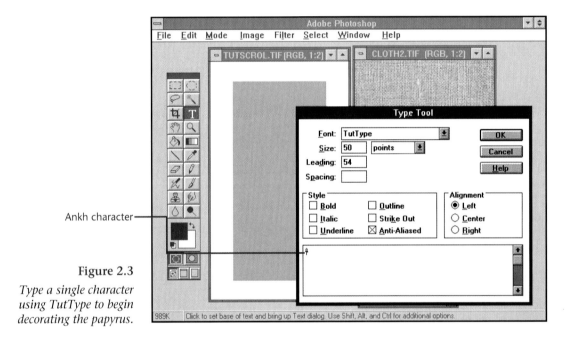

Figure 2.3

Type a single character using TutType to begin decorating the papyrus.

8. Click another insertion point, and the Type tool dialog box will reappear.

9. From here on use your artistic flair to enter different symbols and arrange them in rows. You might want to print a copy of the READ_TUT.WRI file found on the CD. It provides large, clear pictures of the glyphs and the keys to which they are assigned. Or you can use Windows' CHARMAP utility to spot a symbol you like.

10. In figure 2.4, you see the process in action. Type a character, then drag it into place, deselect it, and make another insertion point to continue. For an easy way to add the vertical lines, see the Tip following this exercise.

11. Choose File, Save, and save TUTSCROL.TIF to your hard disk when you have the hieroglyphics arranged so that they appear to say something.

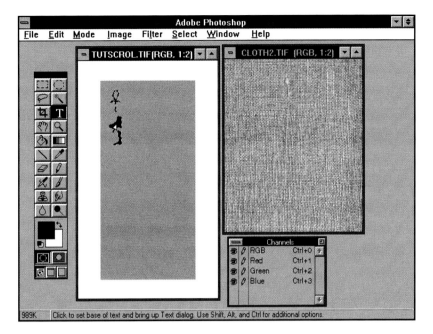

Hieroglyphics often had thoughts separated by a long, narrow line. The forward slash keystroke (/) in TutType contains such a divider, but you might want to use Photoshop's Line tool instead.

To achieve the same sort of relative line thickness as you see in the following figures for the hieroglyphics column dividers, follow one of these methods:

- *Set TutType for* 120 *points when you enter the (/) character*

  or

- *Double-click on the Line tool, and specify* 8 *pixels as the Width. Then click on OK, and click and drag the cursor where you want to draw the divider.*

Using an Alpha Channel To Design Papyrus

CLOTH2.TIF image was scanned as an RGB image, and as such, you can use it in a variety of situations—for a background, a replacement area within a damaged photo, or anything your creative instinct leads you to. For this assignment, however, CLOTH2.TIF's primary value lies in its tonal qualities, the grayscale information that constitutes most of its visual detail.

If you compare the image dimensions of Untitled-1 and CLOTH2.TIF, you can see that CLOTH2 won't exactly cover Untitled-1, but images with repeat designs and randomly distributed objects (such as leaves and sand) can be "tiled" with the Define Pattern command.

When CLOTH2, an RGB image, is sampled to produce a pattern, it can be applied in color to any image's composite color view. But as you'll see, an RGB image is converted to Grayscale mode when it is copied into an Alpha channel. Alpha channels are only capable of holding grayscale information and Photoshop always converts the mode of a selection to accommodate the color-capability of its host image.

Here's how a scan of a cloth napkin is used to create a stylized texture.

1. Click on the title bar of CLOTH2. It becomes the active image window.

2. Choose Select, All (Ctrl+A).

3. Choose Edit, Define Pattern.

4. Double-click on the command button on CLOTH2's image window to close the file. You're done with it now and TUTSCROL.TIF becomes the active window.

5. Press F6 (Window, Show Channels command).

6. Click on the Channel palette's command button, then choose New Channel.

7. Accept #4 as the default name for the channel, but make sure the Color Indicates: Selected areas radio button is selected, then click on OK.

8. Choose Select, All from the #4 channel view of TUTSCROL.

9. Choose Edit, Fill, and then click on the Pattern radio button in the Contents field. Accept the Blending field defaults of 100% Opacity and Normal Mode, and then click on OK.

10. Voilá, instant texture! As you can see in figure 2.5, the pattern of CLOTH2 only repeated a little toward the bottom, and this apparent flaw will not be obvious in the finished image. The pattern of the cloth in the Alpha channel is used by Photoshop as information about how to build selection areas. Photoshop will process the light and dark values to calculate how much each pixel in the RGB color channel should be selected.

11. Press Ctrl+D to deselect the grayscale image, and then choose File, Save.

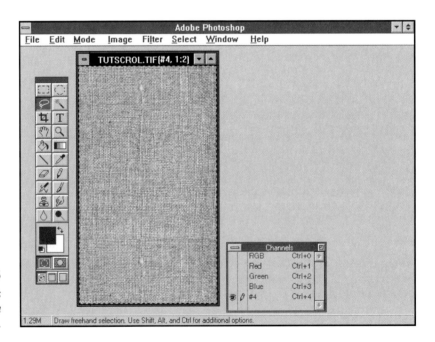

Figure 2.5

A pattern of CLOTH2 fills the Alpha channel with tonal information.

Adding Realism by Saving a Partial Copy of the Scroll

Now that your selection area is defined, it's time to do some editing to the RGB image in TUTSCROL.TIF. You'll load the selection based on the CLOTH2 image, which contains many partially masked (gray) areas, and then copy what's been selected from the RGB composite image of TUTSCROL to the Clipboard. The results will be remarkable. Continue by following these steps:

1. Click on the RGB title on the Channels palette. This returns you to the normal view of TUTSCROL.TIF.

2. The foreground/background colors should still be set at Photoshop's default. If they aren't, click on the Default colors icon button now.

3. Choose Select, Load Selection. Photoshop loads the information about the CLOTH2 pattern fill found in the Alpha channel, as shown in figure 2.6.

4. Choose Edit, Copy.

5. Double-click on the Eraser tool. A dialog box pops up asking if you want to erase the entire image. It's a good question because this is not a commonly used feature of the Eraser tool, and it is a potentially dangerous one.

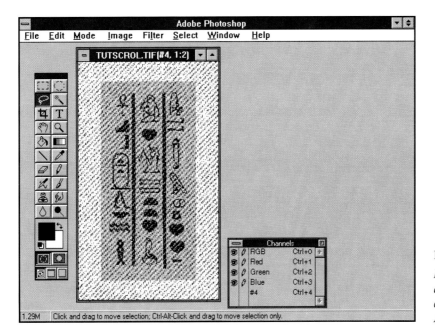

Figure 2.6

Photoshop selects areas according to how dense a corresponding area is in an Alpha channel.

6. Click on Yes, and don't worry about what's happening. Photoshop "cleans the slate," removing the original papyrus and lettering, but you have a modified copy of it on the Clipboard that you'll continue to use.

7. Press Ctrl+D to deselect everything in the TUTSCROL RGB composite channel, and then press Ctrl+A to select the entire image.

8. Choose Edit, Paste. You'll see a lighter, textured copy of your scroll plop into place.

9. Press Ctrl+D, then choose File, Save.

The selection marquee lines are useful for getting a rough idea of the boundaries of a selection area, but don't use them for precise guidelines, especially when partial masks are defined in an Alpha channel. Photoshop will encompass an area with visible marquee lines that are based on 56% or denser Alpha channel areas. This means that areas that are lighter than 56% black can still be partially included in the selection process, but aren't visually indicated by marquee lines. It's only when a selection area is 100% that you can be assured that marquee lines accurately define the shape of a selection border.

Tonally Enhancing the Papyrus

TUTSCROL definitely has a more authentic appearance because the partial mask left certain areas vacant when TUTSCROL was copied, and replaced them with background white color when you pasted the "partial" copy back. But it's presently a little too pale; a lot of the rich peach color was excluded from the selection process because there weren't a lot of dense, black areas in the CLOTH2 pattern for Photoshop to base a complete selection on.

Here's where Photoshop's tonal adjustment features come into play. The Levels command remaps the pixels in an image according to how many color pixels you want at various brightness levels. This produces dynamic results in an image, usually with more overall contrast, which is exactly what TUTSCROL needs.

1. Make sure TUTSCROL.TIF is in a corner of Photoshop's workspace. The Levels dialog box obscures your view of the image otherwise.

2. Press Ctrl+L (**I**mage, **A**djust, Levels).

3. Check the Preview box if it isn't already checked.

4. Click and drag the Black Point slider until the left Input Levels field reads about 98, as shown in figure 2.7. As you can see, TUTSCROLL is taking on more contrast and it's getting darker because you're telling Photoshop that the darkest point in the image should occur at a much higher point. Photoshop takes your instruction and then redistributes all the image pixels according to a new tonal scheme.

5. Click on OK.

*In Photoshop's **F**ile, Pre**f**erences, General dialog box is an option called **R**estore Windows. It's usually a good idea to have this box checked as part of your Photoshop setup. This option allows Photoshop to "remember" parameters such as color selections, tool options such as Feathering and **A**nti-Aliasing, and the Preview option on the Levels, Variations, and other dialog boxes.*

*With **R**estore Windows chosen, all you need to do is check the Levels Preview box once, and it will remain checked in all future Photoshop sessions when you call the Levels command.*

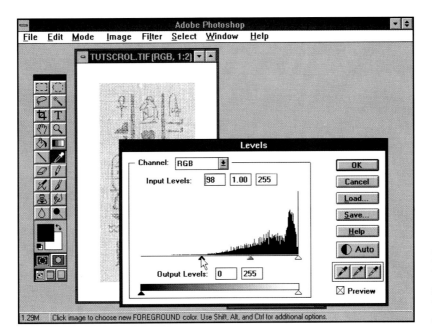

Figure 2.7
The Levels command changes the tonal scheme without affecting color characteristics.

"Distressing" the Papyrus

In the next set of steps, you'll add a second texture, CRUMPL3.TIF, to the TUTSCROL image. CRUMPL3 was created by crumpling a piece of paper and scanning it. When you base a selection on this crumpled paper image, you can add a slight touch of weathering to TUTSCROL, further enhancing the character of this digital papyrus to convey realism.

1. Load the CRUMPL3.TIF image from the *Adobe Photoshop NOW! CD-ROM*.

2. Choose **S**elect, **A**ll (Ctrl+A). This selects the entire CRUMPL3 image, as seen in figure 2.8.

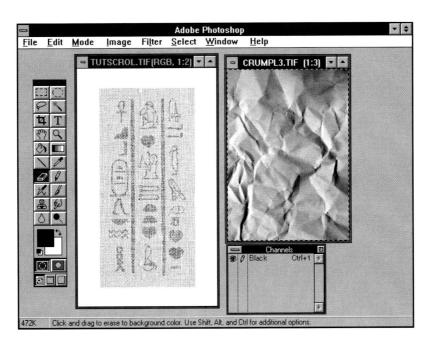

Figure 2.8
Objects containing texture can be scanned, then used in Photoshop with other images.

3. Choose **E**dit, **C**opy. You don't need to define a pattern based on the image this time because CRUMPL3 is larger than the TUTSCROL image. Also, CRUMPL3 doesn't lend itself to seamless tiling like CLOTH2 did.

4. Click on the title bar of the TUTSCROL image window to make it the active image. Then click on the command button on the Channels palette, and choose New Channel from the drop-down list.

5. Accept the default of #5 for the New Channel Name, and click on OK. By default, Photoshop always takes you to a view of a New Channel in the active image window.

6. Choose **E**dit, **P**aste (Ctrl+V). Place a selection tool cursor inside the TUTSCROLL window, and click and drag the CRUMPL3 copy to position it better than the way it pasted in.

7. Choose **S**elect, **N**one (Ctrl+D).

8. Click on the RGB title on the Channels palette to return to the color composite view of TUTSCROL.

9. Choose **S**elect, **L**oad Selection, then pick #5. You'll see the marquee lines vaguely indicating the selected areas Photoshop has read from the darker areas of the CRUMPL3 image in Alpha channel #5.

10. Choose **S**elect, Hide **E**dges (Ctrl+H). The selection marquee becomes invisible so that you can see what's going on in the image while you edit it.

11. Choose **I**mage, **A**djust, Hue/Saturation (Ctrl+U).

12. Check the Preview check box if it isn't already checked.

13. Click and drag the Saturation slider to about +50, and click and drag the Lightness slider to -39. You're accentuating the color properties in the selected area, making them darker. In figure 2.9, the papyrus is taking on some "virtual aging."

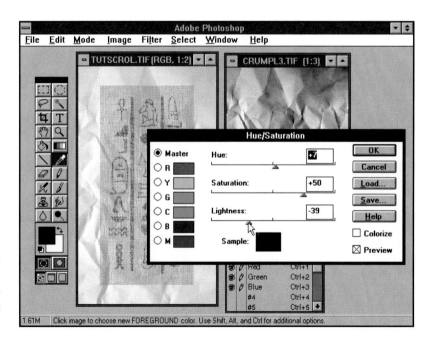

Figure 2.9

The Hue/Saturation command only affects the selected areas in the TUTSCROL image.

14. Click and drag the Hue slider ever so slightly to the right. This makes the selected areas in TUTSCROL shift in color, giving the papyrus a little color variation.

The values used in the last steps with the Hue/Saturation command are fairly arbitrary. They looked good at the time these figures were captured, but you might get equally eye-pleasing results by adding different Hue/Saturation values to the piece yourself. Feel free to experiment.

15. When you're happy with the Hue and Saturation adjustments, click on OK.

16. Press Ctrl+D to deselect the selection area.

17. Choose File, Save to save your work up to this point.

Creating an Ancient Outline for the Ancient Papyrus

The papyrus looks great now, but you need to clean up the border and get rid of the crumpled paper detail evident in the white border in preparation for creating a custom selection around the papyrus. To do so, follow these steps:

1. Choose the Rectangular Marquee tool, and then click and diagonally drag along the papyrus edge so that only the papyrus is included in the marquee border.

2. Choose Select, Inverse.

3. Press the Backspace (or Del) key. Everything except the papyrus is removed and replaced with background white color, as shown in figure 2.10.

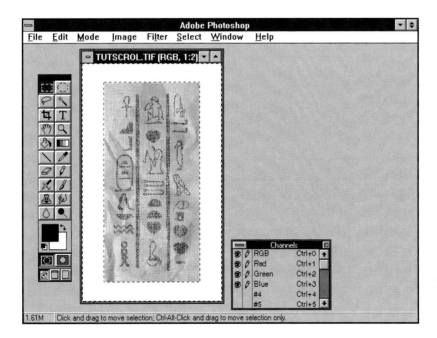

Figure 2.10

Deleting a selection removes it and replaces it with the current background color.

Creating a Freehand Edge to the Papyrus

The next set of steps calls for a creative use of the Lasso tool. You want the border of the papyrus, which looks a few millennia old, to bear a similar appearance. The solution is to trace roughly around the edge of the papyrus, deliberately avoiding perfectly straight lines like the Rectangular Marquee tool produces. Follow these steps:

1. Choose the Lasso tool.

2. Click and drag around the edge of the papyrus in TUTSCROL. Make some sharp turns along the way to simulate nicks and flaws.

3. When you've got a less-than-perfect marquee border around the papyrus, choose **S**elect, Sa**v**e Selection, #4. This overwrites the CLOTH2 pattern in the Alpha channel, but it's okay because you no longer need it. Channels contribute to a larger than necessary image file size, so reusing an Alpha channel this way is a prudent technique.

Emphasizing the Papyrus Edges To Stand Out from the Marble Backdrop

Before copying Tut's love letter to the TUTMARBL image you'll see how to make the selection you just created rough-edged by using a special painting mode applied along a path. *Paths* are vector information that are not part of an image. They're simply mapped to the monitor so that they're visible, and they can be used to define areas without messing up the image. Paths can have a stroke or fill applied to them, and it's only in this way that they contribute visually to a bitmap image.

You can design a path using the Paths palette's Pen tool, but the following is a much easier way, especially applicable to this assignment.

1. Press F9 to call the Paths palette to Photoshop's workspace.

2. Click on the command button on the Paths palette, and then choose Make Path from the drop-down list.

3. Type **.5** in the Tolerance field in the Make Path dialog box, as seen in figure 2.11. Photoshop will create a path based on the freehand selection you created, with a fidelity to the selection not varying more than half a pixel. Click on OK.

4. Choose Save Path from the command button drop-down list on the Paths palette, and accept the default name of Path 1 for your new path. You now have a permanent path in the TUTSCROL image. Clicking on the check mark next to the path title on the palette deactivates it, and clicking a second time makes both the check mark and the path reappear. Leave the path check marked and consequentially visible and active.

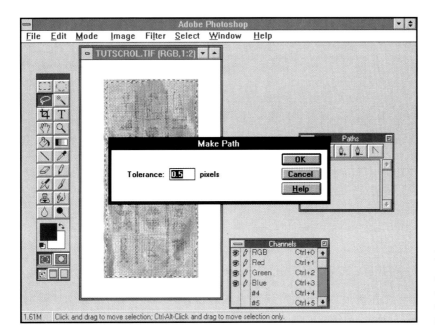

Figure 2.11

Paths can be based on selection areas, but can't be used to select an image area for copying or editing.

Adding a Fringe to the Love Note

Photoshop's Brushes palette puts a lot of different painting and editing functionality at your fingertips. Besides Normal, there are several different modes that you can apply paint with, all accessed from the drop-down list on the palette when a painting tool is active. You won't actually be brush stroking in the next set of steps because the painting modes also can be automatically applied to an image when a path shape has been defined.

The Dissolve mode in Photoshop spritzes a random pattern of foreground color pixels according to a fill or outline defined in an image. This is a great mode for adding a diffuse randomness to image areas, and as you'll see, it also can be used to simulate fraying of an ancient papyrus love letter.

1. Click on the Invert colors icon button. This changes the default colors to foreground white, background black.

2. Choose the Paintbrush tool. This activates the Brushes palette. Choose a medium tip from the second row of the Brushes palette, and choose Dissolve from the drop-down modes list on the palette.

3. Click on the command button on the Paths palette (make sure Path 1 has a check mark next to it—the TUTSCROL path is visible), and choose Stroke Path.

4. The papyrus now has a rough edge and looks more realistic, as shown in figure 2.12.

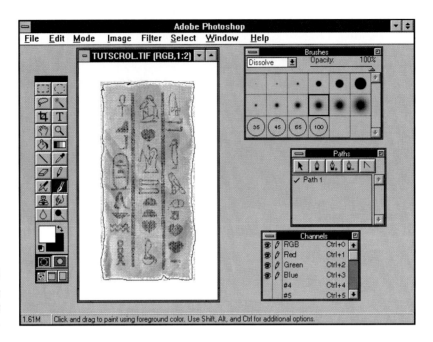

Figure 2.12

Dissolve mode disperses color pixels in a random fashion.

Accurately Selecting a Fuzzy Border

You need to select and copy the papyrus next. This would be a problem with a lot of other image editing software because the outline of the papyrus is now pretty intricate. But this is small potatoes when you're using Photoshop because you can design a selection border in an Alpha channel that closely matches the present outline of the papyrus with the same path and tools you used in the last steps. Here's how.

1. Click on the #4 channel title on the Channels palette. This gives you a view of the rectangle that you defined as a selection earlier around the papyrus image.

   Notice that the path you defined tagged along and is now in view over the rectangle selection.

2. Click again on Stroke Path from the Paths palette's drop-down list.

   The path gets the same foreground white paint treatment as the RGB color view of the papyrus, as shown in figure 2.13. The dissolve around the edges won't be identical to the stroke applied to the color image because Dissolve mode is random. But the selection with Dissolve mode applied basically will match the outline of the papyrus in the RGB view, and will further contribute to the papyrus's realistic look when you copy the image.

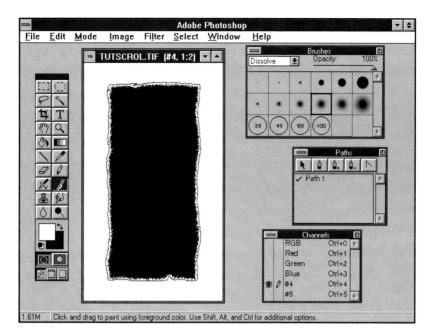

Figure 2.13
Dissolve mode creates a naturalistic border around a selection area in an Alpha channel.

Positioning the Papyrus within the Marble Image

You're basically finished with the TUTSCROL image. In the next few steps, it'll be copied to the Clipboard after the modified selection border has been loaded.

If you decide to save the TUTSCROL image (and there's no reason you shouldn't), it would be a good idea to delete Alpha channel #5 first. Alpha channel #5 contains the CRUMPL3 image, and you no longer need it because it has served its purpose to add aging to the color papyrus image. Channels contribute needlessly to overall image file sizes, and this in turn congests your hard disk space and eats up your RAM.

To delete a channel, first go to its view by clicking on its channel title on the Channels palette. Then click on the command button, and choose Delete Channel. The channel is gone, and you are returned to the RGB color composite view of the image.

You do, however, want to hang on to channel #4, the border you edited with Dissolve mode applied along a path. This is the only way you have of selecting the papyrus out of the white background at a future time.

1. Choose **S**elect, **L**oad Selection, #4. This loads the edited rectangular selection area around the papyrus.

2. Choose **E**dit, **C**opy.

3. Open the TUTMARBL.TIF image that you saved to your hard disk at the beginning of this assignment.

4. Choose **E**dit, **P**aste.

5. Choose **I**mage, **R**otate, Free. A boundary box that sports little corner handles appears around the floating papyrus selection.

6. Place your cursor inside the top left corner handle and click and drag down and to the left ever so slightly (see fig. 2.14). Give the papyrus a casual look as it's displayed against the marble. Leave some room to the left of it so that you have room to add a title to this museum poster.

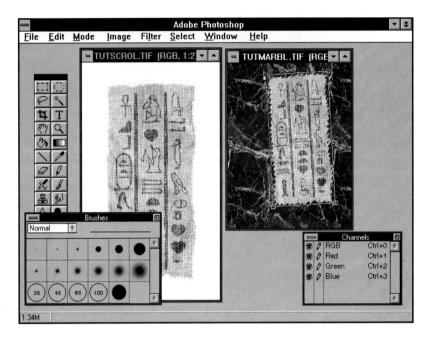

Figure 2.14

Free rotation of a selection can be used to rotate an image to any degree.

7. When you think you've rotated the papyrus enough, click inside the boundary box. Your cursor turns into a gavel, and clicking "nails" the selection to the desired degree of rotation.

8. Choose Select, Save Selection.

9. Choose File, Save As, name the image NOMA.TIF (for Nedrow Museum of Art), and save it to your hard disk. Make sure the Save Alpha Channels check box is marked in the Save As dialog box.

Adding Dimension by Creating a Shadow

The piece looks pretty stunning, doesn't it? But it's lacking a certain dimensionality. This can be fixed by adding a shadow beneath the papyrus. You can copy the selection area you saved last, create a new channel for it to reside while you edit it, and then copy and paste it behind the selection of the papyrus from the color view of the image.

1. Click on the #4 channel title on the Channels palette. This displays the selection area of the papyrus within the NOMA.TIF image.

2. Choose Select, All (Ctrl+A), and then Edit, Copy.

3. Click on the command button on the Channels palette, and then choose New Channel from the drop-down list.

4. Accept the default name of channel #5, and click on OK.

5. Choose Filter, Blur, Gaussian Blur.

6. Set the Radius of the Gaussian Blur to 6 pixels, and then click on OK.

7. The entire selected area fuzzes out, as shown in figure 2.15.

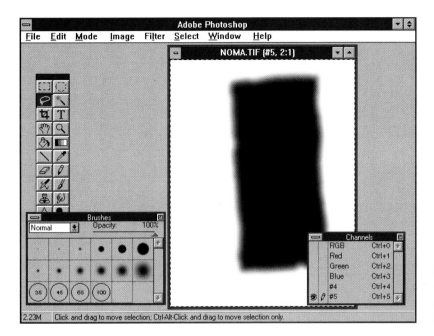

Figure 2.15

The Gaussian Blur is good for creating realistic shadows.

8. With the fuzzy copy of the entire channel still selected, choose Edit, Copy.

9. Click on the RGB title on the Channels palette to restore your view of the NOMA image to its color composite.

10. Choose Select, Load Selection, #4. A marquee border appears around the papyrus as it sits on top of the marble.

11. Choose Edit, Paste Behind. The fuzzy channel copy pastes over the marble, but behind the active selection area of the papyrus.

12. Make sure a selection tool is chosen to activate the Brushes palette's modes feature. I like to use the Lasso tool on such occasions, but you can use any selection tool.

13. Click on the Brushes palette's modes drop-down list and choose Multiply as the active mode. The Brushes palette modes act as compositing tools when a selection tool is active, and this adds a different dimension of functionality to the modes. You'll notice that the white background of the fuzzy selection has disappeared. The Multiply mode has this sort of effect on pure white selection areas.

14. Press the 9 key on the keyboard keypad (or number 9 on the top row below the function keys). This knocks the Opacity of the black portions of the fuzzy copy down to 90 %, as shown in figure 2.16.

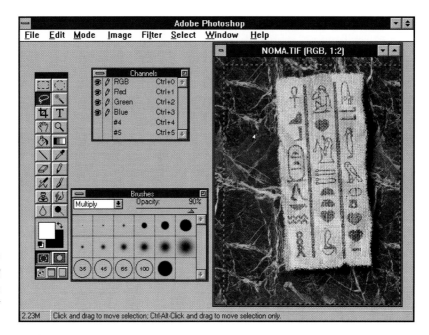

Figure 2.16

Multiply mode can be used in compositing a selection area, or as a painting mode.

15. Click and drag the copy to a point below and slightly to the right of the papyrus area.

16. When you're happy with its positioning, either click outside the marquee border, or choose **S**elect, **N**one to composite the copy into the RGB view of NOMA.TIF.

17. Choose **F**ile, **S**ave. You're done!

In the last steps, an extra Alpha channel was created to make a temporary workspace where a filter could be applied to the image. This was done for convenience's sake, and the blurry copy of the selection area from channel #4 is not used to provide Photoshop with information to create a selection area.

In this instance, the blurry area's purpose was to serve as visual detail to be added to the image, and channel #5 can be deleted at any time now as this workspace is no longer needed.

Measuring and Rotating Type for the Poster

You almost have a museum poster now. The only thing missing from it is some type that tells the audience what this poster is announcing.

Many museum posters run type at a vertical angle to create a "look," and this synthetic museum poster doesn't have to be any different. There's a problem with running type up and down in an image whose dimensions are taller than wider, though. If you enter type the only way Photoshop has provision for—horizontally—and then try to use the Rotate command, the floating selection disappears off the page or at very least, is truncated.

A good solution is to create a New **F**ile based on a selection area you define in the NOMA.TIF image. You can "trick" Photoshop into offering up the image dimensions, and then manually reverse the width and height to provide a landscape workspace for the type. Then you can rotate the type once you're happy with it, and copy it into the NOMA image.

Lithos Bold was used in the following figures, but if you don't own this font, TUTTITLE.TIF is on the *Adobe Photoshop NOW! CD-ROM*. It's a finished type image that was used in the creation of this poster, and you can substitute it the next few steps if you want to create this poster design. Follow these steps even if you don't own Lithos because this is an invaluable trick you'll want to make your own!

1. Make sure that you have black as the background color selected on Photoshop's color selection boxes.

2. Click and drag on the NOMA image window so that some gray area around the image is exposed. You need to select an area of the image that's clear up to the image edge.

3. Choose the Rectangular Marquee tool, and then click and drag an area from top to bottom to the left of the papyrus, as shown in figure 2.17. Make certain you don't include any of the papyrus, though.

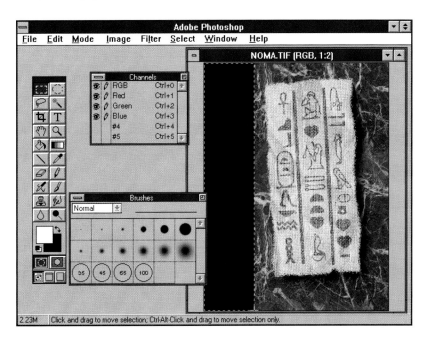

Figure 2.17

Photoshop provides a gray "backing" to an image so that you can fully select areas to their border.

4. Press the Del key. This removes a portion of the marble background, and replaces it with black, which is the future site for our text.

5. Choose Edit, Copy. You won't be using the copied black selection, but you want Photoshop to measure the area to provide new file dimensions you'll be rearranging next.

6. Choose File, New (Ctrl+N). Photoshop anticipates that you want a new file with the dimensions, resolution, and color mode identical to what's on the Clipboard. But Photoshop's only half right on this occasion, and you can avail yourself of the New File info and alter it slightly before clicking on OK.

7. The default Width that Photoshop displays in the New File dialog box should read 780 pixels, and the New File Height is how far you dragged the Rectangular Marquee tool in the last steps. (I selected 160 pixels; you may have a little more or less.) Change these numbers around so that the Width is 160 pixels (or whatever) and the Height is 780 pixels. Leave all other settings alone, and click on OK.

8. Choose **S**elect, **A**ll (Ctrl+A), and then press the Del key. You have an all black Untitled-2 image now, perfect for adding foreground white type to.

9. Press Ctrl+D to **S**elect, **N**one.

10. Choose the Type tool, and then click an insertion point in the Untitled-2 image area.

11. If you have Lithos, choose it from the **F**ont list, check the **B**old Style, choose **A**lignment Centered, **S**ize: 30 points, Lea**d**ing 25 points.

12. Type **THE LOVE LETTERS OF $$$Enter$$$ KING TUTANKHAMEN** in the type entry field, and then click on OK. You'll get your type as a floating selection that you can copy to the Clipboard in whole now, as shown in figure 2.18.

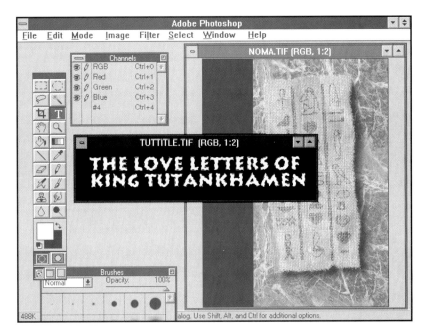

Figure 2.18

Type always appears as entered on an image background as a floating, repositionable selection.

*30-point Lithos with 25-point leading was not a number I picked out of a hat in the preceding steps, but rather an educated "guesstimate" based on a few truths going on here. 160 pixels at 150 pixel/inch resolution is about an inch, which can be discovered by entering this amount in the **I**mage Size dialog box under the Image menu, and switching the Pixels field to Inches. Because an inch has 72 points, 30 point type set on two lines will comfortably sit within the height of the Untitled-2 image space.*

As for the leading, display type (type you use at greater than 18 points), you should always have "tight" leading of anywhere between 85 to 100% of the type size. Smaller font sizes, such as text set at 12 points, typically use looser leading for readability's sake.

Fitting the Type into the Museum Poster

You'll take advantage of Photoshop's power to interpolate data next. Interpolation is the fancy term for the process of stretching and otherwise distorting a bitmap selection. If you've tried pulling on a bitmap image in other image editing programs, you've probably been sorely disappointed by the results, which can look jagged and artificial. Photoshop, however, interpolates an "in-between" pixel based on two neighboring pixels you may stretch apart, and the in-between value smoothes any transition forced by distorting an area.

Using the Scale command, you can "fit" the type in the next steps so that it's a little wider and becomes a more dominant visual element against the black area in NOMA.TIF. The wonderful plasticity of type treated as a graphic becomes evident next.

1. Choose Edit, Copy.

2. You can close Untitled-2 now without saving it. You presently have the image area you need on the Clipboard.

3. Choose Edit, Paste (Ctrl+V), and then Image, Rotate, 90CCW.

4. Choose Image, Effects, Scale, and then place your cursor in the top left corner handle of the Scale boundary box.

5. Play with the two sides of the type selection you're scaling so that the type fills more of the black background area, as seen in figure 2.19.

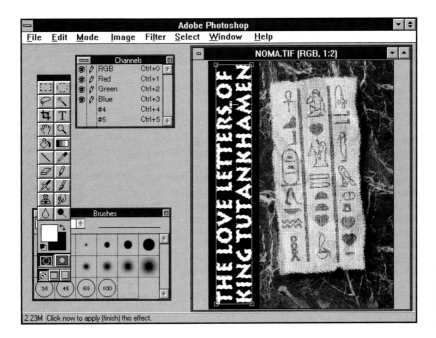

Figure 2.19

The Scale command makes the boundary of a selection area pliable.

6. Click and drag on the other boundary box handles until you have an aesthetically pleasing type selection.

7. Click inside of the boundary box. This "nails" the selection to the desired degree of scaling.

8. Reposition your newly scaled type by placing the cursor inside the marquee border. Center it within the black background area.

9. Click outside the marquee to composite the white type with the black background.

A Finishing Touch to a Museum Piece

You should have some space left at the bottom of NOMA.TIF for a location for the historic unveiling of the Boy King's love letters. In figure 2.20, you can see the finished poster, with text added, and a little logo placed in front of it. Logos can be created as part of a typeface with a number of typeface creation software, such as Fontographer, Illustrator, or CorelDRAW!.

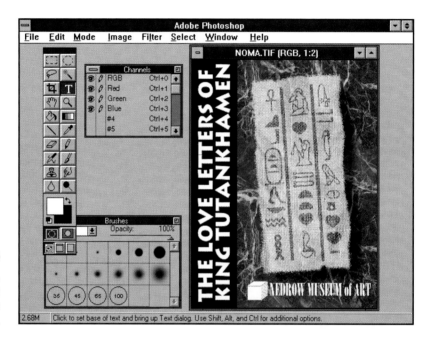

Figure 2.20

The finished poster. Coming next month: FiestaWare Discoveries from the LeBrea Tar Pits.

If you have a drawing-type program, such as CorelDRAW! or Adobe Illustrator, you can add rotated or stretched type, and other graphic designs without even using the Type tool.

Design your graphic in a vector program and then export it as an Encapsulated PostScript (*.EPS) file. Import the graphic into Photoshop and add a New Channel to the image. Copy the EPS image (choose Select, All, then Edit, Copy) into the Alpha channel. The graphic becomes its own selection border this way. When you Load the Selection, you eliminate the white background from it as you copy it, and then it can be placed into your host image!

PART TWO:

Photoshop and Image Types

Chapter 3

Creating a Collage with Scanned Images

The flatbed color scanner opens a world of possibilities for the computer graphics designer. When you have a photo, but not the negative, a scanner is essential. More importantly, a flatbed scanner opens the door to directly sampling real life objects—coins, floor tile, just about anything that's fairly flat.

This chapter's assignment moves away from commercial art in pursuit of the creation of a digital collage for art's sake. Different items were scanned as grayscale and color images, and you'll see on the following pages how expertly Photoshop serves as an integrator of different electronic media.

Breaking Artistic Conventions in Digital Artwork

To illustrate an underwater scene as a collage means that the conventions of photorealism can be largely ignored. Few individuals look at a collage and gasp, "My, what an interesting photograph!" So, unencumbered by having to design accurate perspective and lighting sources like those in everyday assignments, feel free to gather source material for a digital collage from a number of different places.

Different degrees of object depth and relative sizes of things as they appear in real life don't matter here. As source material for the collage shown in this chapter, the only consideration in acquiring images with a UMAX 840 flatbed color scanner is the size of the objects as they relate to each other in the finished piece.

Scanning Different Images with a Beginning Reference Size

The scene in this assignment includes a fish, some seaweed, and some other images to be added to a stylized background that's created entirely within Photoshop. My first scan was of the main attraction in the collage, a rubber stamp impression of a fish. The literal size of the rubber stamp dictates the size and resolution of a background image for the collage that will frame the fish image and leave room for other subterranean artifacts.

The Image on the *Adobe Photoshop NOW! CD-ROM*

In this chapter, you'll learn some valuable tips to use with your scanner, but you don't have to own a flatbed to follow along in the creation of this collage. The *Adobe Photoshop NOW! CD-ROM* has all the sample images that are used in this assignment. Look in the CHAP03 subdirectory when a particular image is referenced in the following steps. You'll be able to participate in the creation of this collage beginning with step 5.

1. First, an old rubber stamp of a tropical fish is inked up and stamped on a sheet of white paper.

2. The rubber stamped image of the fish is scanned at 100% scaling (no pun intended), 150 pixels/inch, and a Grayscale mode is used.

Although rubber stamp images appear to contain only black-and-white information, the ink that leaves a rubber stamp impression soaks into the paper to create fringe areas around a rubber stamped design. These fringe areas contain less than 100% coverage of ink. If your scanner has different settings for different image types, don't use Line Art (or Bitmap, 1-bit per pixel) as the mode with which you scan rubber stamped images. A rubber stamp impression actually is a grayscale type image. To be faithful to the source material, scan it using the matching bit-depth of Grayscale (8 bits/pixel).

3. The scan is completed, and because the flatbed scanner used was TWAIN compliant, the fish image immediately appeared in Photoshop's workspace, as shown in figure 3.1. I pressed Ctrl+R to display Photoshop's Rulers around the fish, and found that Untitled-1 is about 1.7" wide by 2.3" long.

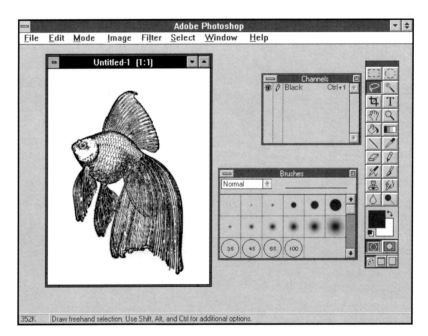

Figure 3.1

Scanners that use the TWAIN interface can be accessed directly by Photoshop.

4. Knowing these dimensions, you can create a properly sized background for the collage. The Untitled-1 scan is saved as FISH.TIF and then closed.

5. Click on the Default colors icon button. This ensures that the new file you create next will have a white background.

6. Choose File, New (Ctrl+N), and enter Width: 3.5 pixels, Height: 2.5 pixels, Resolution: 150 pixels/inch, Mode: RGB Color. Then click on OK.

7. Press F7 to display the Colors palette. Choose the HSB Color model from the Colors palette's drop-down list, accessed by clicking on the palette's command button. You need to specify colors, and the HSB model is the easiest to work with.

Creating a Tropical Background

The concept here is to portray an underwater setting that has a little warmth to it. New foreground and background colors need to be defined that reflect this feeling. To begin the collage work, you'll use the Gradient tool to suggest depth and tonal variation for the background image.

1. Click and drag the sliders on the Colors palette to H: 207°, S: 62%, B: 100%. This is the foreground color for the Gradient fill. This is an arbitrary color; you can select what you feel is most eye-catching.

2. Choose the Paintbrush tool. Then, on the Brushes palette, select a small hard tip, and set the mode to Normal and the Opacity to 100%

3. With the Paintbrush, make a small stroke or two of color on the Colors palette scratch pad.

The scratch pad is a great place to store a color that you don't want to add to the swatches on the bottom of the Colors palette. New swatches must be saved or appended to make them a permanent part of any swatch collection. Unless you select the Save or Append command, when you select a different palette (from the *.ACO files in the Photoshop PALETTES subdirectory), you'll lose the swatches you added to your default Colors palette.

If, however, you have the Restore Windows check box marked under the File, Preferences, General command, your scratch pad area will always retain the colors you place there, from session to session and from palette selection to palette selection.

4. Click on the Invert colors icon button. Then from the Colors palette set H: 101° S: 73%, and B: 38% for the second color to use with the Gradient tool.

5. Stroke a sample of this color on the scratch pad, and then click on the Invert colors icon button to return the pale blue specified earlier to the foreground color.

6. Double-click on the Gradient tool and make sure the Normal Style and Linear Type radio buttons are selected, and Midpoint Skew is set at 50%. Click on OK.

7. Click and drag the Gradient tool (see fig. 3.2). Try to make the break point for the fill occur about a third of the way down on Untitled-2 so that the bottom third of the background piece is fairly murky looking.

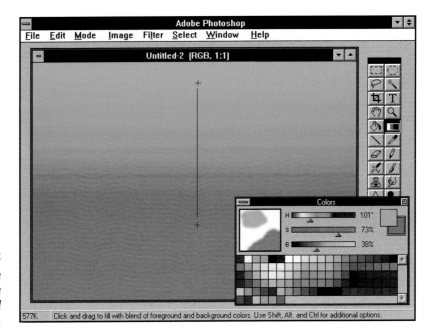

Figure 3.2

The Gradient tool creates a transition between foreground and background colors.

Adding a Doodle to the Background Image

While some underwater creatures will be the highlight of the collage's foreground activity, something can be done to this background image to add a little more visual pizzazz. BLOBS.TIF began its life as a collection of felt-tip doodles on a sheet of white paper, intended to parody the reflections on an ocean's surface seen from underwater. BLOBS.TIF was designed and then scanned so that it was a tad larger than the 3.5" width of the background image. This was done so that these "ocean highlights" would fill the top of the image frame. The doodle was scanned in a Grayscale mode primarily to conserve system resources, but also because its purpose is to serve as selection area information in an Alpha channel, whose color depth never exceeds 8 bits/pixel (grayscale).

1. Open the BLOBS.TIF image from the *Adobe Photoshop NOW! CD-ROM.*

2. Press Ctrl+A, and then Ctrl+C to select and copy the entire image.

3. Press F6 to make the Channels palette visible if it isn't already open in your workspace.

4. Click on the Channels palette command button and choose New Channel from the drop-down list.

5. In the New Channels dialog box, make sure Color Indicates: Selected Areas radio button is chosen, and then click on OK.

6. You're immediately presented with a view of Alpha channel #2. Press Ctrl+V to copy the image of the blobs to this channel.

7. Click on the Black channel title on the Channels palette, then choose **S**elect, **L**oad Selection. The copy of the blobs image in the Alpha channel acts as its own selection border from the main view of the image, as shown in figure 3.3.

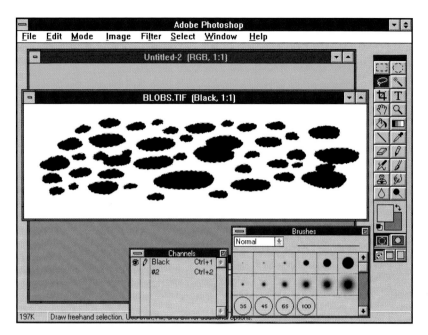

Figure 3.3
Selection information in an Alpha channel can be based on the image you want to select.

8.   Press Ctrl+C to copy the blobs.

9.   Close the BLOBS.TIF image, and don't save it. You're done with it.

10.   Click on Untitled-2's Channels palette command button and choose New Channel.

11.   Press Ctrl+V to paste the blobs into the channel.

12.   Position the pasted blobs toward the upper third of the Alpha channel view, and then press Ctrl+D to finish compositing them into the channel. You'll fine-tune this selection's position next, so don't spend too much time getting them into place now.

13.   Click on the RGB title on the Channels palette, and then choose Select, Load Selection.

14.   Choose a selection tool (the Lasso tool is good). While holding down the Alt and Ctrl keys, place your cursor inside a marquee border, and click and drag the selection area into a pleasing position relative to the top of Untitled-2. You're not moving any image areas, just the selection border.

15.   Choose Select, Save Selection, #4. This overwrites the information you originally pasted into the Alpha channel, replacing it with your properly positioned blobs.

Adding Creative Lighting to the Background Image

Now that the selection area in the Alpha channel is positioned, it's time to use it along with the Gradient tool to make the background image for the collage shimmer.

1.   Double-click on the Gradient tool. In the Type field, click the **R**adial radio button, and then click on OK.

2.   Click on the Default colors icon button, and then click on the Invert colors icon so that the foreground color is white.

3. Click on the Background color selection box on the Colors palette. This makes it active—it doesn't change it to the foreground color.

4. Choose a turquoise color by clicking and dragging on the HSB sliders on the Colors palette. H: 169°, S: 92%, and B: 51% are seaworthy.

5. Choose Select, Load Selection.

6. Click and drag the Gradient tool from the center of the marquee of the blobs to the edge of the Untitled-2 image window, as shown in figure 3.4.

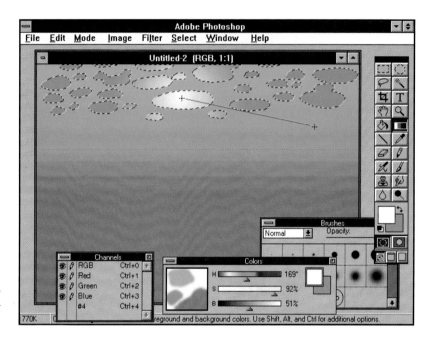

Figure 3.4

The Gradient tool can be used to simulate different types of lighting.

Adding Digitized Flora to the Virtual Ocean

Scanning flat illustrations contributes only one type of medium to this digital collage. I thought it would be fun to use scans of actual, physical objects in this underwater scene. A few sprigs of fern were individually scanned as RGB color images at 50% size. The resolution was set at 150 ppi to keep these rather large fronds in scale with the rest of the Untitled-2 images.

When you open the fern images files in the next steps, you'll note that they appear lackluster when compared to the brilliant, rich hues of the digital background, but you'll correct that shortly. Because the ferns were directly scanned at a fairly high ppi, there's a good amount of digital information to edit, and the corrections will look photographically convincing.

Pennies, ferns with clumps of dirt still lodged in them, and other potential candidates for direct sampling via a flatbed scanner can damage this expensive device unless proper precautions are taken. If you place anything other than a sheet of paper or photo on the scanning surface (the glass plate), put a sheet of Plexiglas or acetate between your source and the plate first. Scanners are extremely sensitive, and a properly cut piece of clean, transparent material should not be visible in the scan.

Also be cautious about the edges of the scanner surface. Most flatbed scanners have a rubber seal around the glass plate to keep airborne materials from leaking through to the delicate electronics, but this seal may not be dirt- or water-tight.

1. Open the PLANT1.TIF image from the *Adobe Photoshop NOW! CD-ROM*. As you can see, the varying thickness of the fern casts a shadow against the white of the scanner's document cover.

2. Choose the Lasso tool. Roughly trace around the outline of the fern image to exclude the broad areas of discolored white background, as shown in figure 3.5.

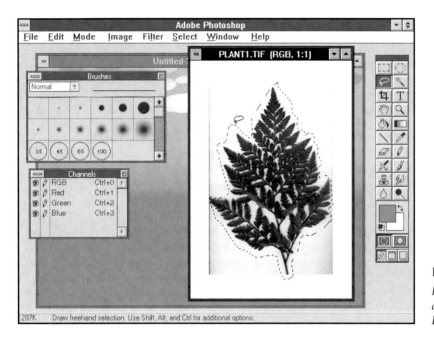

Figure 3.5

Include only the whitest areas of background in the Lasso tool selection.

3. Press Ctrl+C, and then click on the command button on the Channels palette.

4. Choose New Channel, accept the defaults, and then click on OK.

5. Press Ctrl+V. Now press Ctrl+D to copy and then deselect the fern selection in the channel.

6. Double-click on the Magic Wand tool. Set the Tolerance to 40. Click on OK to return to the workspace.

7. Click on a gray area that was included in your copied selection, as shown in figure 3.6. Do not click over any of the fern.

8. Choose Select, Similar.

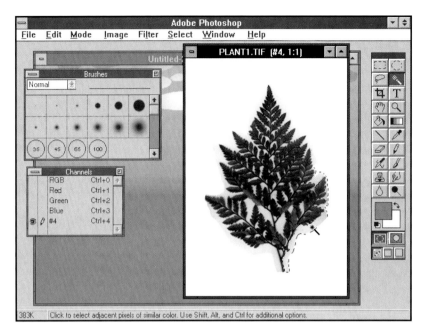

Figure 3.6

The Magic Wand tool creates selection areas based on tonal and color similarities, not geometry.

9. Click on the Default colors icon button.

10. Press the Del key. Congratulations! You now have an accurate selection border for the fern defined in the Alpha channel.

Creating Hyper-Real Seaweed

It's time for a reality check. If you can accept the notion that ferns look similar to seaweed, then you're ready for the next excursion past logic into the world of pure art. As mentioned earlier, the scanned fern looks pretty lifeless compared to the rich-looking virtual ocean. But the ferns do have a lot of *tonal* detail. If you only modify their hue and saturation, the grayscale component in the RGB image remains about the same; consequently, the amount of visual detail remains the same.

To turn a dull, realistic fern into the sort of plastic doodad you use to pepper the bottom of a goldfish bowl, follow these steps:

1. Choose **E**dit, **C**opy (Ctrl+C), and then Save the PLANT1.TIF image to your hard disk. Minimize the image to an icon on the workspace to keep the workspace clear and conserve system resources.

2. Press Ctrl+V, and then click and drag the copied fern to the right of the Untitled-2 image. It's okay to let the bottom of the paste fall out of the Untitled-2 image window. The scan of the rubber stamp fish will be the main attraction in the collage, and room in the center of the background image shouldn't become too crowded as you add other elements.

3. Choose **I**mage, **A**djust, Hue/Saturation (or press Ctrl+U).

4. Make sure the Preview box is checked, and then check the Colorize box.

5. Click and drag the sliders to set H: 115°, S: 100%, and B: 3% (these are arbitrary values and your personal aesthetics may influence these numbers), as shown in figure 3.7.

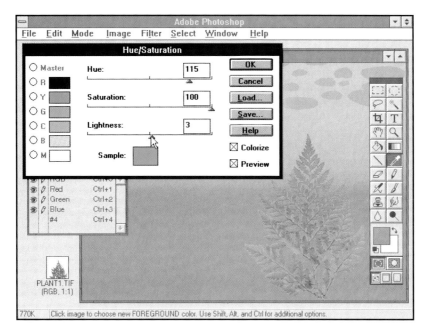

Figure 3.7
The Colorize command assigns a single Hue to an image without affecting relative tonal densities.

6. Choose **S**elect, **D**efringe, enter 1 pixel in the dialog box, and then click on OK.

7. Press Ctrl+D to composite the colorized fern into the background image.

Using the Image To Vary the Vegetation

Additional image files of ferns and other pedestrian growths found on the *Adobe Photoshop NOW! CD-ROM* can be used to cover the ocean floor in this collage. For the finished piece, I used only three plants and applied different shades using the Colorize feature to make them appear different.

I encountered one drawback in directly scanning the ferns, and that was their size. Because most flatbed scanners have a maximum surface size of 8 1/2 by 14 ", it was unfeasible to place the ferns at an angle when they were acquired. The solution to achieving wafting plastic ferns in the ocean seascape is to use some of the treasure buried in the **I**mage menu, as you'll discover in the next few steps.

1. Open the PLANT2.TIF image from the *Adobe Photoshop NOW! CD-ROM*.

2. Follow the same procedures for placing, tracing, copying, and selecting the fern image into a New Alpha channel as you did with the PLANT1 image. (Steps 1–10 in the last exercise.)

3. Click on the RGB channel title, and then choose **S**elect, **L**oad Selection.

4. Press Ctrl+U, check the Colorize box, and this time, play with the hue of the Colorize feature a little. I got pleasing results with Hue settings that ranged from 90 to 130 degrees. Keep the Saturation around 100%, and leave the Brightness at 0. Then click on OK.

5. Press Ctrl+C, and then minimize the PLANT2 image down to icon size.

6. Press Ctrl+V, and paste the fern from PLANT2 into Untitled-2. Then choose **I**mage, **F**lip, Horizontal.

7. Choose Image, Rotate, Free.

8. Place your cursor inside a corner handle of the rotate boundary box, and then click and drag counterclockwise, as shown in figure 3.8.

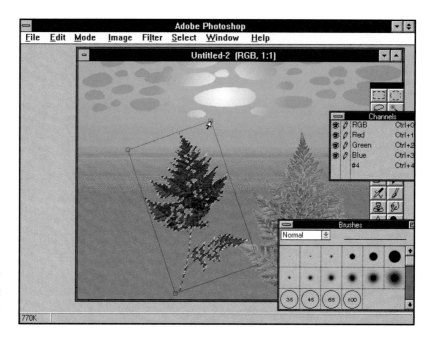

Figure 3.8

Use the Free Rotate submenu item to rotate a selection to any angle.

9. When you're happy with the angle of rotation, click inside the boundary box.

10. Place your cursor inside the marquee borders, and then click and drag the selection to a location toward the bottom of the background image. Allow the bottom of the selection to fall outside of the image window.

11. When the fern is in position, press Ctrl+D to deselect it.

A lot of Adobe literature refers to clicking outside of a selection border to deselect an image area and composite it into a background image. And many experienced Photoshop users have adopted this practice as well.

But be forewarned that this action can have unexpected results sometimes, particularly with mouse users. You always risk the possibility of accidentally dragging a selection area in the process of clicking outside of a selection border. This is the result of working too quickly, and sometimes a little carelessly. If a selection shifts by as little as one pixel when you move outside the area to click, your selection area won't be composited correctly. You should immediately press Ctrl+Z to Edit, Undo.

My personal preference is to let compositing be a "hands-off" procedure for accuracy's sake, and this is why the Ctrl+D keyboard command shortcut frequently is referenced throughout this book.

In figure 3.9, more digitized plant life has been colorized, rotated, and composited into the background image, using the same techniques covered in the last two sections. When you've completed this part, save the image as DEEPSEA.TIF to your hard disk. Be sure to check the **S**ave Alpha Channels check box in the TIFF Options dialog box.

Figure 3.9

The completed background image, awaiting its star.

Creating a Mask for a Fish

The FISH.TIF image you'll use as a foreground element in the DEEPSEA.TIF background needs a touch of glamour. Left as a grayscale image, the fish would be overwhelmed in a sea full of color and plastic ferns.

You create a selection area around the fish in FISH.TIF much the same way you did with the ferns, and use this selection mask for a dual purpose. The first purpose is to create a murky drop-shadow in the DEEPSEA.TIF image.

> *If a part of an image file you want to use in a collage needs enhancing, it's usually a good idea to do this work on it before copying it to a different image background.*

1. Open the FISH.TIF image from the *Adobe Photoshop NOW! CD-ROM.*

2. Choose the Magic Wand tool, and click on the white background area of the image, outside of the fish proper, as shown in figure 3.10.

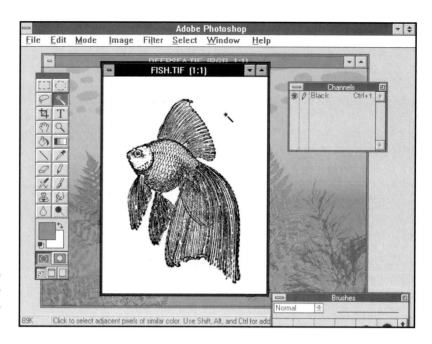

Figure 3.10

The Magic Wand tool selects adjacent pixels, not those inside the fish image.

3. Choose Select, Inverse.

4. Choose Select, Save Selection.

5. Click on the #2 Alpha channel title on the Channels palette.

6. Press Ctrl+C (see fig. 3.11). From the Alpha channel view, you've just copied the black selection area information to the Clipboard, and not the image of the fish.

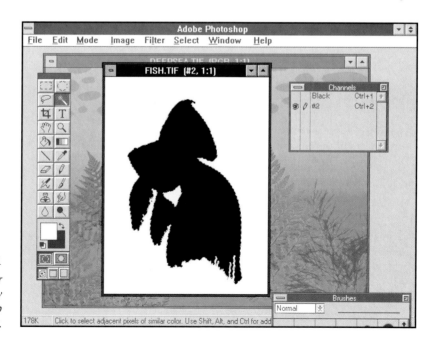

Figure 3.11

You can copy whatever channel view you presently have active in a Photoshop document.

7. Minimize the FISH.TIF image to make DEEPSEA.TIF the active image window.

8. Click on the #4 channel title on the Channels palette. Then double-click on the Eraser tool. When the dialog box asks, Erase entire channel?, choose OK.

9. Press Ctrl+V, and then Ctrl+D to composite the fish silhouette into the Alpha channel and deselect it.

10. Click on the RGB title on the channels palette. Then choose **S**elect, **L**oad Selection.

11. Still have a selection tool active? While holding down the Alt and Ctrl keys, click and drag inside the selection area to position the marquee outline similarly to that in figure 3.12.

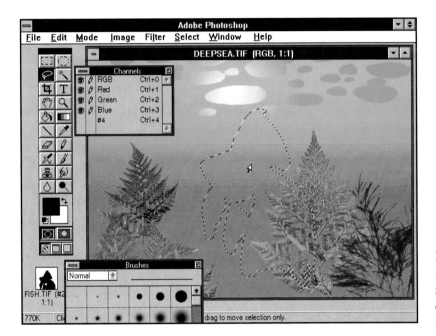

Figure 3.12

The Alt and Ctrl keys make only the selection area, not its contents, repositionable.

12. Choose **S**elect, **S**ave Selection, #4 to store the selection area.

Another way to reposition Alpha channel information from the color composite view of an image is to deselect the pencil icon next to the RGB title and to click on the pencil icon column next to the Alpha channel you're modifying. The pencil icon represents an editable quality assigned to individual channels, and the eye icon is a handy reference as to which channel is visible from your channel view of the document.

So, by making the RGB channel visible but uneditable (and the Alpha channel not visible but editable) you can actually edit between channels. See NRP's Inside Adobe Photoshop for Windows *for more information on working between channels this way.*

Creating Murk out of a Selection Area

As the selection area in the DEEPSEA image is presently defined, it's sharp and crisply matches the outline of the fish. But the purpose of this selection area is to edit the corresponding area in the RGB channel so that it appears murky. Unlike other bitmap image types (such as Indexed Color), you can soften an area's focus in an RGB image so that it looks photographic. As long as this option is here, let's put it to use in the next few steps.

1. Click on the #4 title on the Channels palette to display the view of the selection information.

2. Choose Filter, Blur, Gaussian Blur.

3. Type **4** pixels in the **R**adius field, and then click on OK.

4. Click on the RGB title on the Channels palette.

5. Choose **S**elect, **L**oad Selection. The marquee outline should look like that in figure 3.13. It reflects your application of the Gaussian Blur and has lost the distinct edge it had.

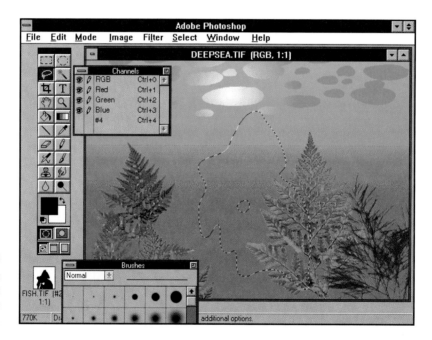

Figure 3.13

A blurred channel creates partially masked areas around the edges of a selection area.

6. Press Ctrl+H. This keeps the selection area active but hides the marquee edges so that you can see the image better.

7. Press Ctrl+L to display the Levels command.

8. Click and drag the Midpoint slider to the left to .71 or enter the value in the center input box. This brings only the selection area's pixels into a narrower range of tones, darkening and increasing the contrast, as shown in figure 3.14. Click on OK to apply the changes.

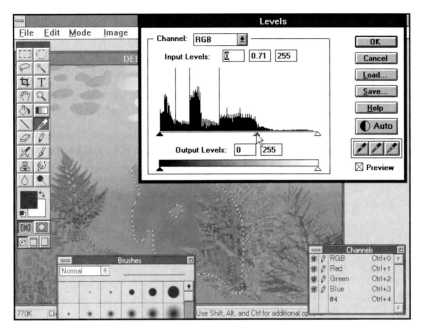

Figure 3.14
The Levels command redistributes the range of the pixels' brightness in a selected area.

9. Press Ctrl+F, the shortcut for applying the last-used filter, which was the Gaussian Blur. As you can see in figure 3.15, this action produces a blurring effect in the shape of the fish that gently tapers off.

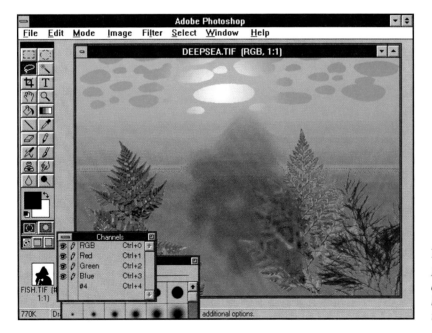

Figure 3.15
Blurred channel selections cause filters/editing to become the least effective toward the edges.

10. Press Ctrl+D, and then Ctrl+S to save your work up to this point.

Selectively Masking the Fish's Grayscale Image Area

It's time to doll up the star of the collage. The grayscale fish will need to be converted to RGB to color it, but before doing this a second Alpha channel needs to be created. The second channel will be used to mask the black lines of the fish so that only the white areas in the image window will be colored in. The Alpha channel created earlier will be used to select the colored-in whites, as well as the black design of the fish image.

1. Restore the FISH.TIF image as the active window in your workspace.

2. Choose the Magic Wand tool, and click on any white area of the image. Outside of the fish is fine.

3. Choose Select, Similar, and then choose Save Selection, New.

4. Press Ctrl+D, and then click on the #5 title on the Channels palette.

The selection process with the Magic Wand tool is an impressive one, but not exactly perfect. As you can see, there are small areas not included in the saved selection, and you don't want them to be missed in Photoshop's selection function.

5. Click on the Invert colors icon button, and then choose the Lasso tool.

6. Click and drag areas that are not completely black as seen in figure 3.16. When you release the mouse button and a marquee appears, press the Del key.

Figure 3.16

Areas deleted from the selection marquee become background black, serving as selection information.

You might want to click on the Default colors icon button, and then use the Pencil tool to clean up spots in the Alpha channel. The Pencil tool is a more appropriate tool for this type of work because, unlike the Paintbrush tool, the Pencil tool has no "spread." It produces clean, sharp, albeit slightly jagged strokes when used.

Creating Rainbow Trout with the Gradient Tool

You'll be using the Gradient tool once again in the next set of steps, this time to apply a brilliant rainbow gradient to our finny friend. Photoshop has the capability to move through the spectrum of hues during a gradient fill. You pick a foreground color, a background color, and a direction (Style) for the spectrum to cycle through, and Photoshop does the rest.

One of the most confusing aspects of assigning a Clockwise or Counterclockwise Style to a Gradient is that the Gradient options box doesn't provide you with any sort of visual clue as to what the effect will look like. Here's a mnemonic and a suggestion for getting the most out of a wonderful effect.

Remember Roy G. Biv from high school science (as in the red, orange, yellow, green, blue, indigo, and violet of a rainbow)? It's the mnemonic most of us were taught to help us remember the initials of the primary hues going counterclockwise on a color wheel. Think of Roy as someone back in high school to remember the counterclockwise order, and this will keep you straight as to which spectrum cycling is which.

If you ever have foreground and background colors that are neighbors in the hue spectrum, choose the direction of the Gradient Style to achieve the best effect. For instance, a foreground Red and a background Orange will produce a Gradient "dud" if you select Counterclockwise as the Style because the colors will cycle from Red to Orange, and then stop. But by choosing Clockwise as the Gradient Style, the colors will cycle as R, V, I, B, G, Y, and then to Orange. Then you're talking serious rainbow.

1. Click on the Black title on FISH.TIF's Channels palette.

2. Choose RGB mode from the **M**odes menu for the FISH.TIF image. You'll immediately be color-enabled with this file, which will increase its file size but still contain the two Alpha channels you created earlier.

3. From the Colors palette, choose a rich mustard foreground color and a pale blue background color.

You can mix different default swatch colors by varying Paintbrush tool opacities and stroking one color over another on the scratch pad. When you do this, you arrive at two shades you can sample with the Eyedropper tool.

4. Double-click on the Gradient tool, and click on the **C**lockwise Style radio button (**R**adial Type should still be selected from earlier). Then click on OK.

5. Choose **S**elect, **L**oad Selection, #5. All the white areas in the RGB view of FISH.TIF are now selected, and the black areas are masked.

6. Click and drag the Gradient tool cursor from the fish's head to the image window frame, as shown in figure 3.17.

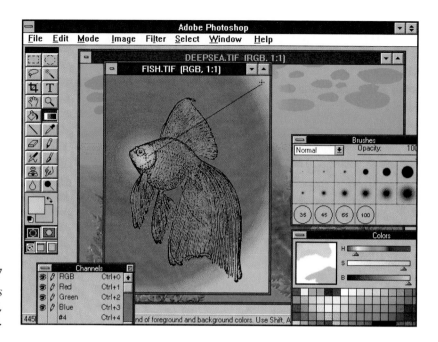

Figure 3.17

The Gradient tool produces a fill cycling Y, O, R, V, I, and ending at Blue.

7. Choose **S**elect, **L**oad Selection, #4. This selects the newly colored fish out of the background. Then press Ctrl+C to copy it.

8. Press Ctrl+Tab to toggle DEEPSEA.TIF back to the active image window.

9. Choose a selection tool. Then press Ctrl+V, and click and drag the pasted fish to the center of the DEEPSEA.TIF image, as shown in figure 3.18. Position it over and to the left of the area you Gaussian blurred earlier.

Figure 3.18

The pasted fish appears to be casting a murky shadow on the collage's background.

10. Press Ctrl+H to hide the marquee edges. If there's a fringe of rainbow color outside the fish border, use the **S**elect, **D**efringe command. A value of 1 pixel, if any, should be all you need to clean up the edge of the paste.

11. When you're happy with the position of the pasted selection, press Ctrl+D to deselect the paste and Ctrl+S to save the image to disk.

Adding a Finishing Touch to the Collage

You now have a pretty interesting collage composed of different source materials that a lot of people don't consider because they think a flatbed scanner is reserved for invoices, faxes, and a few family photos.

This next set of steps is optional, and they are definitely "gilding the lily" as art goes, but this was simply too much fun to resist. I bought a herd of gummi worms at the corner candy store and scanned them as RGB images at 100%. The results were glorious, and frankly, I felt that the rubber stamp fish needed a treat after all this Channel-swimming. To add fish food to the collage, follow these final steps.

1. Open the WORMHERD.TIF image from the *Adobe Photoshop NOW! CD-ROM*, as shown in figure 3.19.

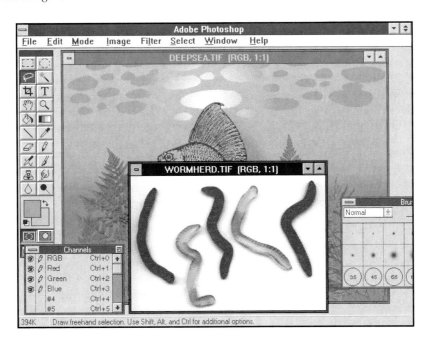

Figure 3.19

WORMHERD.TIF is an example of directly sampling real objects with a scanner.

2. Zoom into a 4:1 viewing resolution of the WORMHERD image. Use the Hand tool to reposition your view so that a single gummi worm is focused on.

3. Double-click on the Quick Mask mode button, and then click on the color selection box.

4. Choose a rich purple from Photoshop's Color Picker as the color overlay for the Quick Mask. Red, green, and other colors the gummi worms have would be poor choices for Quick Mask color because they'd obscure your view of Quick Mask areas. Click on OK.

5. Click on OK in the Quick Mask Options dialog box.

6. Choose the Paintbrush tool. Then choose a very small tip from the Brushes palette, set the Opacity to 100%, and choose the Normal painting/editing mode.

7. Color in a gummi worm with Quick Mask, as shown in figure 3.20. When you've covered most of the worm in view, use the Hand tool to move your view to the rest of the worm and finish coloring.

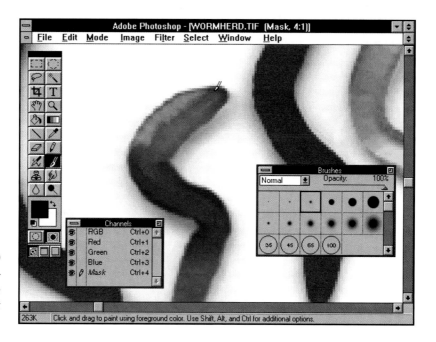

Figure 3.20

Choose a Quick Mask color that contrasts with the underlying image you want to define.

8. Click back to Standard mode when you've finished applying Quick Mask to the gummi worm. Choose Select, Save Selection.

9. Click on the #4 title on the Channels palette, and with your selection area still active, press Ctrl+C.

10. Press Ctrl+Tab to switch to an active view of DEEPSEA.TIF, and then click on the #4 title on the Channels palette.

11. Click on the Default colors icon button, then double-click on the Eraser tool. Click on OK to Photoshop's dialog about erasing the entire channel. You no longer need the selection of the Gaussian Blur.

12. Press Ctrl+V, and then Ctrl+D.

13. Click on the RGB title on the Channels palette, and then choose Select, Load Selection.

14. Hold down on the Ctrl and Alt keys and reposition the selection area to the left of the fish.

15. Follow the same steps used to create the murky fish shadow, and use the Gaussian Blur Filter and the Levels command to create a murky worm shadow.

16. Press Ctrl+Tab to switch back to an active view of the WORMHERD image, click on the RGB title on the Channels palette, and press Ctrl+C.

Photoshop keeps a selection area you've loaded active in an image, even when the image document is minimized or running in the background of another active image window. You can select something in an image, switch to a different image, and then return to it later with the same selection area chosen.

17. Press Ctrl and Tab to toggle back to the DEEPSEA image, and then paste the gummi worm selection on top of the RGB view of the image.

18. Click and drag the worm selection above and to the left of the murky worm shadow.

19. Press Ctrl+D to composite the worm selection into the DEEPSEA background image.

20. Repeat steps 1 through 19 with the other worms in the WORMHERD.TIF file.

In figure 3.21, the finished image has been saved to a different name—SWIMMERS.TIF. If you do the same, you'll now have two versions of a great collage piece.

Figure 3.21

A photographic collage, created with contemporary tools.

Chapter 4

The Depths of Digital Color

In the commercial world of publishing and computer graphics, the Tagged Image File Format (TIFF) is the format of preference when saving an RGB image. TIFF usually is preferred because the format can hold up to 16.7 million different explicit color values, which is typically more than the unique number of colors sampled from a source image.

But sometimes 16.7 million colors (TrueColor) is overkill; they can't all be printed without breaking the budget or, perhaps, the size of the files are too large to be included in an on-screen presentation. Using other, less robust file formats and image types with smaller file sizes is the answer. This compromise to accommodate budgets and presentation graphics programs need not be an artistic compromise. You'll see in this chapter how to stylize an image and create wonderful, eye-catching work when you convert RGB images to other image types.

Features Covered:

- Duotones
- Custom Index Palette
- Selections based on patterns
- Feather command
- Saturation mode

The Image on the *Adobe Photoshop NOW! CD-ROM*

All the image manipulation you'll learn how to perform in this chapter is done with the BARBARA.TIF image on the *Adobe Photoshop NOW! CD-ROM*. You should load it before starting the exercises. The file is referenced by this name throughout the chapter.

The Fashion Look of an RGB Image

An "au courrant" stylizing effect that publications have featured in recent years has been to colorize an area of an image while leaving the rest of it grayscale. Accomplishing this look is easy if you use Photoshop, and it can be performed in a number of ways. One method is to start with a grayscale image, convert it to an RGB image, and then tint areas of the image using the Color mode with the painting/editing tools.

Another way, and the one you'll employ in this chapter, is to use Photoshop's Saturation mode. This mode can apply or remove pure color within an image. When an image area has the color component removed from it, what's left is grayscale. Here's how to create a part RGB/part grayscale image.

1. Open the BARBARA.TIF image from the *Adobe Photoshop NOW! CD-ROM*. Double-click on the Zoom tool, and then click on the scrolless display button. (This display mode will give you a view of the full image.)

2. Choose the Paintbrush tool. Then choose the 45 pixel diameter tip from the Brushes palette, click on the modes drop-down list, choose Saturation, and set the Opacity slider to 100%.

3. Click on the Default colors icon button. When black or white is chosen as the foreground color in Saturation mode, strokes diminish the color components in pixels and heighten the grayscale visibility.

4. Click and drag a stroke at the bottom of the BARBARA.TIF image to get a feel for the amount of spread you have with this size Brush tip.

5. Continue clicking and dragging in areas, avoiding the face of the model and the cameo pinned to her blouse, as shown in figure 4.1. You want to leave the face, hair, hat, and cameo in color.

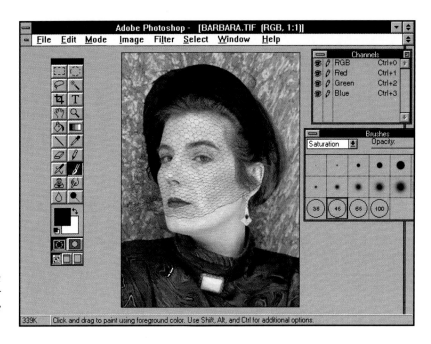

Figure 4.1

Painting in Saturation mode can remove the color component from image areas.

6. When you've finished removing the color from the border areas of the BARBARA image, switch to a smaller Brushes tip (the second row, second from the left tip is good), zoom into a 2:1 viewing resolution, and stroke outside the edges of the model's face, hair, cameo, and hat.

7. Use the Hand tool to scroll around to the other image areas to make certain you've stroked all intended areas with the Paintbrush in Saturation mode.

8. You're done when you have an image that looks like figure 4.2. You've made the focal point of a color image the model's face. Save your file as FASHION.TIF to your hard disk.

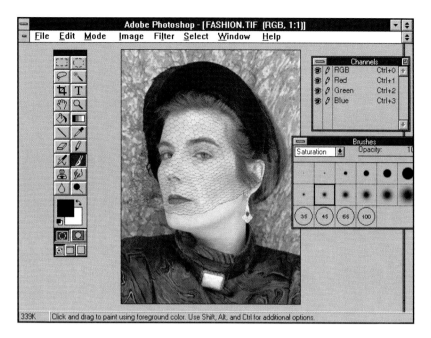

Figure 4.2

Grayscale information happily coexists with color in an RGB type TIFF format.

Making Indexed Color Images for Presentations

Indexed color is another type of image Photoshop recognizes and handles, but in a more limited way than an RGB image. You're usually better off converting an RGB image to indexed color rather than actually creating an indexed image. Indexing is the assigning of RGB color values to a lookup table, which has fixed color values and is limited to 256 unique colors within this image type. With these few colors to play with, Photoshop's Anti-Aliasing feature, the Feather command, and the spread attributed to the Paintbrush tool won't work.

> *Color table, lookup table, and color palette are synonymous terms when referring to indexed color images.*

Using a lookup table to "shorthand" explicit RGB values helps keep the indexed color file size small so that presentation packages and word processing programs can import them with ease.

Color loss is involved when converting RGB images to indexed images; however, Photoshop offers many options to track which colors are lost and which ones represent the lost ones. In the next series of steps, assume the BARBARA.TIF image is destined for a Microsoft PowerPoint electronic slide show. PowerPoint doesn't handle RGB images, but it does make slide transitions between indexed color images beautifully and quickly. Your charge is to make the best possible looking indexed color image from the BARBARA image. Here's how it's done.

1. Open the BARBARA.TIF image from the *Adobe Photoshop NOW! CD-ROM.*

2. Notice that the essential colors in this image belong to the model's face. Click and drag around the model's face with the Rectangular Marquee tool. This is a cue for Photoshop to concentrate on this area in the next steps.

3. Choose **M**ode, **I**ndexed Color.

4. In the Indexed Color dialog box, click on the **8** bits/pixel radio button. Although a greater amount may be specified in other imaging programs, Photoshop toes the line at 256 colors for indexed images.

The limit to a lookup table is not carved in stone as far as indexed color images are concerned. Adobe simply prefers to call a limit to indexed color at 256 unique ones in this type. Anything exceeding 256 colors is labeled an RGB image, whether the image fills 257 of the available color registers or 16.7 million. The reason is that the lookup table for, say, an image with 65,536 (16-bit) colors would require a fairly massive header file to travel along with the image. Bit depth increases exponentially until the point where manufacturers have to say, "This is ridiculous, it takes as much space in a given file format to write a color table for this many colors as it does to write the explicit RGB values." So by convention, indexed color means 8-bit color, or less in this book.

5. Click on the **A**daptive radio button in the Palette field. An Adaptive palette is a unique index that you create for an individual image. By creating a marquee around the model's face (see fig. 4.3), you've told Photoshop to lose the greatest number of unique colors from the area *not* marquee selected and to preserve most of the color values found within the marquee.

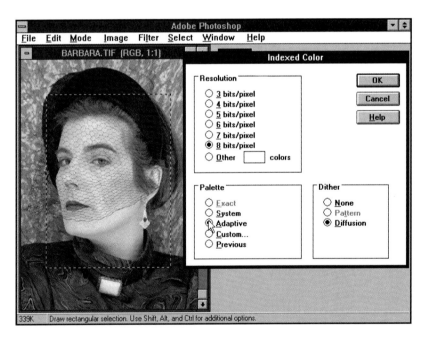

Figure 4.3

An Adaptive palette accommodates the unique color needs of an indexed image.

6. Click on the **D**iffusion radio button in the Dither field. Dithering is the use of available palette colors to "fake" the missing ones. With the Adaptive palette chosen, your choices are **D**iffusion (which is eye-pleasing), and **N**one (which is not).

7. Click on OK, press Ctrl+D to deselect the marquee, and take a look at the BARBARA image transformed into a limited number of colors. It's actually not bad, and will look good on a monitor running a 256-color driver. If you look at the file size on the bottom left of the status bar, you'll see that this image is a third the size it was when it was an RGB image.

Testing Photoshop's Indexing Prowess

Try a little experiment if you doubt that the image has been optimally reduced in color depth to portray the colors inside the marquee border the most faithfully.

1. Choose **M**ode, and then choose Color **T**able (a grayed-out option unless you're displaying an indexed color image).

2. This is the lookup table you custom designed by marquee selecting the model's facial area, as shown in figure 4.4. Notice that there is heavy emphasis on skin and hair colors, while only a few greens are reserved to represent all the background patterns. Click on OK to exit the Color Table.

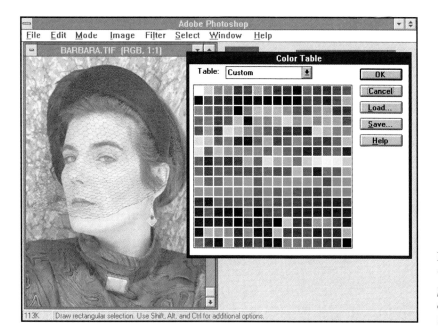

Figure 4.4

The Custom Color Table for BARBARA.TIF shows all the colors used in the indexed color image.

Photoshop's Color Table can be edited. While it is not recommended that you edit an indexed color image extensively by altering the lookup table, you can tweak an indexed image without changing the image back to RGB.

For instance, if you wanted to change a shade of green in the BARBARA image, you'd click on that color on the lookup table and choose a different shade from the Color Picker.

Plan your conversions from RGB to indexed carefully, and make sure you work with a copy of an image. Converting from one image mode to another is a translation of image data, and the more times you do it, the more the mode change degrades the quality of the image.

3. Save the image in PCX format to your hard disk. PCX file formats are compressed (they load larger into RAM than their stored file size) and handle all the visual information in a 256-color image as well as the TIFF format does for TrueColor images.

4. This is optional: Load a new copy of the BARBARA.TIF image from the *Adobe Photoshop NOW! CD-ROM* and perform the same indexing steps you did before. This time *don't* marquee select the model's face. Then check out the Color Table. You'll see more background colors because Photoshop's Adaptive palette gave equal preference to all image areas.

If your imaging work involves presentations, and you want the best quality image when converting from RGB to indexed, marquee select the most important areas in the image first and then choose the Adaptive palette.

Creating a Duotone Image

Duotone is a printing process by which two different versions of the same grayscale image are printed to paper using different inks. Commercial presses can't always render all 256 shades found in grayscale images as halftone dots, so the Duotone process was used initially to reinforce tonal areas of grayscale images.

But Duotones, Tritones, and Quadtone images (three and four passes of different inks) have evolved into an art form all their own, and they are used in publications for an eye-stopping effect.

Let's take a look at how a Duotone can be created. You'll change BARBARA.TIF into an authentic sepia tone portrait in the next few steps.

1. Open BARBARA.TIF from the *Adobe Photoshop NOW! CD-ROM.*

2. Choose **M**ode, **G**rayscale. This is the first conversion step for producing a Duotone. Click on OK when Photoshop asks you about discarding colors.

3. Choose **M**ode, **D**uotone.

4. Click on the **L**oad button in the Duotone Options box.

5. Using the **D**irectories and Dri**v**e windows, find Photoshop and scroll down its sub-directory tree to the DUOTONES\DUOTONE\PMS subdirectory.

6. Choose 159-1.ADO, and then click on OK.

7. As you can see in figure 4.5, The Duotone Options box now displays two different mapping curves for printing inks. Click on OK to see the Duotone as an on-screen display of how the image should print.

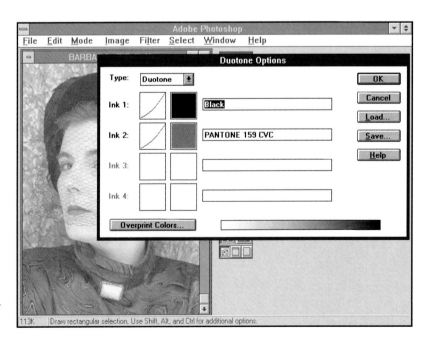

Figure 4.5

A Duotone uses one image, two grayscale variations of it, and two different inks.

You can edit the density curves of any of the inks in the Duotones Options box by clicking on the density curve. Do not confuse this graph with Photoshop's Curves command, however. A Duotone curve has a scale of densities for inks from 0 to 100%, while the Curves command graphs tonal brightness on a scale of 0 to 255. A Duotone actually is an image type belonging to commercial presses, and Photoshop maps an approximation of how it will print to your monitor.

The DUOTONES subdirectory that Photoshop installed is a sample collection of pre-sets that have been carefully plotted by commercial printers and Pantone, Inc. You should try these settings before venturing into creating your own Duotone maps because they are complex and merit your examination before imitation.

Converting Duotones to RGB Images

As mentioned before, the Duotone image as displayed on-screen is a representation of how the image would print. Photoshop plots different density curves for the inks. You can only save a Duotone image in the proprietary *.PSD format if you want to continue to work on the image.

You might want to place a Duotone image in a desktop publishing document to send to a commercial printer. Before you do, you need to prepare the image properly for export to the DTP program.

If you use Aldus PageMaker as your DTP program, for example, first press Ctrl+K to display Photoshop's General Preferences dialog box and make sure that Short Pantone Names is checked. Click on OK. You then can save the image as an EPS file that will import into the DTP program and print as expected. This procedure works with many PC-based DTP programs, but check your DTP program's documentation, or call their technical support people before you send your file off to a commercial printer.

If you are printing to a high-end Scitex publishing system, the procedure is different. First, from Photoshop's Mode menu, convert the image to Multichannel, and then from Multichannel to CMYK. Then save the file in Scitex CT format. It'll look strange, but print beautifully.

The Duotone images can be converted back to an RGB image without much loss of color fidelity. Do this next so that you can share this image with someone who doesn't own Photoshop.

1. Choose **M**odes, **R**GB Color.

2. Save the image as DUO159-1.TIF to your hard disk, as shown in fig. 4.6. You no longer have accurate printing instructions for a two-color press, but a converted Duotone can be rendered to a film recorder or 4-color press in its present state just fine.

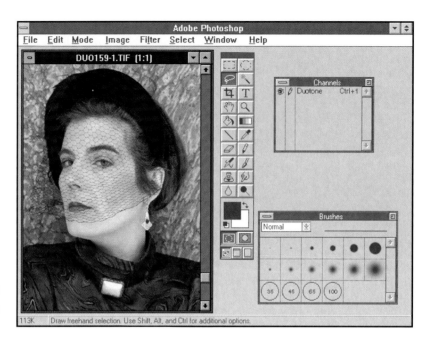

Figure 4.6

Save a Duotone with a file name you will remember.

The cryptic file names in the Duotone, Tritone, and Quadtone subdirectories refer to the Pantone color-matching system's specifications for inks to be mixed and printed onto different types of paper with varying absorbency values. None of which helps you remember the Duotone selection you really like when you want to retrieve it!

Whether you save an image like this as a TIF or as a PSD, why not use the name of the Photoshop *.ADO file as the name for your image?

Creating a Tinted Indexed Color Image

As you saw earlier, you can edit the index of an indexed color image by using the Color Table command. The Color Table comes with several predefined tables you can use that range from Black Body (which produces an image similar to a thermogram) to Windows' system table (which any Windows program can tap into). It's worth your time to explore the uses for these predefined tables and to develop your own custom tables. But for now, try this sure-fire technique for creating monochrome tinted images. You'll see how you have more control when you tint a Color Table than you have when using the Hue/Saturation command's Colorize option.

1. Open BARBARA.TIF from the *Adobe Photoshop NOW! CD-ROM*.

2. Choose **M**ode, **G**rayscale. You want to tint a grayscale image, not remap a lookup table that already contains color information.

3. Choose **M**ode, **I**ndexed Color. The image won't appear to change much after the conversion.

4. Choose **M**ode, choose Color **T**able.

5. Click and drag your cursor from the top-left color swatch to the bottom-right, as shown in figure 4.7. This tells Photoshop that you want to remap the entire gamut of available colors.

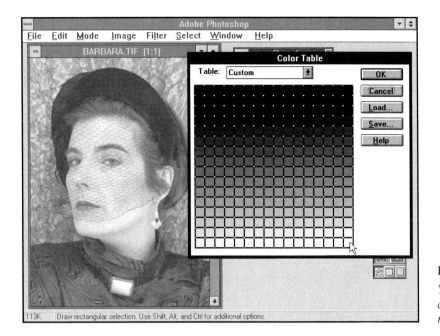

Figure 4.7

You can select one or all colors in the Color Table to re-map.

Selecting all the lookup table colors makes Photoshop display the Color Picker. Notice it reads Select first color:. This refers to the one that will occupy the upper-left swatch in the Custom Color Table you're designing.

6. Click and drag the Hue slider to the purple range, and then click and drag the circle in the spectrum area to the bottom, center. H: 285°, S: 50%, and B: 0% is a good selection, as shown in figure 4.8.

Figure 4.8

Your first color for the Custom Color Table should have 0% Brightness.

7. Click on OK, and the Color Picker is redisplayed for you to choose the last color in the range. Click and drag the circle in the spectrum straight up until your H and S values are the same as before, but Brightness is now 100%. Click on OK.

8. As you can see in figure 4.9, the Custom Color Table has all 256 registers (swatches) filled with shades of purple. Click on OK to apply your changes to the image.

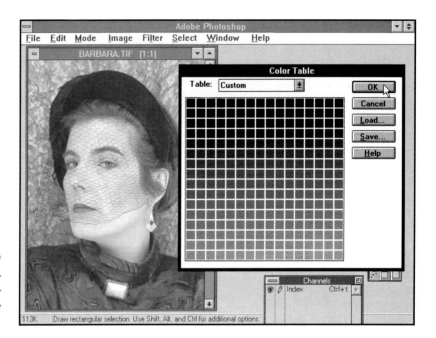

Figure 4.9

A Photoshop indexed color image can have a color gamut of 256 unique colors.

9. Save the image before closing it, but read on for your format options.

Photoshop provides the following options for saving indexed color files:

- If you'd like to use the image as Windows wallpaper, choose the BMP file format. BMP is like the PCX format in that they are compact formats for storing indexed color images. BMPs are used exclusively by many Windows applets, and Desktop Wallpaper must be in the BMP format.

- If you want to pass an indexed color image along to a Macintosh user, choose the PCX format. Be aware though, that the PCX format was openly published, and different manufacturers use different versions of PCX format. Photoshop writes to the Version 5 standard, and some older software programs may not understand it.

- When in doubt, use the TIFF as the format to save an image file. TIFF images have immense header information, but their color-handling capability is equally immense. And it's the only format besides Photoshop's PSD that can handle multiple Alpha channels.

As you can see in figure 4.10, the tinted indexed color image has been saved as LAVENDER.PCX and takes up only 113 KB of hard disk space. Images in Photoshop are malleable until you save them to a specific file format, so always choose a format that has the same color capability as the mode of the image you created.

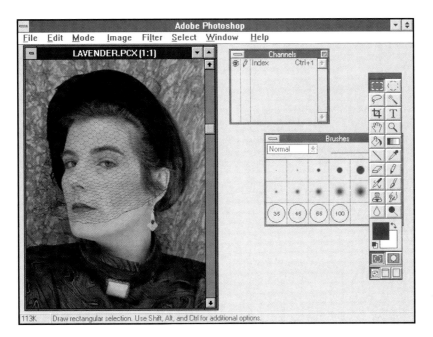

Figure 4.10

PCX files can handle 256 colors, the amount found in indexed color images.

Designing an Imitation Rotogravure

Before halftone screens for commercial printing presses were invented, literature that contained an image had to be manually etched onto a press plate. Images that were photographic in nature were lovingly, painstakingly reproduced by keen eyes and steady hands that vanished along with the craft as technology progressed.

But the rotogravure image is iconized in our society; it's seen on oatmeal boxes and on folding money. An effect that faithfully imitates rotogravure is our final step in exploring how Photoshop handles the color in digital images.

1. Open the BARBARA.TIF image from the *Adobe Photoshop NOW! CD-ROM*.

2. Choose File, Open, and then find the PATTERNS subdirectory under Photoshop on your hard drive.

3. Pick the WAVES.AI file from the list of patterns, and then click on OK.

4. WAVES.AI is a vector file that must be rasterized to a bitmap format for use in Photoshop. When the EPS Rasterizer dialog box pops up, enter .4 in the Width field, *not* the 1.596 it offers by default. Check the Anti-Aliasing and Constrain Proportions boxes, enter 150 pixels/inch in the Resolution field, and accept Grayscale as the mode. Then click on OK.

5. In figure 4.11, you can see that the WAVES.AI pattern is sized properly to imitate the etching lines found in rotogravure images. Press Ctrl+A, and then choose Edit, Define Pattern.

Figure 4.11

AI images are vector images that can be smoothly scaled for a variety of uses.

Many of the Photoshop patterns were designed as "repeat" patterns that can be used to fill in a large area seamlessly. Use the steps in this section with other Adobe Illustrator files to create different visual effects.

But unlike the WAVES image you use here, most of the Adobe Illustrator files produce unflattering results when applied to portrait images.

6. Click on the title bar of BARBARA.TIF. Then choose **M**ode, **G**rayscale, and press OK in Photoshop's query dialog box.

7. Press F6 to display the Channels palette if it's not already visible.

8. Click on the Channels palette's command button, and then choose New Channel from the drop-down list.

9. Accept the default name of channel #4, click on the Color Indicates: Selected Areas radio button, and then click on OK.

10. Choose **S**elect, **A**ll (Ctrl+A). Then choose **E**dit, **F**ill.

11. Click on the Pattern radio button, set Opacity to 100%, mode Normal, and then click on OK.

12. Press Ctrl+D to deselect the pattern in the Alpha channel.

As shown in figure 4.12, you now have a seamlessly tiled pattern in an Alpha channel. This is the basis of a very elaborate selection you'll use to create the rotogravure effect.

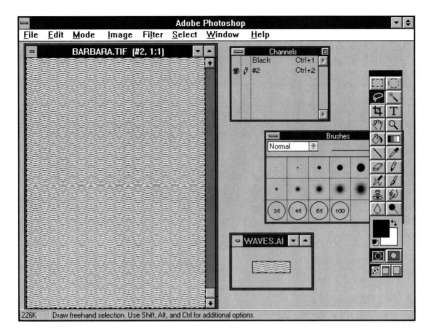

Figure 4.12

Alpha channel information is used to select parts of the main image.

Applying the Rotogravure Effect

Remember, as bitmap images go, successive changes made to them continue to alter them further and further from the original. In other words, there is no going back to an edit you performed three or four steps ago.

We'll make this reality work to our advantage in the next steps by repeatedly applying variations on an image edit to create a composite of the WAVES design and the grayscale image of the model.

1. Click on the Black channel title on the Channels palette.

2. Choose **S**elect, **L**oad Selection. Immediately, the image sprouts a billion marquee lines. Calm down and press Ctrl+H to hide these lines, but keep this phenomenally complex selection border active.

3. Press Ctrl+B to display the Brightness/Contrast command.

4. Enter –11 for the Brightness and +42 for the Contrast (or use the sliders). As you can see in figure 4.13, selective areas in the image are affected by the Brightness/Contrast edit, and the model begins to take on a more illustrated look.

5. You may want to repeat the same step a second or third time, varying the Brightness and Contrast values. This will make the effect more pronounced. Make sure that the Preview box in the Brightness/Contrast command is checked and that you have a good view of how far you're taking this editing.

6. Stop when you feel you've achieved the effect with some subtlety and grace.

7. These next steps are an artistic embellishment but produce a neat effect nonetheless. Make sure you have the whole image in frame first, and then choose the Lasso tool.

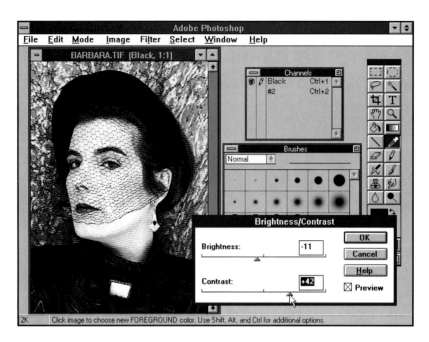

Figure 4.13

*Brightness/Contrast affects
image areas corresponding
to the black lines in the
Alpha channel.*

8. Click and drag a marquee from the top left of the image to the bottom right. She's framed in an oval now, right?

9. Choose **S**elect, **I**nverse. Then choose **S**elect, Fea**t**her.

10. Enter 9 in the **R**adius field, and then click on OK.

11. Click on the Default colors icon button (just to make sure).

12. Press the Del key. As you can see in figure 4.14, the woman wearing the cameo is now *herself* a cameo.

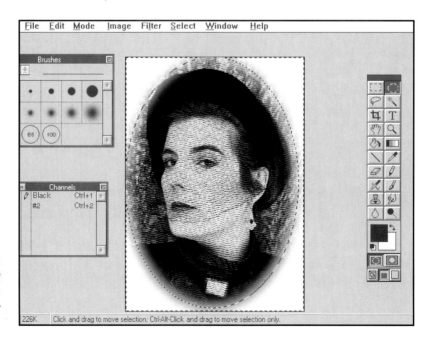

Figure 4.14

*Use the Feather command
to soften the edges on
painting, selecting, or
editing work.*

13. If you feel you're finished with this image forever, save it as a PCX or BMP after you've deleted the Alpha channel. Even though you can save RGB images to these formats, they don't support Alpha channels. If you'd like to play with the image some more, save it as a TIFF and check the $\underline{S}$ave Alpha channels box in TIFF Options.

In figure 4.15, I've opened a copy of the original to compare it to the rotogravure piece. There are two very different looking images here, yet Photoshop handles the visual information for the different modes and formats the same way. It's all little ones and zeros, the binary code, and Photoshop is quite capable at helping the artist sort them out.

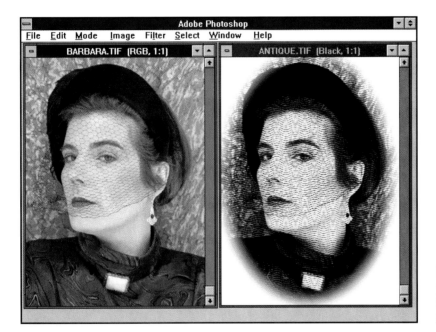

Figure 4.15

You can take image data in any direction with Photoshop.

Chapter 5

The EPS Image

Although Photoshop handles more than a dozen bitmap-type image formats, there's one non-bitmap type you'll want to become more familiar with to complete your digital imaging set of tools. The Encapsulated PostScript (EPS) format is a wonderful "bridge" between the bitmap and vector types of computer graphics. EPS images are resolution-independent—they can be smoothly scaled to any size without producing rough, jagged edges. After an EPS image has been rasterized, it can be used exactly like a TIFF, PCX, or other bitmap image, and Photoshop's full complement of filters and tools can be applied to it.

When working with computer graphics, it's important to understand that different image types have unique strengths and weaknesses. To successfully bring a great graphic idea to life, take advantage of the different image types' strengths. Simply put, the right tool for the right job makes your imaging work easier and more professional looking.

Features Covered:

- Paths
- Importing an EPS image
- Channels
- The From Saved option
- Patterns
- Partial masks

Embellishing Image Areas with EPS Files

The main image used in this chapter to complete a photorealistic scene came through a milieu of software programs known as *modeling and rendering* applications. The scene in figure 5.1 is a hidden wireframe view of the corner of a child's room that was created by modeling, and then combining a number of *primitives*—simple geometric shapes that are extruded, lathed, and swept to form recognizable, dimensional images that can be manipulated in 3D space.

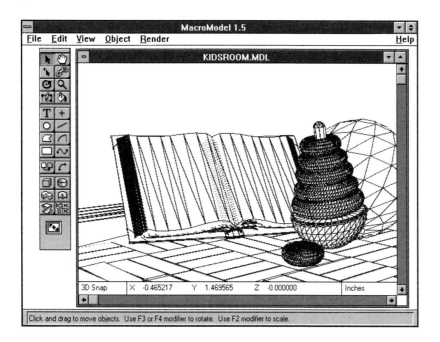

Figure 5.1

Modeling software has features that help create dimensional, photorealistic scenes.

After you assign lighting for the scene and materials to the dimensional objects, you must render the model to an image format that other programs, such as Photoshop, can accept. The rendering process commences, and in a little while, a file in the Tagged Image File Format (TIFF) is written to hard disk. KIDSROOM.TIF, as shown in figure 5.2, is a remarkably lifelike "virtual" image, and yet it lacks a few necessary elements that complete the artistic expression of this children's room.

Figure 5.2

KIDSROOM.TIF is a computer graphic model that has been rendered.

Rendering and modeling programs excel at portraying lifelike 3D objects, but they cannot effectively handle 2-dimensional design work, such as text in a book or patterns found in wallpaper. As you can see in the preceding figure, the book in the KIDSROOM image looks stark, and an inky void exists where the walls should be. Photoshop shines at creating and working with 2D patterns, such as wallpaper, which makes Photoshop the perfect program to finish this image.

The modeling program did create an Alpha channel mask that defines the area of the image where the walls should be. You'll use this mask in Photoshop when you fill the gaps in this picture with wallpaper you can create.

Adding text to the open pages of the book in KIDSROOM will be the first step in completing this image. Using the Alpha channel mask to "apply" the wallpaper will be a separate set of steps.

The Images on the *Adobe Photoshop NOW! CD-ROM*

If you'd like to get in on the action as the steps are covered in this chapter to manipulate EPS images, you can utilize files from the *Adobe Photoshop NOW! CD-ROM*. Before beginning, you'll need to load the materials used in this image—KIDSROOM.TIF and KID-STYPE.EPS. Additionally, you will need to load the typeface Elephants and Bears from the companion CD into Adobe Type Manager, the type management utility that comes with Photoshop.

The typeface Elephants and Bears was created by using CorelDRAW!, a vector design drawing program. One of CorelDRAW!'s many capabilities allows it to take a simple vector design and define it as a character in a Type 1 or TrueType typeface. The typeface then can be used in Photoshop or any other Windows program.

Using a Clipping Path as a Template

The first part of this assignment is to create an outline of where the text should lie on the open pages of the book in this image. You'll notice that facing pages of the book are not flat, and the angle at which the book was "photographed" causes the book's top to recede from the viewer. If this had been a simple, planar distortion of an image surface, Photoshop's Distort or Perspective **I**mage command, when applied to text created with the Type Tool, would fit the bill. But the pages are wavy and they recede, so this calls for a different application, in this case CorelDRAW!.

To ensure that the wave and the degree of recession of the text matches that of the open pages, a path of the book's outline is created in Photoshop and exported to a vector-based package to use as a template. CorelDRAW! can indirectly use this information to create and shape graphical objects as was done with the simple cartoon and text used in the following exercise. The properly shaped text is then exported back to Photoshop as an EPS image that can be placed on top of the open pages of the book. To do so, follow these steps:

1. Choose the Zoom tool, and then click once over the book area of the KIDSROOM image to zoom into the image for a close look at the book's page. A 1:1 viewing resolution is good.

2. Press F9 (or choose **W**indow, Show P**a**ths) to call the Paths palette to Photoshop's workspace.

3. Select the Pen tool. Start in the upper left corner and click with the Pen tool in a clockwise direction until you're back at the starting point. You're creating Anchor points with path segments being filled in automatically. When you get back to the beginning point, the Pen tool cursor suddenly sprouts a tiny circle toward its bottom right. Make sure that the path you create leaves a margin on the page because this path serves as a template for text on the page, and text naturally has a margin.

4. Because path segments created by single-clicking Anchor points are straight, they need to be converted to curved path segments. This is done with the Corner tool. Select the Corner tool, then click and drag an Anchor point in a clockwise direction (the direction you created the path). This action causes direction points to appear, and you'll find you are no longer clicking and dragging an Anchor point but rather a direction point that governs the degree of curvature of the two adjacent path segments.

5. Release the direction point, then click and drag on it again. Photoshop's convention for path segments and direction properties is that an initial click and drag on an Anchor point produces a direction point that symmetrically reshapes the two adjacent path segments. Clicking and dragging on the resulting direction point "breaks" the symmetrical property of the direction point, and the direction lines (the short lines that connect direction points to an Anchor point) can operate independently. This is your big opportunity to shape a path segment to follow the flow of the book page, as shown in figure 5.3.

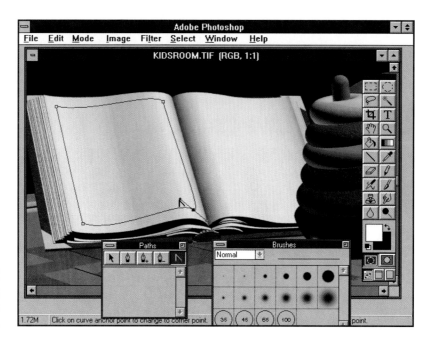

Figure 5.3

Change smooth direction point properties to sharp ones with the Corner tool.

The "single-click" method of defining a path in Photoshop is a little more involved but more straightforward for some graphic designers. If you're familiar with manipulating Bézier curves, like the ones found in Adobe Illustrator, CorelDRAW!, or Micrografx Designer, you might want to click and drag Anchor points using the Pen tool. This produces curved path segments complete with direction lines and points right from the beginning.

You still need to use the Corner tool, whose purpose in Photoshop is to toggle the direction point's properties between smooth (symmetrical direction lines) and corner (independently adjustable direction lines). My personal preference is to use the single-click method for defining straight path segments, then curving them with the Corner tool. This takes equal or less time than Bézier drawing, and it's less of a hassle.

6. After a direction point has been given a "corner" property, and the two adjacent path segments can be manipulated independently, choose the Arrow Pointer tool for final path refinements. The Arrow pointer tool is used to reposition Anchor points that you have drawn, and to reshape path segments by clicking and dragging on direction points.

You'll get more than a little frustrated if you try to adjust path segments with the Corner tool. Clicking on an Anchor point or direction points also might produce undesired results because the Corner tool's only purpose is to edit the properties of an Anchor point from smooth to sharp.

7. After the left page has been accurately outlined with a path, it's time to save the path by clicking on the Paths palette's command button, and selecting Save Path from the drop-down menu. A Save Path dialog box appears. Generally, no special name for a path is necessary unless you're dealing with a huge number of different paths. Click on OK to accept the default name, Path 1, and the outline of the left book page is preserved.

8. Repeat the same procedure for the right book page. Don't worry about the child's toy obscuring your view of the right page's lower right corner. Just click in this corner where you imagine the edge *should* be. Bend the path segments to follow the lines of the page's edges. Don't forget that this path outline should define an imaginary page margin, the point at which text on the page will end.

One of the nice things about Photoshop's paths, is that any additional path segments you create after saving one are sort of tallied up as being part of the same saved path. In other words, the right page outline you define is still considered part of Path 1, as long as you don't uncheck the path title on the palette before proceeding. Unchecking a path makes a path disappear from view. Any subsequent paths you create are considered to be separate from the unchecked saved path.

Exporting the Clipping Path

Now that the first and second page outlines have been defined as paths, it's time to export them in an EPS format that can be imported into another program for it to use. CorelDRAW! is used in the next few steps to create an "envelope" around an existing text block or two that conforms to the shape of these paths. The CorelDRAW! work then can be exported as an EPS file that Photoshop can use. After the shaped text is imported into Photoshop, it can be composited into the KIDSROOM image.

If you don't own CorelDRAW!, you still can take part in this next adventure. The resulting CorelDRAW! EPS files are on the *Adobe Photoshop NOW! CD-ROM*, and the next steps simply describe how to import and export EPS information files. If you own another vector design program, such as Adobe Illustrator, you might have a design of your own that you would like to experiment with here. Follow these steps:

1. Make sure the check mark is visible next to the Path 1 title on the Paths palette. If the path title isn't checked, the subpaths you just created aren't visible.

2. Choose File, Export, Paths. An Export paths to file: dialog box appears, as shown in figure 5.4.

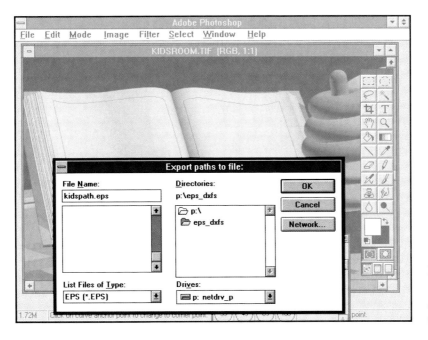

Figure 5.4

You can export a path as an EPS image for use in other design programs.

3. In the File **N**ame text box, type the name **KIDSPATH.EPS**. Using the Dri**v**es and **D**irectories fields in the dialog box choose a directory on your hard disk where you want to save the exported file.

4. Click on OK, and you're done exporting the paths. Now choose **F**ile, Sa**v**e As, and save KIDSROOM.TIF to a directory on your hard disk. Choose **F**ile, E**x**it. The Photoshop work, for the moment, is through. Now it's time to concentrate on shaping text according to your new EPS template.

Using a Drawing Program as a Photoshop Partner

As you can see in figure 5.5, Photoshop has been closed, and CorelDRAW! is now the active Windows application. Save the KIDSROOM.TIF image to your hard disk if you're following along with the *Adobe Photoshop NOW! CD-ROM* image at this point. The figure shows a simple illustration and storybook text that were created with vector-type drawing tools. Vector art is scalable, and the ideal candidate for one of CorelDRAW's effects, the envelope. Designs created with vector-type software are built with lines and nodes, which are very similar in concept to Photoshop's path segments and Anchor points. CorelDRAW! can reshape a vector design according to a different vector shape. This is what the imported Photoshop EPS path will be used for.

Figure 5.5

A vector-type image contains information about the design's geometry.

In figure 5.6, the automatic process of enveloping the picture and text is performed by selecting the graphics and text, and then clicking on the Create From button. This makes the cursor change into a special arrow that is clicked on the KIDSPATH.EPS that was imported into Photoshop, as seen in figure 5.6.

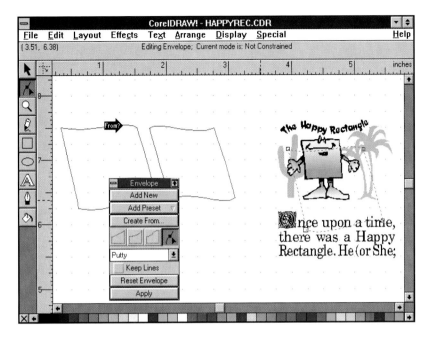

Figure 5.6
CorelDRAW! bases the shape of an envelope on a user-definable shape.

The Apply button is then clicked, and as you can see in figure 5.7, the CorelDRAW! graphics and text assume the shape of the first page outline you designed in Photoshop.

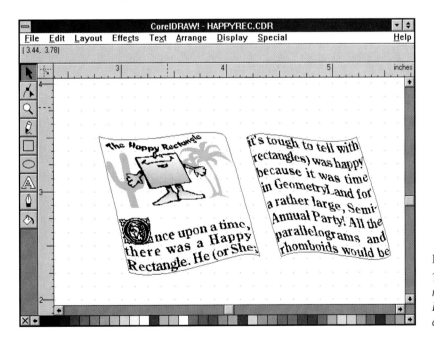

Figure 5.7
The CorelDRAW! design reshaped to match the Photoshop paths, ready for export.

Creating an EPS Mask for Export

The CorelDRAW! graphic, funny little cartoon, text, and all, now looks like it will dimensionally match the angle of the book image's page in KIDSROOM.TIF. But the enveloped graphic is half of what needs to be EPS-exported to complete the book.

When an EPS is rasterized in Photoshop, it takes on a foreground and background property, unlike vector graphics that can exist as geometry surrounded by blank space. The CorelDRAW! design will be rasterized as a grayscale image on a white background. You don't want a white background for the book's graphics; the graphics need to be placed without any sort of background so that the book's pages show through.

The solution is to create an identical copy of the enveloped graphic and to attribute black to all of its components. When the EPS of the tonal graphic is rasterized in Photoshop, the silhouette copy will be placed in an Alpha channel of the tonal image. As the black areas in the Alpha channel will be seen as selection information, the tonal image of the graphics and text will be masked away from their white background. Then, selecting only the graphic and text to composite on the book's page will be a simple matter.

To see how to use the results of these exported EPS images, load KIDSROOM.TIF from your hard disk, and then minimize it on the workspace (you'll use it soon). Then load both the HAPYMASK.EPS and HAPYTYPE.EPS images found on the *Adobe Photoshop NOW! CD-ROM* into the Photoshop workspace. This is how it's done.

1. The HAPYMASK.EPS file needs to be rasterized so that it can be manipulated in a bitmap format. Choose File, Open, and the EPS Rasterizer dialog box appears. Photoshop usually is pretty intuitive about setting the proper dimensions for rasterizing an EPS file. If it offers you 3.264 by 2.167 for HAPYMASK, take it—this is correct for this assignment's purpose. Also, select a Resolution of 150 pixels/inch. This is the resolution of the KIDSROOM image, and the two image resolutions should match.

2. Choose Grayscale as the mode HAPYMASK is rasterized to. Even though these CorelDRAW!-exported EPS images will be used as part of the RGB KIDSROOM.TIF image, Photoshop automatically converts pasted image types to match that of the background image at the time it's pasted. Make certain that the Anti-Aliased check box is marked before you click on OK in the EPS Rasterizer dialog box to ensure that the EPS image is rasterized with smooth, photographic-quality edges. Then click on OK.

3. HAPYMASK's only purpose is to create an accurate selection border around the HAPYTYPE.EPS image so that the white background in HAPYTYPE isn't selected—only the design of the cartoon and the text. Choose Select, All (Ctrl+A), then choose Edit, Copy (Ctrl+C) to copy the image to the Clipboard. You now have the HAPYMASK image set to paste into the HAPYTYPE.EPS file, as shown in figure 5.8.

4. Close the HAPYMASK image without saving it. You're done with the file. Open the HAPYTYPE.EPS file, and specify the same image dimensions, resolution, and image type that you specified for HAPYMASK.EPS.

Figure 5.8

A black-and-white copy (no grays) of the cartoon and text serves as a selection area for the HAPYTYPE.EPS image.

5. Press F6 (or choose **W**indow, Show C**h**annels). Photoshop treats rasterized EPS files the same as TIFF or other image types, so HAPYTYPE.EPS can be assigned an additional channel—an Alpha channel that Photoshop uses to build image selection areas.

6. Click on the Channels palettes command button, and choose New Channel from the drop-down list.

7. A Channel Options dialog box pops up. Click on the Color Indicates: Selected Areas radio button. Accept the default name #2 for the new Alpha channel, and then click OK.

8. You're immediately shown a view of this Alpha channel within the HAPYTYPE file. Choose **S**elect, **A**ll (Ctrl+A) now. This selects the entire Alpha channel #2, and you'll see marquee border lines running around the active image window. This tells Photoshop that this is the target area for the copy of the HAPYMASK image that is currently loaded on the Clipboard.

9. Choose **E**dit, **P**aste (Ctrl+V). The HAPYMASK copy on the Clipboard drops into the selected area of the Alpha channel. Press Ctrl+D (**S**elect, **N**one), and the HAPY-MASK image is in place and will be used by Photoshop to define a selection border in the next step.

10. Click on the Black channel title on the Channels palette. You're returned to the grayscale image of the CorelDRAW! cartoon and text. Choose **S**elect, **L**oad Selection, and then choose **E**dit, **C**opy. You're copying only the graphic, and none of the white background (see fig. 5.9).

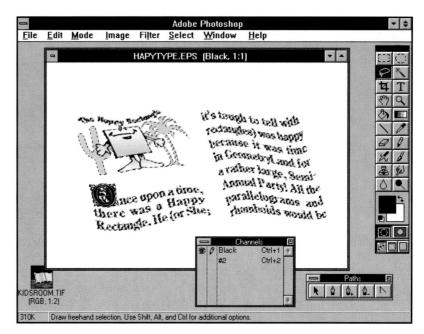

Figure 5.9

*The selected areas in
HAPYTYPE.EPS are based
on the information in
Alpha channel #2.*

After the selected areas of HAPYTYPE.EPS have been copied to the Clipboard, it is no longer necessary to keep the file open. You can close the file without saving. The fewer image windows you have open simultaneously in Photoshop, the better off you are memory-wise.

Using the Original Path as a Guideline

Because paths you create in Photoshop don't go away unless you deliberately delete them, Path 1 is still in the KIDSROOM.TIF image. The path serves a second purpose now that you've used it to reshape the CorelDRAW! graphic. Now that the copy of the EPS graphic is loaded on the Clipboard, it's time to restore the KIDSROOM icon on Photoshop's workspace, and finally add some copy to this bare book.

You will use the Paths palette extensively throughout the rest of the assignment, yet the workspace is going to get a little cluttered with the image and all of these palettes open. Make certain Path 1 has a check mark next to it on the Paths palette, then click on the minimize/maximize button on the palette's upper right corner. This reduces its size and functionality for the moment, and you'll notice that the original paths in the KIDSROOM image have reappeared.

1. Click on the Lasso tool.

It's not a mandate that you have a selection tool active before you paste a selection from the Clipboard, but it's good Photoshop practice. You can access the Arrow pointer from other tools by holding down the Ctrl key, but this is sometimes courting disaster.

For instance, you can reposition a pasted floating selection with the Paintbrush tool active if you hold down the Ctrl key and click and drag. The problem with this arises when you decide that the floating image needs to be repositioned once more. If you instinctively click and drag with the Paintbrush but forget to hold down the Ctrl key, you paint the floating selection. Always use selection tools to reposition and save your headaches for other software.

2. Choose **E**dit, **P**aste, and then click and drag inside the marquee border of the HAPYTYPE image so that its outline fits neatly inside the paths displayed on the KIDSROOM image, as shown in figure 5.10.

Figure 5.10

Use the path you exported to position the imported EPS file it was based upon.

3. You might want to use the arrow keys to nudge the pasted area up, down, or across to perfectly position it. An arrow keystroke equals moving a floating selection by one screen pixel. Make certain that the marquee border is still active around the pasted image. Clicking outside the marquee border of a paste composites the paste into the background image, which spells problems most of the time.

4. When you're happy with the positioning of the cartoon and text, choose **S**elect, **N**one. You're half done with the kid's room now, but do not save the image to your hard disk yet.

As you've noticed, the bottom right corner of the pasted selection now sits on top of the child's toy, which is incorrect. An important Photoshop lesson, however, is that nothing is irrevocable in the land of digital images. Photoshop loads multiple copies of an image when you call it into Photoshop's workspace, which means a copy of your most recently saved image is always hidden away in system RAM and on part of your hard disk as a temporary file Photoshop swaps in and out of memory. You should always pack your machine with additional RAM and hard disk space when dealing with high-quality bitmap images, and herein lies the reward.

Photoshop gives you access to a copy of an image you're working on through a number of tools. The one used in the next steps is the Rubber Stamp tool. It can be set to clone from a saved version of an image file, but only if you haven't saved it recently, so don't save KIDSROOM to your hard disk quite yet. You still have to remove a character or two from the bottom of the child's toy.

5. Double-click on the Rubber Stamp tool. This displays the Rubber Stamp Options dialog box. Photoshop installs with the default of Clone (aligned) as the Rubber Stamp's option, but you can change this. Choose From Saved from the Option: drop-down list, then click on OK.

6. Choose a medium Brushes palette tip for the Rubber Stamp (figure 5.11 shows a good choice). Press Ctrl++ to expand your viewing resolution to 2:1, and start cloning over the type that's on top of the child's toy. The Rubber Stamp "erases" the area back to the last-saved version of this image, which contained no CorelDRAW! cartoon or graphic.

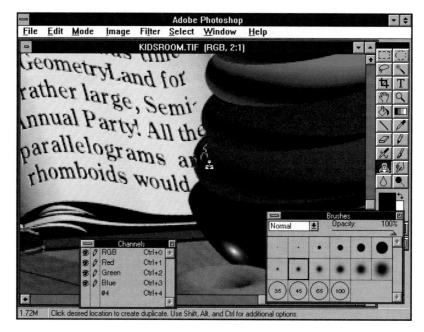

Figure 5.11

Using the Rubber Stamp option of Last Saved "erases" an image area back to its previous condition.

7. Press Ctrl+– when you're finished to get a better perspective of your handiwork. If it looks like figure 5.12, you've made a small child very happy.

*When you're done, you might want to consider resetting the Rubber Stamp's Option back to its default of Clone (aligned). I have Photoshop's environment set up on my PC to **R**estore Windows (from General Preferences under the **F**ile menu). This means that every time I start a new Photoshop session, the tools, palettes, and settings remain as I left them when I last exited the program. It's good in a way, but it'll mess up your work if you start using the Rubber Stamp to clone over an image, only to find it's set to restore from your last-saved version of an image. Cleaning up after you're done also applies to the Gradient tool, the Type tool, and feathering attributes you might have defined with the selection tools.*

Figure 5.12

The type now looks as though it were always on the book's pages.

Defining a Background Area To Paste Into

As mentioned earlier, an Alpha channel was created at the time the child's room image was rendered to mask the black background from the toys and book. This makes it a simple matter to load the selection area later and use Photoshop's Paste Into command to drop a wall or two into the appropriate area.

But you're not reading this book because you want simple, right? How about if the walls behind the toys have a wallpaper design and they have some perspective and some lighting, as well?

To create fancy, dimensional, realistic wallpaper using Photoshop, you must define the areas where the walls will be pasted so that they can be lit and put in perspective before being pasted in place. You'll use the Paths palette to define the area, and then copy it for use as a template in a new image.

1. Path 1 needs to be unchecked on the Paths palette, making it idle and invisible. As this path is no longer necessary, you might want to delete it by clicking on the Path title, and then selecting Delete Path from the command button drop-down list. The only thing that's important is that Path 1 is not active so that the new path you're about to create won't be appended to Path 1.

2. Using the Pen tool, click Anchor points to define the corners of where you'd like the first panel of wallpaper to go. I've guessed where the walls meet behind the book and the toy, and completed the path to match the first area that needs covering (see fig. 5.13).

Figure 5.13

A path can be copied to a new image file, or exported to other applications.

3. Save the path by choosing Save Path from the palette's command button drop-down list, and accept its default name of Path 2.

4. Choose **E**dit, **C**opy. Paths can be copied to the Clipboard as easily as image selection areas. The only difference between paths and image selection areas is that a path is selected by virtue of its presence in an active image window—you don't have to select it with the Arrow tool prior to copying it.

5. Minimize the KIDSROOM image to icon size. You won't need it for the moment, and you'll spare your monitor some ergs redrawing an image you don't need at present.

6. Choose **F**ile, **N**ew, and then choose **W**idth 5", H**e**ight 3", **R**esolution 150 pixels/inch, and RGB Color mode. Then click on OK. This new image window is where you build the wallpaper.

7. Choose **E**dit, **P**aste, and voilà, the Path #2 copy plops into the center of the new image file. The Path #2 copy is simply a set of coordinates that is visible because Photoshop mapped it to the monitor. It's not actually part of the bitmap image, and it won't get in the way of painting or editing the image background.

Remember that Paths belong to the vector-family of graphics, and as such, don't mingle with bitmaps until they've been rasterized into something more tangible.

8. Choose the Rectangular Marquee tool, and click and diagonally drag a selection area in the center of Untitled-1 (the new file image) that's about one quarter of the total image window size.

9. Click on the Foreground color selection box. This calls Photoshop's Color Picker, and set H: 240°, S: 44%, and B: 99% in the HSB color model entry fields. This mixes up a light pastel blue, which also can be approximated by clicking and dragging the little circle in the spectrum model on the left side of the Color Picker box. An accurate shade is not critical here—pick any shade that you want. This is the color of the wallpaper background. You'll apply a foreground pattern later. Click on OK to accept your color selection.

10. Choose the Paintbrush tool, and make sure the Opacity is set to 100%, Normal mode on the Brushes palette. Then Choose the 100-pixel diameter tip on the Brushes palette, and with one swoop or two, cover the rectangular selection area in Untitled-1. You also can choose Edit, Fill to achieve the same result, but I've found painting to be quicker than accessing another dialog box. Notice how you can color straight across Path #2, and the path offers no resistance or complaint (see fig. 5.14).

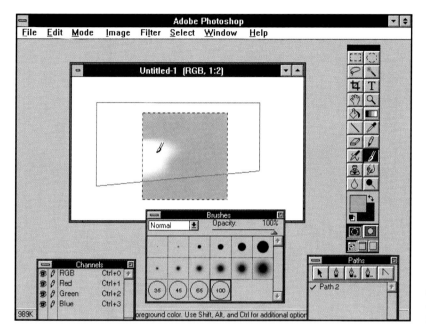

Figure 5.14

Paths sit on top of a bitmap image; the two never interact.

You've just created a small swatch you'll use to create an entire patterned wallpaper image. The Path will guide you as to how the wallpaper should be distorted to reflect the angle it's supposed to be at in the KIDSROOM image. Now it's time to pick a pattern for the kid's room.

The Type Tool Uses PostScript, Too

Decorative typefaces are very popular these days, and it doesn't take a rocket scientist or a large budget to get into the business of creating "home brew" fonts by yourself. Elephants and Bears is a Type 1 font on the *Adobe Photoshop NOW! CD-ROM* that I created for this assignment. It consists of some original symbol designs that were created freehand, pen and paper-style, scanned, cleaned up, and then exported as individual characters in the Adobe Type 1 PostScript font format using CorelDRAW!.

Adobe Type Manager rasterizes Type 1 typefaces on-the-fly—the split-second you type a character, it is mapped to the monitor. For a task like the upcoming one, this is a time-saver over having to import another EPS design from a vector application to create the wallpaper pattern for the KIDSROOM image. With Elephants and Bears loaded in Adobe Type Manager for Windows, here's how to create a repeating design for the wallpaper.

1. Before using the Type tool, you need to set a different foreground color, one that's darker than the pastel blue, to use as the pattern color. Click on the Invert colors icon button, then click on the Foreground color selection box again to call the Color Picker.

2. Setting these values—H: 240°, S: 98%, and B: 56%— creates a warm navy, and it works well with the pastel blue. Make these settings now, and then click on OK.

3. It's time to add the elephants and bears. Click an insertion point within the pastel blue swatch by using the Type tool. This calls up the Type tool dialog box. Select Elephants and Bears from the **F**ont drop-down list of available system fonts.

4. Set **S**ize to 60, Lea**d**ing to 72 and Alignment to **L**eft. In the Style field, only **A**nti-Aliased should be check marked. (The size and leading settings are fairly arbitrary calls in this assignment. They worked for this illustration, but feel free to experiment here.) I found 60 points on 72 produced workable symbol images (see fig. 5.15). This produces about a 3/4" tall character in a 5-by-3 image area. After you've entered these settings, type an uppercase **E** (for elephant) in the text entry box at the bottom of the dialog box, and then click on OK.

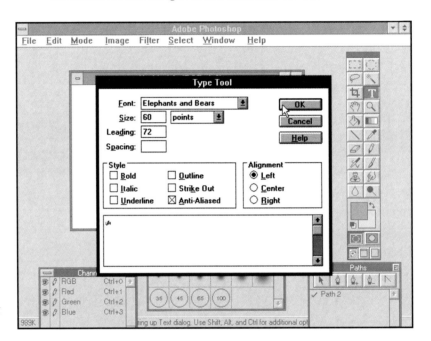

Figure 5.15

The Type tool dialog box "remembers" your last entry.

5. Now you should have an elephant as a dark navy floating selection in Untitled-1's image window. Click and drag the floating selection so that it occupies the upper left quarter of the pastel blue background rectangle. Then click outside the elephant's border. The floating selection is composited into the background.

6. Click an insertion point again in Untitled-1 with the Type tool. The Type tool dialog box is displayed again. The settings for **F**ont, **S**ize, and Lea**d**ing were retained, so all you need to do is to type in a **B** (for Bear) in the text entry field, and then click on OK.

7. Position the bear floating selection to the right of the elephant image. When it's in place, deselect the bear by clicking outside the marquee border. Repeat the insertion point/Type tool dialog maneuver twice so that you wind up with an alternating bear and elephant pattern in the pastel background rectangle, as seen in figure 5.16.

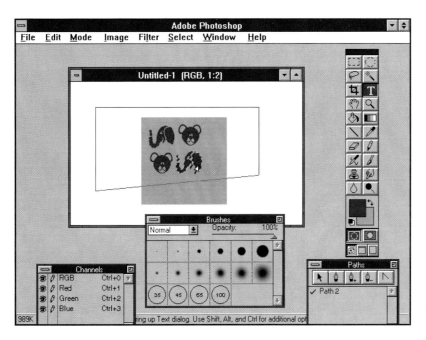

Figure 5.16

Larger patterns can be made out of mini-patterns.

Making a Pattern from a Selection Area

Creating patterns is something every graphics application should have the facility to do. Photoshop is more than amply suited for this task. Here's the trick to creating a complex wallpaper pattern while exerting an embarrassingly small amount of energy.

1. Choose the Rectangular Marquee tool.

    The Rectangular Marquee tool is the only Photoshop selection tool that you can use to define a pattern in Photoshop. You also can use the Select, All command if you want a ponderously large (still rectangular) pattern sampled from an entire image. But why?

2. Click and diagonally drag the cursor until you have only the bear and elephant "pattern" selected in the Untitled-1 image area. Leave a little extra room, or bleed, around the outside edges.

3. Choose Edit, Define Pattern. Your marquee border will vanish, and the area you defined with the Rectangular marquee tool is now registered with Photoshop as a pattern.

4. Choose Select, All (Ctrl+A). All of Untitled-1 is now selected. The Path is unaffected by the next series of steps because it's not a bitmap image, only a representation of an outline that's mapped to your monitor.

5. Choose Edit, Fill. This brings up the Fill dialog box, where you want to choose Pattern for the contents, Opacity 100%, and a Normal mode. Then click on OK.

6. Bingo! You now should have a rather limited edition of a zoo occupying Untitled-1's window, as shown in figure 5.17.

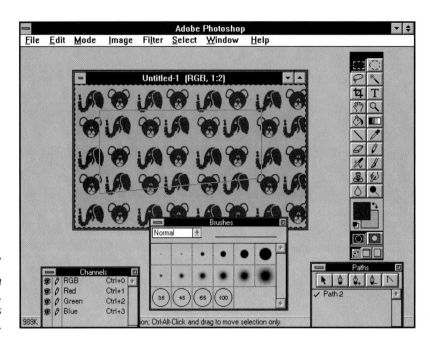

Figure 5.17

Pattern fills will cover an entire selection area, replacing the previous image.

Distorting the Wallpaper To Add Dimension

Path #2 will now serve as a template for using Photoshop's Distort Effect to reshape Untitled-1's image area. You'll twist the selection of the wallpaper to suggest that the right side of the wallpaper is receding from the viewer's eye. With RGB images, the type of image used in this assignment, Photoshop can tap into 16.7 million colors to interpolate "in-between" color pixels that smooth the edges of neighboring pixels. Interpolation is essential when pixels are bent out of shape with fancy effects, like the Distort command.

You cannot successfully perform the distort effect with image types such as Indexed or Bitmap. Photoshop can't smooth the transition with the limited number of colors available in these image types, and you wind up with a distorted bitmap image that contains harsh, unappealing jagged edges.

You will paste a copy of this modified wallpaper behind the scene of the floor and toys shortly, so when you perform the next few steps, don't use Path #2 as an exact outline to follow, but rather as the general "feel" for the geometry that should be matched. The idea is to leave enough extra image area around the outside so that you have some leeway in positioning the wallpaper behind the toys.

1. Choose **S**elect, **A**ll (Ctrl+A). Then choose **I**mage, **E**ffects, Distort. An effects boundary box will surround the selection area, with four hollow boxes at each corner.

When you place your cursor over a corner box, the cursor turns into an arrow that can be used to drag the corner in any direction. When the cursor is outside the boundary box, it turns into a tiny international "do not" symbol. Clicking when the cursor is a "do not" symbol will cancel any edits you've made to the boundary box, and the effect is canceled. When you place your cursor inside the boundary box, the cursor changes again—this time it turns into a gavel. Clicking the cursor when it is gavel-shaped locks the effect into place, so don't do that until you've achieved the effect that you want.

2. Start with the upper left Distort box corner. Click and drag it toward the corresponding upper left corner of Path #2. Stop when you're around one-fourth of an inch away from it. This effect is processor-intensive, so don't expect the change to be immediately visible. Let Photoshop process this move before continuing and don't click outside the Distort boundary box or inside the boundary box until you've finished the effect.

3. Do the same thing with the other three corners of the Distort boundary box, until you have a shape similar to that shown in figure 5.18.

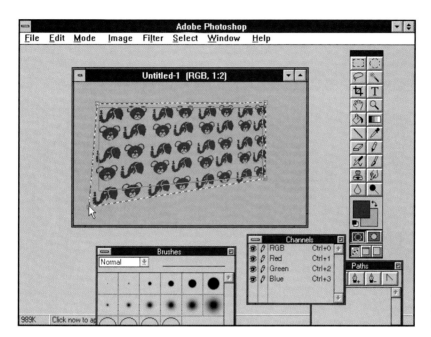

Figure 5.18

The Distort command creates a feeling of dimension out of a flat image.

4. When you're happy with your distorted wallpaper, click inside the Distort boundary box. Your cursor turns into a tiny gavel, and "nails" the image to the desired degree of distortion. The active marquee border is not deselected, however. You must press Ctrl+D, or choose Select, None to finish the move.

Adding Shading to the Wallpaper

MacroModel and RenderMan created a beautifully-lit virtual scene, and it would be a crime to drop an evenly illuminated wallpaper background into the scene now. The solution to "lighting" the wallpaper before copying it into KIDSROOM.TIF is to use a partial mask. You can create a selection area based on the brightness levels of pixels in an Alpha channel. If you have Color Indicates Selected Areas set for an Alpha channel, Photoshop will evaluate black pixels as ones to be included in a selection and white pixels as ones to be ignored.

But what about gray areas? These are partially selected areas that Adobe calls *partial masks*. The Gradient tool can be used to create a smooth transition from one color to another, and this includes a number of grays along the way. It makes a nice lighting effect when applied to an image's color channel, but when a gradient fill is applied to an Alpha channel, it creates a selection border that smoothly trails off into nothingness. This is the way lighting should behave on our virtual wallpaper in this virtual room, and this is what you'll do next.

1. Click on the Default colors icon button. This makes the foreground Photoshop color black, and the background white.

2. Click on the Channel palette's command button, and choose New Channel from the drop-down list. Channel #4 is okay as the default name, but make sure that the Color Indicates Selected Areas radio button is selected, and then click on OK.

3. You're now presented with the Alpha channel #4 view of Untitled-1. Double-click on the Gradient tool and make sure that the options are set to Style: Normal, and Type: Linear before proceeding. Click on OK to confirm the settings and exit the Gradient Tool Options box.

4. Click and drag clear off the bottom of Untitled-1's image window with the Gradient tool cursor, as shown in figure 5.19.

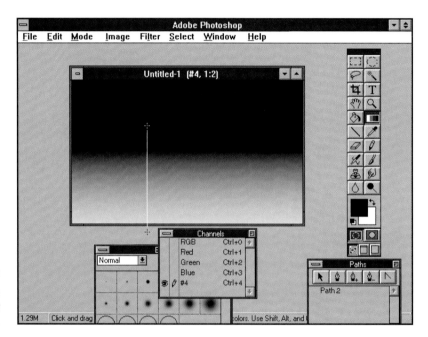

Figure 5.19

A Gradient fill in an Alpha channel creates an elegant partial mask.

5. Click on the RGB title in the Channels palette. This gives you the color composite-view of the elephant/bear wallpaper.

6. Choose Select, Load Selection. A marquee appears in Untitled-1's image window, but it won't encompass the entire wallpaper image. That's okay. Marquee borders don't directly correspond to selection areas defined as partially masked ones. And this ruined your evaluation of a selected area if you rely on the marquee as a clear indicator of a selected area.

7. Choose Edit, Copy (Ctrl+C). This copies the selection to the Clipboard. Remember that the lighter areas you defined with the Gradient fill are only partially transported to the Clipboard, and you'll get an unexpected, but pleasant surprise when you paste the copy into the KIDSROOM image.

8. Minimize the Untitled-1 image, and restore KIDSROOM.TIF by double-clicking on its icon.

9. Choose **S**elect, **L**oad Selection. The mask that was created in the rendering of this image now displays an active marquee border around the blank wall area.

10. Choose **E**dit, Paste **I**nto. The wallpaper is now behind the toys but in front of the blank space the loaded selection in KIDSROOM defines.

11. Choose a selection tool now—the Rectangular Marquee tool is fine. Place the cursor inside the pasted selection, and move it around until you have the left wall covered with pattern. Don't worry about the unpatterned area of the selection on the right side of the image, as shown in figure 5.20. Instead, let it fall where the right wall appears to be. You will remove it shortly.

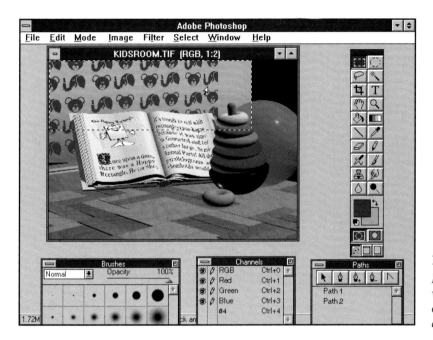

Figure 5.20

Position the wallpaper with the unpatterned areas outside of the left wall area.

The Eraser Tool and Last-Saved Image Versions

You still haven't saved KIDSROOM.TIF, and superficially, it might seem like a good idea right now. But hold off for a millisecond, and clean up the right, unpatterned side of this gloriously dimensional wallpaper. The trick here is similar to when you wiped the lettering off the child's toy with the Rubber Stamp tool, but the choice of tools for this activity doesn't need to be as elaborate.

The Eraser tool becomes a Magic Eraser tool when you hold down the Alt key and click and drag it. This means you can go straight up the edge where the wallpaper overlaps the right "wall" that you'll soon be covering. Press the Shift key while holding the Alt key and click and drag to constrain the Eraser to a straight line.

1. Choose the Eraser tool.

2. Hold down the Shift and Alt keys simultaneously.

3. Position your cursor at the bottom of where the pattern ends on the right. This should be the location where you want the right side of the wall to begin.

Photoshop will resist when you start to click and drag straight up because it takes a moment to read the last-saved version of KIDSROOM.TIF into memory.

4.   Click and drag straight up until you reach the top of the image. You're done.

Encore Performance for the Wallpaper Artist

The following is an abbreviated list of steps for creating the second, final piece of wallpaper for this image. The procedures are the same as those you just did, with a minor variation here or there. You're almost done. You should have a good feel for the tools explored, and now you should be creating possible scenarios in the back of your mind for the uses of EPS images in your own assignments.

1.   Deselect Paths #1 and #2 on the Paths palette. They should not be visible in the KIDSROOM image. Using the Pen tool on the Paths palette, outline the remaining black background area in the KIDSROOM image. Again, it makes no difference whether you go into the border of the toys, as shown in figure 5.21, because the channel #4 mask in KIDSROOM.TIF protects this area when it's time to paste a wallpaper selection into the image.

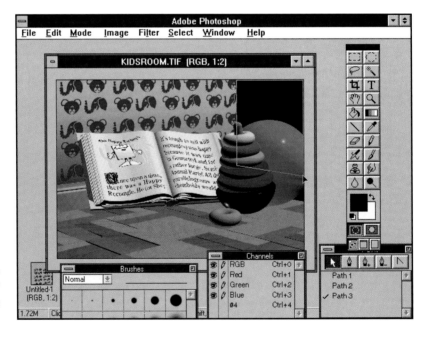

Figure 5.21

Define the area to be covered with virtual wallpaper with the Pen tool.

2.   Save the path by choosing Save Path from the Path palette's command button drop-down list (this should be Path #3 now). Then copy the path to the Clipboard.

3.   Double-click on Untitled-1's icon to restore it to the workspace as the active image window.

4.   Choose Edit, Paste. Path #2 is no longer visible in Untitled-1's window because it's not selected on the Paths palette. It's a weird phenomenon to have named, saved paths synchronously appearing and disappearing in different images, but it works.

5. You still have the Bear/Elephant wallpaper defined as a pattern, so choose **S**elect, **A**ll, then **E**dit, **F**ill to flood the Untitled-1 image window with pattern.

6. Choose the **I**mage, **E**ffects, Distort command, and shape the Distort boundary box to conform to the general shape of Path #2. You have very little KIDSROOM left to wallpaper, and Path #2 should suggest the "feel," not an exact guideline for distorting the wallpaper, as shown in figure 5.22. Be sure to allow for "play" when you eventually paste it into KIDSROOM.TIF.

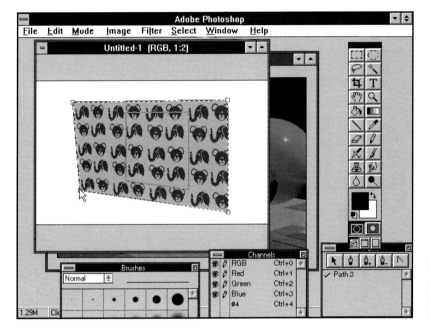

Figure 5.22

Loosely shape the selection area of wallpaper with the Distort boundary box.

7. Click on the Channel #2 title on the Channels palette to reveal the Alpha channel with the gradient fill in it. Choose the Gradient fill tool once more, but this time sweep the gradient from left to right to suggest that light is being cast on this wall differently. It also breaks the monotony of identically shaded left and right panel wallpaper.

8. Click on the RGB title of Untitled-1, and choose **S**elect, **L**oad Selection.

9. Choose **E**dit, **C**opy, then press Ctrl+Tab to toggle back to the KIDSROOM image as the active Photoshop window.

10. Choose **S**elect, **L**oad Selection. This loads the entire Alpha channel #4 selection again. But you don't want the entire selection active—only the remaining black background area.

11. With the Rectangular marquee tool, press Ctrl then click and diagonally drag the left side of the active marquee border from where the wallpaper ends to the left side of the KIDSROOM image. The Ctrl key combination removes from an active selection area, as the status bar at the bottom of Photoshop's workspace indicates. Only the remaining black background area remains.

12. Choose **E**dit, Paste **I**nto. Then position your cursor inside the marquee selection area, and move the pasted wallpaper copy around until it is positioned aesthetically.

13. Try to position this pasted wallpaper so that the little bears and elephants line up, as shown in figure 8.23. You might want to use the arrow keys to nudge the paste a pixel or two before finishing.

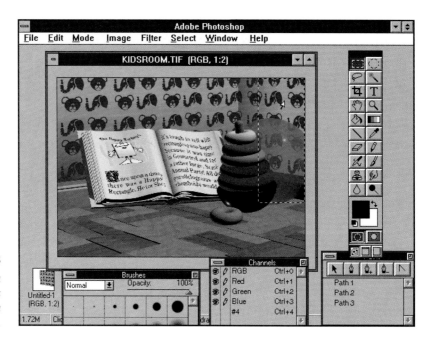

Figure 5.23

The Ctrl key used with a selection tool subtracts from an existing selection area.

14. When the wallpaper looks properly positioned, choose **S**elect, **N**one, and then immediately choose **F**ile, Sa**v**e As, name your work, and save it to a directory on your hard disk.

Not bad work for an afternoon, eh? Wallpapering the children's room has never been such a personally gratifying experience for a designer, and Photoshop's brand of pasting has it "hands down" over any other type of wallpaper paste. Figure 5.24 is of the finished image, lighting and imagery created through rendering and modeling; humanity, warmth, and a slight sense of humor accomplished by knowing some fancy moves with Adobe Photoshop.

Figure 5.24

KIDSROOM.TIF—the completed image.

Chapter 6

Combining Images

Photoshop excels at helping to combine common images to create an uncommon photo. Its power lies in the precision tools with which a user can create selection borders around a bitmap image for the purpose of compositing an area to a new background image.

But you should plan your photography carefully before combining images to make sure that lighting, perspective, camera angle, and resolution are identical. That's really the only hard part, as you'll see in this chapter about how to take a miniature model car and a country road to build an image people can't tear their eyes away from.

The Images on the *Adobe Photoshop NOW! CD-ROM*

ROAD.TIF and MINICAR.TIF are the images used in this chapter, and you can access them from the CHAP06 subdirectory on the *Adobe Photoshop NOW! CD-ROM*. If you would like to follow along in the creation of this piece, refer to these files throughout this chapter.

A Little Planning

The goal in building the image in this chapter is to create an image that "resonates" in the viewer's mind. A miniature car is placed on a full-sized road, complete with accurate lighting and shadows. The finished image looks photographically correct, yet there's something wrong with it, and this is what keeps the viewer intrigued.

Actually, you'll learn the tricks here for placing *any* miniature in a full-sized background, but there are a few rules you must accept that have bearing on how successfully you can use Photoshop in creating the scene.

- Use a standard 50-55mm lens when photographing the full-size background, but use a macro close-up lens when photographing the miniature. Make certain the miniature occupies the same field size through the lens that you intend it to occupy in the background image.

  When you digitize the two images (either through scanning or having a PhotoCD made of them), there must be enough digital information about the miniature to fill its intended space in the background image. Don't cheat on this one because if the resolution (the sampled pixels per inch) of the miniature is less than the background, you will be forced to use Photoshop to increase the resolution. Interpolated visual data usually results in obviously large pixels, an undesired side effect.

- Make sure the lighting in both photos is identical. The miniature car was photographed within minutes of the photo of the background image. The angle and position of the sunlight was the same, making the final composite scene more believable.

- Take the photo of the miniature at the same height and altitude as a viewer of the background image would see it. As you can see in figure 6.1, the MINICAR.TIF image was captured at a slightly inferior (lower) angle than a photographer would instinctively capture it, on a makeshift cardboard platform on the side of the road. A low horizon in a photo of a miniature suggests the miniature was too large for the photographer to "get on top of" the subject, hence it appears larger.

Figure 6.1

The background image and the subject are of equal resolution and proportionate size.

Accurately Selecting the Mini-Car

The Paths palette is used in Photoshop for designing smooth, extremely accurate templates that can be used to base a selection, to have color applied along its edge, or for use in other design programs as a guide (a *clipping path*). Unlike other Photoshop palettes, the Paths palette has its own discrete design tools that operate independently of toolbox tools.

Your goal is to define an accurate outline around the miniature car using the Paths palette tools. After the path is created, you'll make a selection border based on the path and use the selection to copy the car into the road background. Using paths takes some getting used to, but you'll discover that when it comes to selecting image areas that have borders of straight lines and smooth curves, the Paths palette has the tools you'll want to use.

1. Open the MINICAR.TIF image from the *Adobe Photoshop NOW! CD-ROM*.

2. Press F9 to display the Paths palette.

3. Choose the Zoom tool, and marquee zoom to a 4:1 viewing resolution above the windshield of the miniature car. A path needs a starting point, and this is where you'll begin.

4. Choose the Pen tool on the Paths palette, and click a point on the car's outline where the windshield meets the hood.

5. Click a second point to the right of the first, where the border of the hood meets the engine block. Continue in a clockwise direction, clicking on points of the car's front where a sharp directional change occurs. As shown in figure 6.2, several Anchor points now exist along the outline of the car, with path segments automatically connecting with each successive click of the mouse.

Figure 6.2
Click Anchor points where sharp changes in direction occur.

It's okay if the path segments formed between Anchor points don't perfectly match the outline of the car—in fact, you can see several instances in the last figure where a path segment clips an image area of the car. These straight paths will have their properties changed to curved path segments in later steps.

It's only important that you continue to travel in the same direction (clockwise in this case) as you started and that an Anchor point be defined where there's a sharp change in the course of the car's outline.

Perfecting the Path Outline around the Mini-Car

In time, you'll learn to ignore the obvious "wrongness" found in paths that don't initially conform to the exact outline of an underlying bitmap image. But there's nothing wrong with a little diversion during path creation to reshape a path segment before you've completed an outline. Unsaved Paths, like the one you're designing, will stay on top of your bitmap image until you've saved them or deliberately pressed the Backspace key to delete them. As vector information, Photoshop displays them *resolution-independently*, which means you can zoom closer into the MINICAR image, and the path you're building will remain the same width.

Let's refine the path at this point, using a different Paths palette tool, and remove some of the visual distraction these straight path segments present.

1. Choose the Zoom tool, and marquee zoom to an 8:1 viewing resolution over the area where the path segment lies between the first two Anchor points.

2. Choose the Corner tool from the Paths palette, and then click and drag, clockwise and down, on the second Anchor point, as shown in figure 6.3. Suddenly, you're not dragging on an Anchor point anymore, but a direction point instead.

When you use the Corner tool to create direction points and lines, you should click and drag in the direction you created the path. The path in this chapter's assignment is built in a clockwise direction, and you should create the direction lines and points by dragging in a clockwise direction. If you don't, the Anchor points will have inverted direction points, which is a fancy way of saying that you would produce weird, uncooperative, curved path segments.

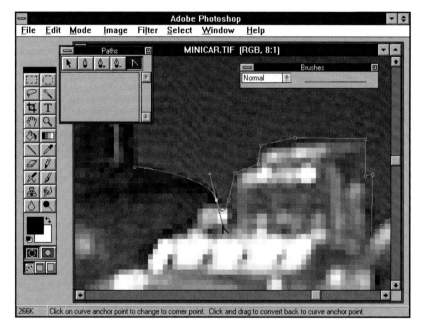

Figure 6.3

The Corner tool produces direction points from an Anchor point that connect straight path segments.

3. Click and drag on the top direction point (at the end of the direction line, *not* the Anchor point) with the Corner tool. This changes the property of the Anchor point from smooth to corner.

4. While holding the Ctrl key, click and drag on each direction point to shape the two adjacent path segments, one at a time, to conform to the outline of the car, as shown in figure 6.4.

Figure 6.4

The Ctrl key toggles the function of the Corner tool to the Arrow pointer tool.

Designing Curves around the Mini-Car

In some instances, you might want to forego clicking on points to produce Anchor points and straight path segments, and instead adopt a different technique with the Pen tool to create curved path segments from the get-go. The Bézier method of drawing involves creating a direction line for a path segment (and curving the segment) at the time you create an Anchor point.

As you move clockwise around the miniature car, building the path around its outline, you soon come to the front tires. This is an excellent place to experiment with the Pen tool and curved path segments. Tires are round shapes, and their curves have symmetrical properties anyway, right?

1. After clicking the Anchor point where the front-left tire meets the fender, click and drag with the Pen tool. As seen in figure 6.5, the cursor is holding a direction point at the end of a direction line. Don't release the mouse button yet.

2. Drag the direction point until the path segment belonging to the last Anchor point fits the outline of the tire.

3. If the placement of the Anchor point is wrong, or if you want to reposition the opposing direction point, press the Ctrl key to switch the Pen tool's function to that of the Arrow pointer tool. Unlike the Corner tool, the Arrow point is only for positioning, not modifying Anchors and direction points.

4. Click and drag a second and a third Anchor point, using the same techniques as described before to shape the path segments belonging to the smooth Anchor points to the outline of the front-left tire.

5. When you reach the area where the tire meets the undercarriage of the car, go back to clicking only with the Pen tool to produce straight path segments. Then resume clicking and dragging when you reach the front-right tire.

Figure 6.5

*Clicking and dragging with
the Pen tool produces a
smooth Anchor with a
curved path segment.*

*If you'd like a preview of how a particular path segment will result from clicking an Anchor
point, double-click on the Pen tool. In the Pen Tool Options dialog box, check the Rubber
Band box. You'll then be shown a view of every path segment preceding an Anchor point
click. This is a personal preference option, and some users shun the Rubber Band option
because it turns your path-designing work into something resembling a county fair taffy
pull.*

Finishing and Refining the Path

As you work your way in a clockwise direction around the car, you'll eventually meet the
first Anchor point that you clicked. You do want to close the path because selection borders become wildly inaccurate when created from an open path.

When you reach the first Anchor point, a tiny circle will appear to the bottom-right of the
Pen tool signifying that you're about to close the path. After the path is closed, use the
following steps to refine the path around the car.

1. Any path segment that is straight where it should be curved requires a click and
    drag, clockwise, using the Corner tool.

2. After the connecting path segments are curved, you can move on to the next step,
    if you want a smooth Anchor point in a particular place.

    If you want a sharp directional change at this Anchor point, however, release the
    mouse button, and then click and drag on a direction point. You now can fit one
    path segment to the car's outline, and the direction point no longer controls path
    segments on both sides of the Anchor point.

3. Press the Ctrl key, and click and drag on the opposing direction point. The Arrow pointer tool is used for editing a path segment or Anchor point, but it doesn't change the properties of either.

4. An unsaved path can be saved at any phase of the path's completion—and now seems to be a good time. Click on the command button on the Paths Palette, and choose Save Path from the drop-down list. Accept the default name of Path 1, and click on OK.

5. You should have a saved path around the car's outline that looks like figure 6.6.

Figure 6.6

The completed path around the outline of the miniature car.

Adding Car Windows to the Car Outline

If you continue to use the Pen tool while a check mark appears beside the saved path's title on the Paths palette, a saved path will continue to adopt additional path segments. In the next steps, you'll make this feature work for you, to add noncontiguous geometric areas—the outlines of the windows to the car to Path 1. You don't want the background information in the MINICAR.TIF image peeking though when the selection of the car is placed on the ROAD.TIF background image. Creating a subpath around the windows takes care of this problem.

1. Zoom in to the front window area of the MINICAR image. A 4:1 viewing resolution is good.

2. Click on points along the inside edge of the outline of the front car window, as shown in figure 6.7.

Figure 6.7

A subpath is created whenever you add to a closed path.

Subpaths to a path can be created in either a clockwise or counterclockwise direction. To produce and edit direction points, it doesn't matter which route you choose, only that you click and drag on an Anchor point in the same direction the subpath was created.

3. Close the subpath, and use the Corner tool to create curved segments and to change the property of the Anchor points to sharp corners.

4. Press the Ctrl key to access the Arrow pointer tool. Refine the subpath using the direction points so that the subpath closely matches the outline of the front window.

5. Repeat the last steps to create additional subpaths around the rest of the car windows. These subpaths are automatically saved as components of the saved Path 1.

6. When all the subpaths are completed, click on the command button on the Paths palette, and choose Make Selection from the drop-down list.

7. Enter 0 in the Feather **R**adius field in the Make Selection dialog box, check the **A**nti-Aliased box, and then click on OK. Photoshop creates a very precise selection border from the path and subpath information, as shown in figure 6.8.

Don't panic when your elaborate path (and subpaths) disappear from view when you make a selection based upon it. Photoshop switches off your view of the path when a selection is made, but the path still exists. Adobe presumes that you no longer want a path to be visible after a selection has been based on it, and the path simply becomes invisible at the time. If you want to make the path visible and editable again, click to the left of the path title on the Paths palette. A check mark appears, and the path becomes visible. This check mark can be switched on or off at any time, as long as a path is saved.

Figure 6.8

A selection area based on paths and subpaths is created by using the Make Selection command.

8. Press Ctrl+C to copy the selection area of the car to the Clipboard, and then minimize the MINICAR image to an icon on the workspace. You'll need it again later.

Adding the Selection to the Background

I overlooked something when photographing the two images used in this chapter. Although I matched the lighting and resolution in both the MINICAR and ROAD images, the area of road in the ROAD image goes downhill from left to right. The miniature car was photographed on an even surface. Consequentially, you'll need to rotate the car after it's been copied.

Additionally, a copy of the car's shadow will be placed in the ROAD image, and it, too, will need to be rotated. Photoshop's Arbitrary Rotate command will be the best choice of the available Rotate commands because with it you can specify identical values for the selection of the car and shadow.

1. Open the ROAD.TIF image from the *Adobe Photoshop NOW! CD-ROM*.

2. Press Ctrl+V to paste the selection of the car into the background ROAD image.

3. Choose the Lasso tool (or any selection tool), place the cursor inside the floating selection, and click and drag the car selection onto the road (see fig. 6.9).

4. Press Ctrl++ to zoom your view to a 1:1 resolution. When the car is positioned as shown in figure 6.10, choose Image, Rotate, Arbitrary.

5. Enter 1.5 in the Angle: field, click on the CW radio button, and then click on OK. (1.5 is a value I came by through trial and error.)

6. Choose Select, Defringe. Then enter 1 pixel in the Width field, and click on OK.

Figure 6.9

Reposition the pasted selection of the car.

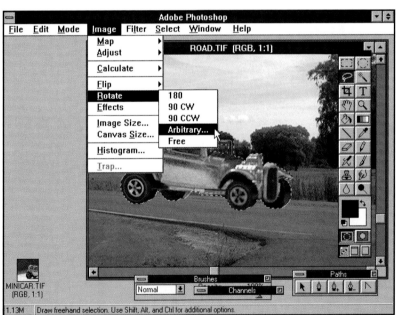

Figure 6.10

Arbitrary rotation can be specified up to 1/100th of a degree.

Even though a selection is created without a Feather Radius, an antialiased selection still might contain pixels with semitransparent, sometimes unwanted color around the edges. In the example in this chapter, the car selection has dark brown edge pixels from its native background. They might not be apparent if the car was pasted into a similarly colored background, but the ROAD image sports a bright blue sky. Defringing by 1 or 2 pixels usually solves the problem of contrasting edge pixels. Zoom in closely on a floating selection, press Ctrl+H to hide the marquee edges, and see if a floating selection in your own work requires the Defringe command. Always use the Defringe command before saving a selection.

7. Choose **S**elect, **S**ave Selection, and then save your work up to this point to your hard disk.

Using the Magic Wand Tool To Pick Up a Shadow

You'll see in other chapters how a shadow is created using the Gaussian Blur filter, but in this assignment, you actually can use most of the car's shadow as it was cast on its surface in the MINICAR image. As you've seen, the shadow in this image is flat and lacks tonal variation. This makes the Magic Wand tool a good choice for selecting the shadow area. The shadow is an intricate one, and it's much easier to select it and refine it for use in the ROAD image, than to render a shadow for the car by hand.

1. Restore the MINICAR image on Photoshop's workspace.

2. Double-click on the Magic Wand tool, enter 26 in the **T**olerance field for pixels, and then click on OK. This is another "trial and error" value.

3. Click the Magic Wand cursor on part of the shadow beneath the car. It's okay if the Magic Wand picks up part of the car tire, as shown in figure 6.11. This actually is desired because you'll be pasting the shadow behind the saved selection of the car in the ROAD image. You can use the tire as a guide for lining up the car and shadow.

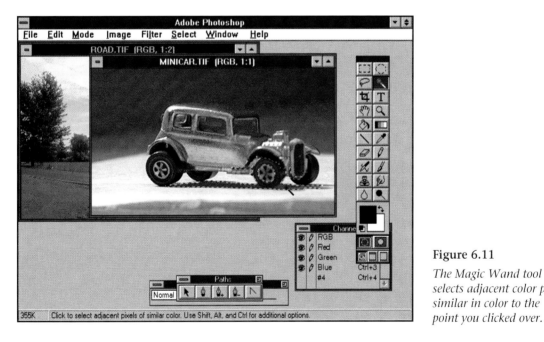

Figure 6.11

The Magic Wand tool selects adjacent color pixels similar in color to the point you clicked over.

4. Hold the Shift key, and click a second time in a shadow area that wasn't selected with your first Magic Wand click. Nonadjacent image pixels can't be selected by the Magic Wand tool; they must be added to a selection area.

5. Press Ctrl+C when you have most of the shadow marquee selected, and then minimize MINICAR again to make ROAD.TIF the active image window.

Pasting the Shadow behind the Car

In the next steps, you'll see how useful the apparently unwanted tire portion of the selection you copied is as a visual reference for the placement of the shadow.

1. Choose Select, Load Selection, and then choose Edit, Paste Behind.

2. Place your selection tool inside the marquee border, and then click and drag it until it's visible beneath the car.

3. Choose Image, Rotate, Arbitrary. Click on OK. Photoshop "remembers" your last entry into this and other dialog boxes.

4. Click and drag the floating shadow selection until the marquee border around the tire area precisely aligns with the tire of the car it's pasted behind.

5. The shadow is a little intense and the wrong shade to be realistically cast on the ROAD image's pavement. Click on the Mode drop-down list on the Brushes palette, and choose Multiply.

6. Press the number 5 on the keyboard. While a pasted selection is a floating one, and you have a selection tool active, you can select the Opacity of the composite paste directly from your keyboard in 10% increments. As shown in figure 6.12, a half-transparent, Multiply mode composite makes the shadow look realistic in tone.

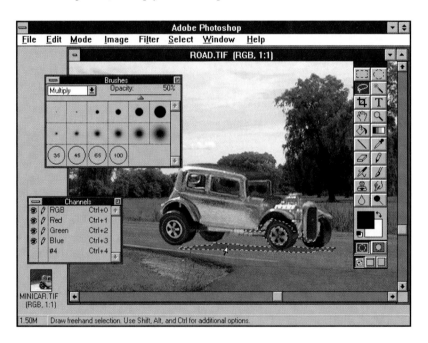

Figure 6.12

Multiply mode accentuates the darker areas of a pasted selection.

Retouching the Shadow

The shadow definitely adds a dimension to your photo-fakery, but it needs some polish around the edges to display the same refinement as the rest of the visual detail in the ROAD image.

Fortunately, shadows alone don't contain much visual interest; they basically allow visual detail from what they're on top of to show through, and they have soft edges where light meets shade. Two painting modes come in handy to finish the image, the Darken and the Multiply modes.

Photoshop modes are found in various locations and can be applied in a number of different ways. The editing tools, such as the Smudge and Dodge/Burn, can operate in modes that are set on the Brushes palette. Stroking and filling a selection or path also can be done in a mode. And the combining of two images (compositing) can be performed in a mode, accessed either through the Brushes palette or the Edit, Composite Controls command.

If you hold down the Alt key prior to choosing Edit, Paste, the Composite Controls will be displayed automatically. (Pressing Alt before Ctrl+V works too, but it's a real finger-twister.)

1. Choose the Paintbrush tool. Hold down on the Alt key and click over a shadow area. The cursor changes into the Eyedropper tool, and you've sampled the shadow foreground color.

2. Choose Darken mode, and click and drag the Opacity slider to 29%. Choose the far left, middle-row tip from the Brushes palette, and stroke along the hard edge of the shadow.

3. As you can see in figure 6.13, the Darken mode adds the foreground color only to areas lighter than the shadow color. This blends the edge of the pasted shadow into the background image, while the 29% Opacity allows visual detail to show through wherever you color.

Figure 6.13

Soften the edges of the pasted shadow using the Paintbrush set to Darken mode.

4. When you've finished retouching the shadow, you might want to use the Multiply mode for the Paintbrush to increase the tonal density slightly where the base of the wheels touch the ground. Shadows naturally are more intense at the base of the object casting a shadow, and Multiply mode progressively saturates an area with foreground color when using a painting tool.

5. When you're happy with the shadow work, delete the Alpha channel from the image, and save the image as DRAGSTER.TIF to your hard disk. As you can see in figure 6.14, there's something contradictory, yet absolutely authentic about the finished piece. Did someone actually build a 1:1 scale toy car, or are those bonsai trees in the background?

Figure 6.14

Front-end alignment notwithstanding, Photoshop combines different images perfectly.

PART THREE:

Image Corrections and Enhancements

Chapter 7

Restoring an Image Area

It's often the experience of professional photographers that an important picture is impossible to choreograph. If you have five minutes to capture a portrait of a senator, movie star, or even a relative, you take as many photos as possible, and still hope to find only one that's usable later.

Later, you might find that the best image you have of someone contains a flaw you wish you could remove. With Photoshop you can. In this chapter, you'll see how to restore a portrait whose subject is partially obscured by his own hand.

Retouching Is Serious Business

You shouldn't take the tricks shown in this chapter lightly; retouching a portrait photo can be fun, but the results can range from invisible to phony-looking. It all depends on your artist's eye, how much retouching needs to be performed, and if you have a good working knowledge of Photoshop's tools. The example in this chapter is an exaggerated one, and hopefully you'll never see such a sorrowful image pass your desk. But the following techniques can be used in a number of situations where you need to rescue an image from an unusable state to one of near-perfection.

The Image on the *Adobe Photoshop NOW! CD-ROM*

The retouching you'll perform in this chapter uses the REG_EDIT.TIF image on the *Adobe Photoshop NOW! CD-ROM*. You should load the image before participating in the steps. The file will be referenced by this name throughout the chapter.

Assessing the Image Areas for Retouching

Our fictitious Congressional hopeful, Reginald "Reg" Edit, had an itchy cheek when he was photographed. He needs a campaign poster, but as you can see in figure 7.1, his portrait captures a less-than-perfect pose.

At this point, you need to take a look at what's wrong with the picture, and what can be done to fix it. Reginald's finger, hand, and forearm are obscuring part of his cheek, the background, and his left shoulder. Fortunately, there seems to be enough similar, unobscured image areas available in the image to use as source material to replace the area currently occupied by his hand. Each obscured area of this image will require a specific approach to retouch the image.

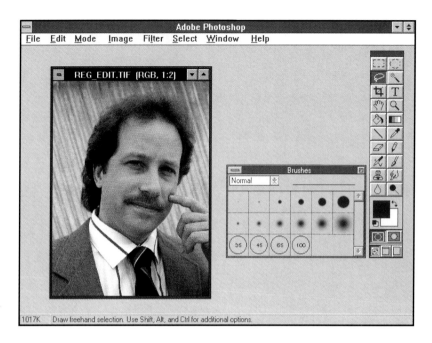

Figure 7.1

A poor pose in a photograph can be corrected with Photoshop.

Isolating the Border of the Face

First concentrate on Reg's face. You need to remove the finger from his cheek and replace it with another image area that is of similar color and texture. Because the area where Reg's cheek meets the background is a smooth one, a path can be used to define this area so that it can be modified.

1. With the REG_EDIT.TIF image in Photoshop's workspace, choose the Zoom tool, and marquee zoom to a 2:1 resolution around the area where Reg is poking himself in the face.

2. Press F9 to display the Paths palette.

3. Choose the Pen tool, and then click an Anchor point where Reg's cheek meets the background, above his finger.

4. Click a second Anchor point on Reg's cheek line, below his finger.

5. Continuing clockwise, click a third and forth Anchor point so that the path segments Photoshop draws between Anchors loosely encompasses Reg's cheek where his finger intrudes.

6. Click a fifth time on your first Anchor point. This closes the path (see fig. 7.2). This path will be refined and then serve as a basis for creating a selection area.

7. Choose the Corner tool, and then click and drag downward on the first Anchor point. This produces direction points from the Anchor, one of which your cursor is now holding.

8. Drag the Anchor's direction point so that the path segment along Reg's cheek conforms to the curvature of his cheek.

9. Repeat the last steps with the second Anchor point. The goal here is to match the path segment to Reg's cheek line accurately.

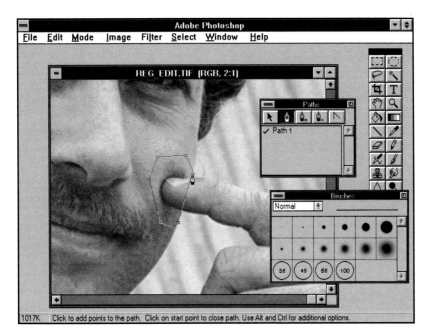

Figure 7.2
Leave room around the finger when you design the path.

10. Click on the Path palette's command button, and choose Save Path from the drop-down list.

11. Accept the default name of Path 1, and click on OK in the Save Path dialog box.

Creating a New Cheek Line for Reginald

The selection area based on this saved path will be used for two purposes. First it will be used as a selection area that encompasses the area of Reg's cheek that needs to be restored. You'll concentrate first on his cheek line. Naturally, there's two sides to a line, so to complete this part of the retouching work, the selection area will be inverted to retouch the background that's obscured by his hand. Let's get the edge of Reg's face restored, then concentrate on background restoration.

1. Click on the command button on the Paths palette, then choose Make selection from the drop-down list.

2. In the Make Selection dialog box, enter 0 in the Feather Radius box, make sure the Anti-Aliased box is marked, and then click on OK.

3. Choose the Zoom tool, and marquee zoom into a 4:1 viewing resolution of the active selection area.

4. Double-click on the Rubber Stamp tool, and choose Clone (aligned) from the Options drop-down list. Then click on OK.

5. On the Brushes palette, choose Normal mode, 100% Opacity, and then choose a medium Brushes tip from the second row.

6. Alt+click on the area close to Reg's cheek line, above the selection marquee. This sets the sampling point for the Rubber stamp tool.

7. Click inside the selection marquee starting above Reg's fingertip, and drag through the finger. As you can see in figure 7.3, you are replacing the fingertip with image area sampled above the area obscured by the finger.

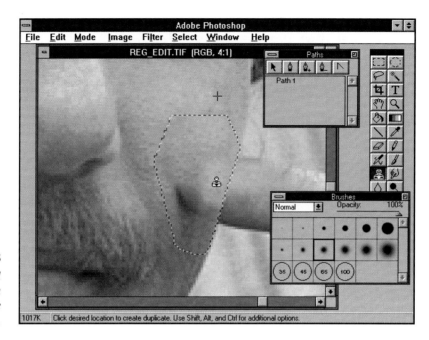

Figure 7.3

The Rubber Stamp tool replaces image areas with samples from other image areas.

Don't overwork the Rubber Stamp tool in one area. Repeated strokes and back-and-forth motions will continue to replace the selected area with identical samples, and the result will be unaesthetic and tell-tale of retouching. Strive to make short, single strokes, and frequently reset the sampling point for the Rubber Stamp tool so that the area you're cloning over contains a variation of sampled texture values.

Also, don't try to clone over the entire selection area. Your first goal is to define a new cheek line for Reg. Don't concern yourself with exactly matching the skin tones at this point, as you'll refine your work later.

8. After you have the top half of the right side of the selection border cloned, Alt+click in a very light area of the candidate's five o'clock shadow to set a new Rubber Stamp tool sampling point.

9. Click and drag inside the bottom right of the selection area, and move upward along the selection edge of Reg's cheek line. You'll get a somewhat hard edge where his five o'clock shadow stops, but it's okay; you'll fix it later, and your objective is to give Reg a restored cheek line.

10. After a maximum of three or four strokes, your cloning work along Reg's left cheek should be completed. Save the image to your hard disk as REG_EDIT.TIF.

It's not always necessary to save a selection area when you already have a path saved that was used to create the selection area. Saved selections increase image file sizes by a third, whereas saved paths add only a 1 or 2 KB, depending on the complexity of the path.

Restoring the Background, Removing the Hand

The finger should still be visible on Reg's cheek, but his cheek line should be completely redefined. It's time to concentrate on the other side of the path area you defined to remove a good part of Reg's hand from the scene.

As you would do in traditional painting, learn to work from the general to the specific in retouching work. Start with the coarse work, and then move to refining specific areas. Concentrating on details at an early phase of retouching will place unequal emphasis on specific image areas, thus attracting attention, which is not wanted!

1. After saving the image, your selection marquee still should be active. If it's not, choose Make Selection from the Paths palette's drop-down list again.

2. Press Ctrl+– to zoom out to a 2:1 viewing resolution. You'll be concentrating on the area to the right of the selection border. Scroll over to the hand if you don't have a clear view.

3. Choose **S**elect, **I**nverse. Everything *except* Reg's cheek area now is selected.

4. Choose a larger, second row Brushes tip (keep Opacity and mode the same). Then Alt+click directly on a dark portion of the diagonal striped background area.

5. Click directly on a different dark, diagonally striped area close to Reg's cheek line, and then drag around the hand, as shown in figure 7.4.

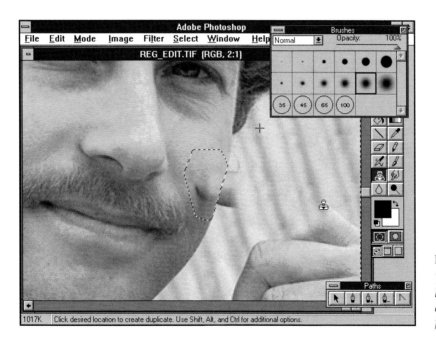

Figure 7.4

You can re-create a background pattern if you clone a similar location from the sample location.

6. The Rubber Stamp presently is locked in to sample and clone areas that match the pattern of the background. Continue clicking and dragging along the edge of Reg's cheek until you restore the area.

   For the sake of the figures in this book, the marquee borders around the selection are visible. But marquee borders hinder the visibility of Photoshop retouching work, so you might want to press Ctrl+H at various points in this assignment to hide the edges of the marquee.

Replacing Reg's Cheek

Reg clearly has a beginning and end to his cheek now, which leaves his fingertip to clone over. Skin has many variations in both texture and tone, and this has proven to be a most frustrating challenge for the traditional photo-retoucher. In the chemical world of photography, an airbrush with semi-opaque dyes would cover this area, and pores, freckles, and other visual detail would be lost. But by locating an area on Reg's face with almost identical tone and texture values, the Rubber Stamp tool once again can be used to replace what his finger covered up in the photo.

1. Press Ctrl+D to deselect the marquee area. You lose the selection, but it can be created again with the Paths palette command. You won't be doing any edge work here, so the selection area isn't required.

2. Press F8 to display the Info palette, click on the Eyedropper icon on the top palette field, and select HSB Color.

3. Run your cursor over parts of Reg's cheek close to, but not directly on, the remaining fingertip area.

4. Write down the HSB values displayed on the Info palette on a piece of paper if you're like me and can't memorize them.

   This is a very subjective part of the assignment, and you might find values on Reg's cheek that differ from those stated in the steps. For example, H: 60°, S: 20%, and B: 75% was one value I took from the cheek area. I then sampled an area that had similar values. If your values are different, use the values you get in the next steps.

5. Run your cursor around Reg's opposite, unobscured cheek area until you find a corresponding HSB value. When you do, Alt+click to set the Rubber Stamp sampling point.

6. Click and drag over the remaining fingertip in one or two strokes.

7. Set the Brushes palette to 50% Opacity, and change the mode to Lighten. You'll be both cloning and lightening Reg's five o'clock shadow next.

8. Click and drag downward, starting from above the area where Reg's five o'clock shadow begins. This creates a smoother transition between skin areas, as shown in figure 7.5.

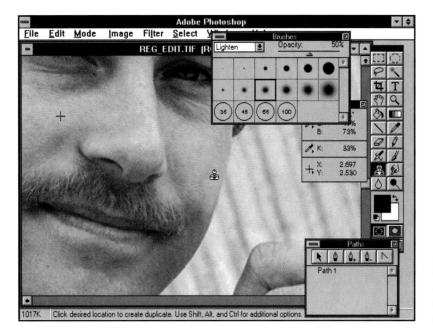

9. Set the Brushes palette back to Normal mode and 100% Opacity. Then Alt+click over an area near where you've been cloning over.

10. Finish Reg's cheek by clicking and dragging areas very close to your sampling point. This evens out rough transition areas, and adds a little skin texture. Aim for getting the skin color right. You'll finish the visual detail—the texture of the skin—in the next section.

11. Save your work to your hard disk.

Softening the Edgework, Adding Visual Detail

You've lost some focus in the cheek you are working on through the many steps applied to the image area. A quick fix for restoring some visual information to Reg's cheek is to add a little contrast to the area. This must be done with some subtlety, so here's how to bring out the detail, but keep the edgework in this area hidden.

1. Click to the left of the Path 1 title on the Paths palette. This makes the path visible again.

2. Click on the command button on the Paths palette, then choose Make Selection, enter 4 in the Feather Radius field, and click on OK. The resulting selection area now will have a very soft transition edge to it between selection and masked area.

3. Choose Filter, Sharpen, Sharpen. As you can see in figure 7.6, the Sharpen command added contrast to Reg's cheek, drawing out skin detail, while the border of the selection area tapers off smoothly into the other facial areas.

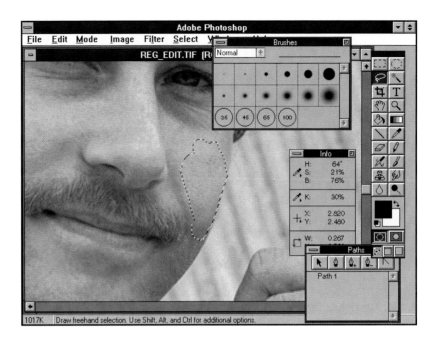

Figure 7.6

A Feather Radius makes a smooth transition between selected and masked areas.

While useful at times, the Feather command also ruins image detail depending on how you use it. Use the Feather command to create soft borders, but don't use the command when you want to edit the edge of a selection area precisely. For more information about the many uses of the Feather command, see NRP's Inside Adobe Photoshop for Windows.

4. Save your work to your hard disk.

Defining an Edge to Reg's Suit

Because our candidate had an itch that couldn't wait, his hand covers his lapel and shoulder. Fortunately, the image texture and color of the hidden areas are almost identical to the rest of his suit. To restore this area, you'll first use the same technique for defining an edge as you did with Reg's cheek.

1. Double-click on the Zoom tool to zoom out to a 1:1 viewing resolution of the image.

2. Choose the Pen tool on the Paths palette, and then click an outline of path segments so that the bottom of the path can be used to define Reg's shoulder, as shown in figure 7.7. Save the Path as Path 2, and use the Corner tool to create a natural-looking slope to the shoulder.

3. Create a selection area from Path 2 using the Make selection command on the drop-down list on the Paths palette.

4. Choose the Rubber Stamp tool, and then Alt+click over a dark diagonal area in the background.

5. Start clicking and dragging over a diagonal line, and then click and drag completely within the selection area. This removes Reg's hand and adds an edge to his shoulder.

Figure 7.7

Define the area above the shoulder with a path.

Replacing the Hand with a Fabric Pattern

This leaves you with the remains of Reg's hand intruding on his jacket. Rather than using the Rubber Stamp to clone the area by sampling from other parts of the jacket, you'll use the From Pattern option. The fabric of Reg's jacket is a fine weave with lots of texture, but little remarkable detail, so a small sample from a clear area of his jacket is the ideal source for this part of the retouching assignment. Don't worry about matching exact shades found on the surface of the jacket—the hard part of this retouching is done. A well-executed retouch of Reg's face takes the focus of the image away from the area you'll work on next.

1. Choose **S**elect, **I**nverse, and then choose **S**elect, **S**ave Selection. You need to access a selection tool next, and this would lose the selection area you now have defined as including the jacket and other areas, and masking the background area you just retouched.

2. Choose the Rectangular Marquee tool, and then marquee select an area of jacket below Reg's right shoulder, as shown in figure 7.8.

3. Choose **E**dit, **D**efine Pattern.

4. Double-click on the Rubber Stamp tool, and choose Pattern (non-aligned) from the Op**t**ion list. Then click on OK.

The difference between Pattern (aligned) and Pattern (non-aligned), is that a non-aligned pattern starts the Rubber Stamp tool's sampling point from the same point every time you click and drag. Conversely, the aligned option samples synchronously from the sample pattern; you click and drag up, the sample point moves up within the invisible pattern sample.

Figure 7.8

Select an area that will best match the area that needs retouching.

5. Click and drag in small areas over the remains of Reg's hand, as shown in figure 7.9. Every time you release the mouse button and click and drag again, Photoshop resets the sample point for the pattern, so take care that your strokes are random as you retouch.

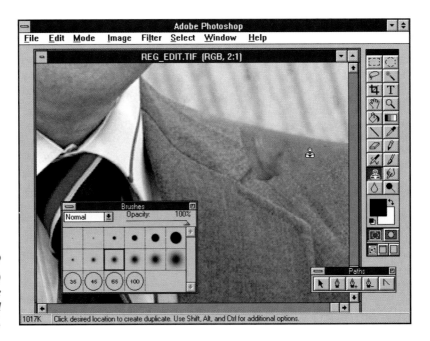

Figure 7.9

The Pattern (non-aligned) option samples image areas from a pattern stored in system RAM.

6. When you've retouched every area except the point of Reg's collar, you're done for the moment. Save your work to your hard disk.

Tailoring Reg's Collar

Retouching the point on Reg's left collar is easy if you think about this one. In the next steps, you'll simply sample from a clean edge of the collar, then continue cloning until the two collar lines meet.

1. Double-click on the Rubber Stamp tool, and set the Option to Clone (aligned). Then click on OK.

2. Zoom into a 4:1 resolution of the collar point.

3. Alt+click over a part of the bottom collar line that doesn't need retouching, and then click and drag in a straight line in a two o'clock direction and angle, as shown in figure 7.10.

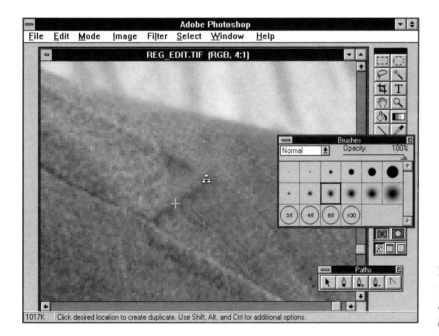

Figure 7.10

The Rubber Stamp tool resamples areas that you just cloned.

In the last step, the traveling sample crosshair of the Rubber Stamp tool samples areas you've already cloned to complete the bottom collar line, as you did with the dark diagonal lines in the background image.

Resampling this way is useful for re-creating unimportant visual areas, such as backgrounds and minute trim on images, but don't make this a Photoshop practice unless it's absolutely necessary. The idea behind retouching with the Rubber Stamp tool is to avoid creating obvious patterns, and recycling image areas by repeating samples unfortunately creates this.

4. Repeat the process of sampling the top collar line, then clicking and dragging over the line in a four o'clock angle and direction.

5. Save your work when you've connected the collar lines at the point. As you can see in figure 7.11, the cloned jacket area looks restored albeit a little soft in focus.

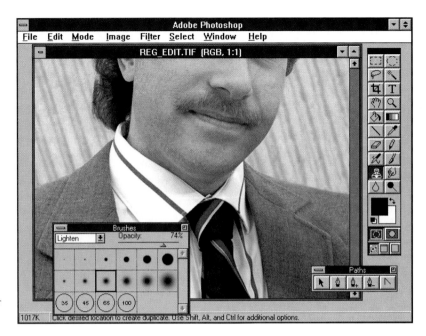

Figure 7.11

Invisible mending in one hour, courtesy of Photoshop!

Sharpening Selected Jacket Areas

The loss of detail in Reg's jacket was inevitable because dimensional objects in an image move in and out of focus according to the focal plane of the camera's lens. This can be compensated for, though, by using the same techniques you used to correct Reg's skin texture. In the next steps, you'll use the Paintbrush tool and the Quick Mask mode to define the areas that need sharpening the most.

1. Choose the Paintbrush tool, and pick a medium Brushes tip from the top row of tips that have no spread attributes.

2. Double-click on the Quick Mask mode button, and choose the Color Indicates: Selected Areas radio button.

3. Click on the Color selection box, and choose a color that really clashes with Reg's jacket so that you can see the Quick Mask overlay. Green is good.

4. Click on OK, and then click on OK to return to Quick Mask mode and the image.

5. Click and drag over areas of the jacket that contain little visual sharpness, as shown in figure 7.12. Do not try to fill the entire cloned area, but rather let your strokes be "painterly" and follow some of the contours and shades of the jacket.

6. Click on the Standard mode button. Choose **S**elect, Fea**t**her, and enter a Radius of 4 pixels. Then click on OK.

7. Press Ctrl+H to hide the marquee edges, and then choose **S**elect, Sharpen, Sharpen.

8. Press Ctrl+D to deselect the selection area, and then choose the Blur/Sharpen tool.

If the Blur/Sharpen tool is presently set to Sharpen, double-click on the tool to reset it to Blur in the options box. You also can hold down the Alt key to toggle from Sharpen to Blur, but why work in a design program with both hands tied up?

Figure 7.12
Apply the Quick Mask overlay in the area you want to add contrast to.

9. Click and drag across the edge of Reg's shoulder to soften the artificial border you created between background and shoulder earlier. In figure 7.13, you can see the result of some carefully planned time spent removing a photo flub most people would consider impossible.

Figure 7.13
Use the Blur/Sharpen tool to soften the edge of the shoulder to get a photographic look.

10. You're done, and it's clean-up time. Delete the two saved paths by displaying them (clicking on the path title on the Paths palette), and then click on the command button and choose Delete Path.

11. Save your image as WIN_REG!.TIF to your hard disk. Do not check the Save Alpha Channels box in the TIFF Options dialog box as you don't need the saved selection area any more.

What you've done is a fairly extensive transformation of image data. In noncomputerese, you've performed miracles, something our candidate might need to swing an election. In figure 7.14, I added a snappy banner beneath the finished image, and opened REG_EDIT.TIF again from the *Adobe Photoshop NOW! CD-ROM*.

Figure 7.14

Your finished image should look like an entirely different photo.

Hopefully, you'll never need to edit an image as extensively as the one in this chapter. If you do, you've acquired a fine arsenal of tricks and techniques to accomplish the task. Nevertheless, with as much visual information missing from the original as you had in this chapter, your labors reconstructed the image, but not flawlessly. That's why it's always an option to throw bright colors and splashy type next to the image to complete the piece, as I did in the last figure. It's a diversion, for sure, but it might be just the one you'll need sometime to successfully convey an image as appearing unretouched at a casual glance.

Chapter 8

Reshaping a Picture's Contents

It wasn't long ago in the PC environment that if you pulled on a corner of a bitmap image in an application, you'd wind up with a jagged, stair-steppy image reminiscent of a 1980s video game. But, with the advent of 24-bit TrueColor imaging and the capability of Photoshop to interpolate pixel values, a bitmap image can be as malleable as a vector-type graphic. In this chapter, you'll see how to mold a bitmap image to create powerful, striking imagery.

Creating a Magazine Photo-Illustration

This chapter's assignment is to build a graphic that illustrates a magazine article on drought. It's a topical theme, and through the course of the following steps, you'll learn how to create a 3D photorealistic box from a flat photograph. You can use the technique on RGB images of a wide variety of subject matter, and you might decide to expand upon this idea to create other photorealistic polygonal shapes.

To begin, digitized images of the sky and of parched land are source materials for the piece. Additionally, an EPS image was created in a drawing program to serve as a guide for reshaping the sky image into a box.

The Images on the *Adobe Photoshop NOW! CD-ROM*

This is exciting stuff you're going to get into, and even if you don't have an assignment to illustrate drought, you'll want hands-on experience with the techniques shown in this chapter. The *Adobe Photoshop NOW! CD-ROM* contains all the image files used in this assignment.

Measuring the Background Image for a Foreground Element

In figure 8.1, you see the DROUGHT.TIF image with Photoshop's rulers bounding the image window. This is the first step in creating a foreground element: to press Ctrl+R. Because the width of DROUGHT.TIF is about three inches, the box you'll create out of clouds should be two and one half inches to fit within the background image.

Features Covered:

- Channels
- Distort command
- Paths palette
- Last-saved versions
- Levels command

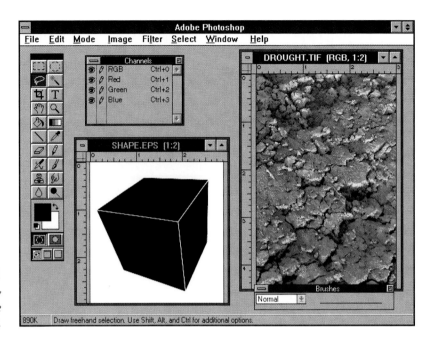

Figure 8.1

Press Ctrl+R to display rulers around the active image window.

SHAPE.EPS, the box shape created in a drawing program, was designed to fit comfortably within the DROUGHT image. You'll be using the EPS image with STORMSKY.TIF, also found on the *Adobe Photoshop NOW! CD-ROM*, in the next steps as a template for transforming a photographic sky image into the shape of a building block.

Adding the Template to the Sky Image

An EPS image is terrific for basing a selection area upon. Encapsulated PostScript images typically are grayscale, containing 8 bits per pixel color information. Which, coincidentally, is the maximum bit-depth of an Alpha channel that holds selection information. Here's how it's done.

1. Open the STORMSKY.TIF, and then the SHAPE.EPS image from the *Adobe Photoshop NOW! CD-ROM*.

2. The EPS Rasterizer dialog box appears. The **W**idth should be 2.889 inches, and H**e**ight 2.958 inches. Set the **R**esolution to 150 pixels/inch, and choose Grayscale mode. Then click on OK.

3. Press Ctrl+A, and then press Ctrl+C to copy the entire SHAPE image to the Clipboard.

4. Press F6 to display the Channels palette if it isn't already open in your workspace.

5. Press Ctrl+Tab to toggle to STORMSKY.TIF as the active image window.

6. Click on the command button on the Channels palette, and choose New Channel from the drop-down list.

7. Click on the Color Indicates: Selected Areas radio button, accept the default name of #4 for the channel, and click on OK.

8. Press Ctrl+V to paste the SHAPE image into the Alpha channel.

9. Press Ctrl+D to composite the pasted SHAPE image. You'll be moving the location of the SHAPE selection area later, so don't be too concerned about its placement right now.

Adding the Template to the Sky Image

10. Click on the RGB title on the Channels palette to display the color view of STORM-SKY.TIF.

11. Choose File, Save As at this point, and save the STORMSKY.TIF image with its new Alpha channel to your hard disk (check the Save Alpha Channels box on the TIFF Options dialog box).

Creating a Vector Template from Selection Information

You are not actually going to use the selection area in the Alpha channel to modify the RGB image. It's purpose is to base a path on the area. Paths are geometric, vector-based information that Photoshop maps to your monitor, but they *aren't* mapped to the image they overlay. It's this unique property that enables you to see a "blueprint" of a shape, and to base your image editing on it without the path ever interfering with the bitmap image. Selection areas are for active editing work, and you need to do a little planning before editing.

1. Press F9 to display the Paths palette in your workspace.

2. Choose Select, Load Selection. The selection area based on the SHAPE image in the Alpha channel becomes visible.

3. Choose a selection tool. Then, while pressing the Ctrl and Alt keys, click and drag the selection area to the right so that the selection is positioned similarly to that seen in figure 8.2. The right side of STORMSKY.TIF is visually more interesting, so you'll want to use that section of sky in your design.

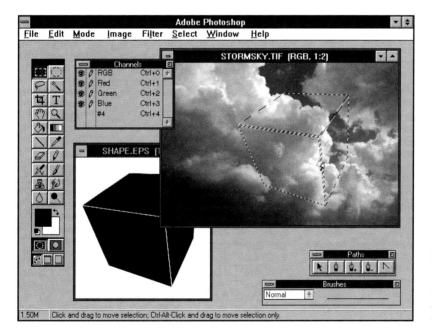

Figure 8.2

Clicking and dragging a selection while holding the Alt and Ctrl keys moves only the selection border.

4. Click on the command button on the Paths palette, and choose Make Path from the drop-down list.

5. Type **0.5** in the Tolerance field for pixels. This is the lowest value (the closest approximation) a path might be automatically built from selection information. Click on OK.

6. When the path is created from the active selection area, click on the command button on the Paths palette and choose Save Path from the drop-down list.

7. Accept the default Name of Path 1 for the path, and click on OK.

Think of paths as ghosts; you can see them, but you pass right through them to do your editing work on a bitmap image. And if a path ever obstructs your view, click on the Paths palette to the left of the title. When the check mark disappears, so does the path, only to return when you click again next to the path title.

Building the First Side of the Sky Block

The Path presently displayed will serve as an invaluable guide for distorting parts of the STORMSKY image. To create a dimensional facade, you'll begin by selecting a square area to shape into the front portion of the path.

1. Click on the Default colors icon button.

2. Choose the Rectangular Marquee tool, and while holding down the Shift key, begin your click and drag at the vertices of the path where the three shapes that make up the path meet, as shown in figure 8.3. Drag all the way to the bottom of the image window.

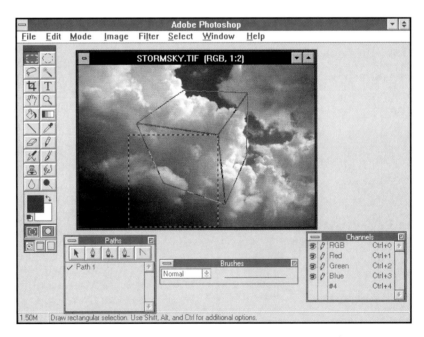

Figure 8.3

Rectangular marquee selections are constrained to a square when you hold the Shift key.

3. Press Ctrl++ to Zoom your view to a 1:1 resolution, filling the workspace. Scroll down so that you can clearly see the square selection and the path area that represents the front of the block shape.

4. Choose Image, Effects, Distort.

5. Place your cursor inside a corner handle of the Distort boundary box, and then click and drag the corner so that it is over the corresponding corner of the path. In figure 8.4, three of the corners have been fitted to the corresponding path area, with the fourth being moved into place.

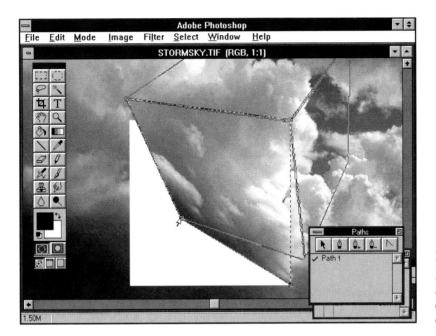

Figure 8.4

Make the Distort boundary box conform to the four corners of the "front" part of the path.

Because of the construction of the path based on the SHAPE selection, gaps exist where the three facets of the box meet. When continuing to create this block of cloudy sky, butt the edges of the distorted cloud selection areas to their nearest neighboring selection. When creating this image, I placed the two top-corner Distort boundary handles in the center of the gap. In subsequent steps, I brought the other two distorted selections up to the edge of this first distorted selection area, ignoring the path lines altogether. The path segments are supposed to be guides, but not absolute ones.

6. When you think the Distort boundary closely matches the front facet of the path, click inside the boundary box to lock the Distort effect to the desired degree of distortion, as shown in figure 8.5.

7. Press Ctrl+– to zoom out and get a perspective on your work.

8. Choose Select, Save Selection, New to save the modified selection area.

9. Press Ctrl+D to deselect the image area. Do not save your work at this point, though. You need an unsaved version of the STORMSKY image to completely retouch this image.

Figure 8.5

The Distort effect adds perspective to a dimensionally flat image.

Creating the Second Side and Adding to a Selection

The "pickin's" will diminish in terms of available STORMSKY image area left to work with as you create the second and third sides of the cloud box—with every trip to the buffet, the pie gets smaller. You'll have to perform an amazing Photoshop feat to distort the top side of the cloud box, but amazing feats are all in a day's work with plastic, digital images.

Tackle the second side first, and discover an effortless way to add to the selection area you saved in the last steps.

1. Hold the Shift key, and using the Rectangular Marquee tool, start your click and drag at the vertex of the paths, and drag a square over the right facet of the path.

2. Press Ctrl++ to zoom back to a 1:1 viewing resolution of STORMSKY.TIF. Scroll so that both the selection area and the path guide for the right facet are completely in view.

3. Choose **I**mage, **E**ffects, Distort.

4. Click and drag each corner of the Distort boundary box to match the four corners of the corresponding path segments, as shown in figure 8.6.

5. Click inside the Distort boundary box to complete the effect when you have all four corners in place.

6. Press Ctrl+– to zoom out for a moment.

7. Click on the Invert colors icon button so that the background color is black.

8. Click on the #4 title on the Channels palette.

9. Press the Del key. The second distorted selection area is now black and combined with the selection area you first saved, as shown in figure 8.7.

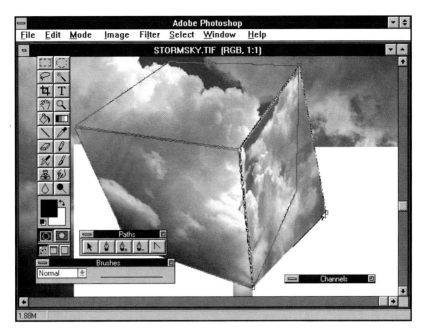

Figure 8.6
Because of massive number crunching behind the scenes, the Distort effect takes a moment.

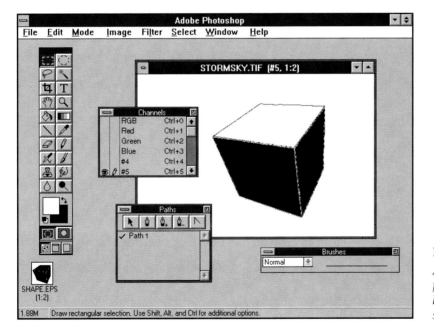

Figure 8.7
Adding black (deleting the foreground to expose black background) redefines your selection area.

10. Press Ctrl+D, and click on the RGB title on the Channels palette. The change you made in the selection area doesn't require a separate Save Selection command.

Creating the Third Side of the Box

Because digital copies of image files are completely identical, you can work with a little more ease on the third, top, final side of the cloud box. If you're following along using the *Adobe Photoshop NOW! CD-ROM* images, you'll see that you have a tricky problem; the upper corners of the left and right distorted sides prevent the creation of a square selection out of original image area to distort into the top side of the box.

The solution, then, is to copy the two sides to the Clipboard (using the selection area you defined last), and then restore the image area of STORMSKY you need to make the selection. Restoring the image destroys the first two sides you labored on, but you'll paste the copy back when you're through. Take a deep breath.

1. From the RGB view of STORMSKY.TIF, choose **S**elect, **L**oad Selection, #5, as shown in figure 8.8.

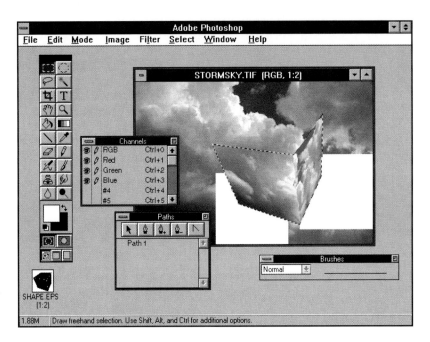

Figure 8.8

The combined selection areas create a marquee border encompassing all image editing to this point.

2. Choose **E**dit, **C**opy (Ctrl+C).

3. Click on the Default colors icon button.

4. Choose the Eraser tool. Then, while holding down the Alt key, click on a point in the STORMSKY image. Photoshop will read the last-saved version of the image into system RAM.

5. Click and drag all over the place while holding down the Alt key. The Eraser is now in Magic Eraser mode, and returns the background and the edited areas of the image to its last-saved state, as shown in figure 8.9.

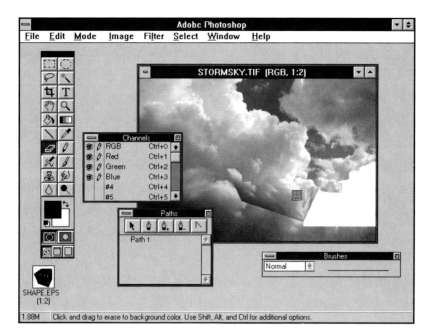

Figure 8.9

The Alt key in combination with the Eraser tool erases image areas to their last-saved version.

6. When you have restored enough of the original STORMSKY image around the top part of the path, choose the Rectangular Marquee tool, hold the Alt key, and drag a selection area starting at the vertex of the path segments and ending at the top of the image window.

7. Zoom into the area making sure you have a total view of the selection and the path you'll use as a guide.

8. Choose Image, Effects, Distort, and match the boundary corners to the top path segments the same way you did with the first two sides (see fig. 8.10).

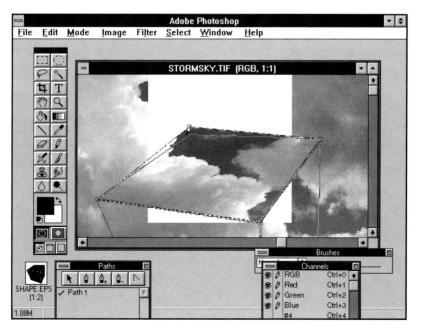

Figure 8.10

A restored background image offers plenty of unaltered area to use.

9. When you're finished tweaking the Distort boundary box, click inside of it to finish the effect.

10. Choose Select, Save Selection, and then choose New to save it to channel 6. You don't want to alter the combined selection area in channel 5 yet.

11. Choose Select, Load Selection, #5.

12. Press Ctrl+V to paste the first two sides of the cloud box back into the image, as shown in figure 8.11.

Figure 8.11

An image copy will land precisely within a loaded selection border.

13. Click on the check mark next to Path 1 on the Paths palette to make it invisible, and then press Ctrl+H to hide the marquee edges. *Now* you can exhale.

Pasted selections are "attracted" to active selection marquee borders. This is why it's necessary to have a selection border that's identical to a copied selection active when you paste a copy back into an image.

With no selection border active, by default, Photoshop pastes a copy into the center of an active image window.

Cleaning Up the Dimensional Sky Image

You still don't have one complete selection border defined in a channel to select the whole cloud block image. Let's spend a brief moment correcting this and removing superfluous image areas so that you can get a better look at the work.

1. Click on the #5 title on the Channels palette.

2. Click on the Invert colors icon button.

3. Choose Select, Load Selection, #6. In channel 5, a marquee outline will appear around the black selection areas of the left and right sides in channel 5.

4. Press the Del key.

5. Click on the #6 title on the Channels palette. Then click on the Channels palette's command button and choose Delete channel from the drop-down list.

6. Click on the #4 title on the Channels palette. This is the SHAPE.EPS copy, which was the "safety net" if anything went wrong during the operation. But you're home free now, so click on the Channels palette's command button and choose Delete channel from the drop-down list.

7. Click on the RGB title on the Channels palette.

8. Choose Select, Load Selection, #4, the channel of combined selection areas, which moved up a notch when the SHAPE.EPS channel 4 was deleted.

9. Choose Select, Inverse.

10. Click on the Default colors icon button.

11. Press the Del key to remove everything in the RGB channel *except* the cloud block, as shown in figure 8.12.

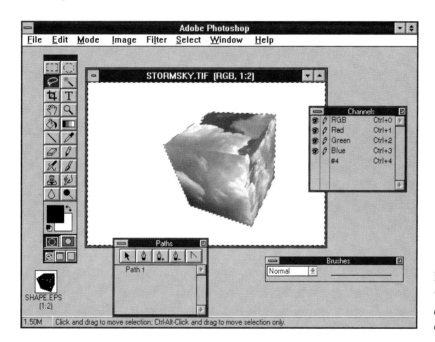

Figure 8.12

The Select, Inverse command turns selection areas into masked areas.

12. Choose the Rectangular Marquee tool, and click and drag a comfortable crop around the cloud box image.

13. Choose Edit, Crop.

14. Choose File, Save As and save the file as SKY_BOX.TIF.

Softening the Sky Box/Adding Realism

The only thing missing from an otherwise splendid photorealistic image is that the box's edges look a little too perfect. Nothing that's captured with a camera lens has lines this sharp. The solution? Stroke a few paths along these edges using Screen mode. Here's how.

1. Double-click on the Zoom tool to get a 1:1 viewing resolution of the cloud box.

2. Make sure Path 1 is invisible now (no check mark next to the title on the palette).

3. Select the Pen tool on the Paths palette.

4. Click an Anchor point on the bottom of the box where the left and right facets meet.

5. Click a second Anchor point where the edge between left and right facet stops at the top facet of the box.

6. Choose the Paintbrush tool, and then click on the Invert colors icon so that your foreground color is white.

7. Choose the left, middle row tip on the Brushes palette, set the mode for Screen, and click and drag the Opacity slider to about 60%.

8. Click on the Paths palette's command button, and select Stroke Path from the drop-down list. The Paths palette performs the command based on your active painting tool, and partially bleaches the area beneath and to each side of the path segment, as shown in figure 8.13.

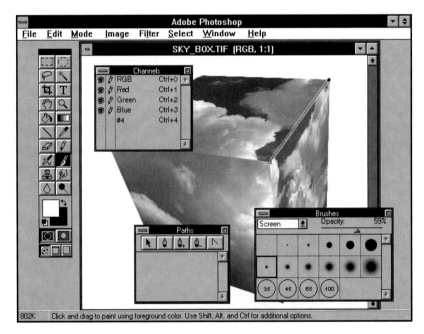

Figure 8.13

Stroking a path in Screen mode bleaches an area toward the foreground color.

9. Press the Backspace key twice to eliminate the path segment.

10. Repeat the last steps with the other two edges of the box.

Creating Irregularities in the Screened Strokes

Because SKY_BOX was saved since you applied the strokes to the path segments, the screened strokes now can be removed with the Magic Eraser tool. Or, they can be partially erased by using an option of the Rubber Stamp tool. The latter is what you'll do next to create minute imperfections in the screened strokes.

Photographic flaws are important to include in images that were created mostly digitally. A clean look suspends disbelief in the viewer's eye when looking at computer graphics.

1. Double-click on the Rubber Stamp tool, and choose From Saved from the Options drop-down list. Then click on OK.

2. Set the mode on the Brushes palette to Normal, Opacity to 55%, and choose the 34 pixel diameter tip.

3. Click and drag over portions of the screened strokes, as shown in figure 8.14. This partially removes the strokes by restoring the last-saved version of SKY_BOX.TIF. You're done when the image displays highlights along the edges, rather than uniformly rendered lines.

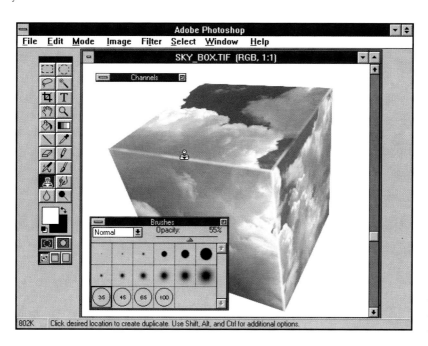

Figure 8.14

The From Saved Rubber Stamp tool option is more sophisticated than the Magic Eraser.

Integrating the Sky Box with the Background Image

Now the SKY_BOX image needs to be placed on top of the DROUGHT.TIF image. You'll create a dimensional effect using the Channels palette and a hand-rendered shadow so that the box image appears to be hovering slightly above the parched earth.

1. Choose Select, Load Selection, and then press Ctrl+C to copy only the image of the box to the Clipboard.

2. Open the DROUGHT.TIF image from the *Adobe Photoshop NOW! CD-ROM.*

3. Press Ctrl+V. Then with the Lasso tool, place the cursor inside the floating selection and click and drag to position it, as shown in figure 8.15.

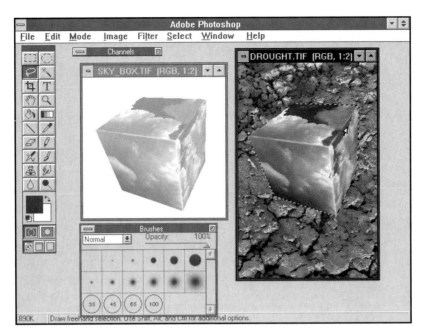

Figure 8.15

Leave room for a drop shadow and some type at the bottom of the DROUGHT.TIF image.

4. When you're happy with the positioning of the floating selection, choose **S**elect, **D**efringe, and then type a value of 1 pixel in the dialog box. Click on OK.

5. Choose **S**elect, **S**ave Selection, and then press Ctrl+D to composite the floating selection into the background image.

Adding a Drop Shadow Effect to the Sky Box

The next series of steps calls for a little artistic flair. Use the top facet of the box as a model for creating a shadow area beneath and slightly to the left of it. You can see that the
lighting in DROUGHT.TIF is from above and to the right, so a shadow should be in the converse direction to the image area that's supposed to be casting it. Don't worry about creating a selection border that includes part of the box. The area you'll design is only a selection area that will be placed behind the box.

1. While holding down the Alt key, click a point on the box that represents the back-left corner of a shadow.

2. Click a second, third, and fourth point to define the other corners of the box's shadow. Holding down the Alt key constrains the Lasso tool's selection edges to straight lines, as shown in figure 8.16.

3. Release the mouse button when you have the fourth point clicked, and then choose **S**elect, **S**ave Selection, #5. Press Ctrl+D to deselect the selection area.

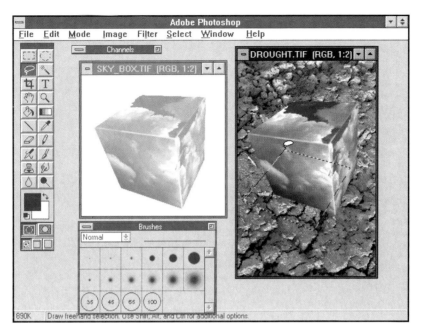

Figure 8.16

The Lasso tool can create a straight-edge (nonparallel line) selection area.

4. Click on the #5 title on the Channels palette, and choose **I**mage, **A**djust, Brightness/Contrast (Ctrl+B).

5. Click and drag the Brightness slider to about +3⊘, and then click on OK. The drop-shadow should be a light, subtle one.

6. Choose Fi**l**ter, Blur, Gaussian Blur. Enter 8 pixels as the **R**adius for the blur, and then click on OK.

7. As shown in figure 8.17, the light, blurred selection area is done and ready to be copied behind the selection of the box, but in front of the DROUGHT image.

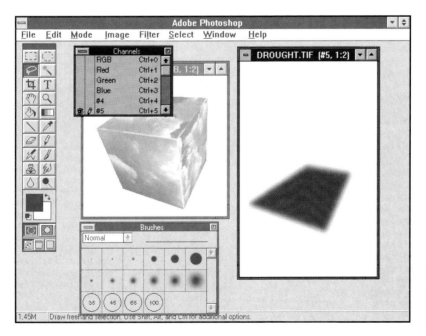

Figure 8.17

A light, blurred grayscale image area makes an ideal shadow.

8. Press Ctrl+A and then Ctrl+C to copy the #5 channel contents to the Clipboard.

9. Click on the RGB title on the Channels palette.

10. Choose Select, Load Selection, #4.

11. Choose Edit, Paste Behind.

12. With the Lasso tool still active, choose the Multiply mode on the Brushes palette, and then click and drag the selection of the shadow to a point beneath and to the left of the box, as shown in figure 8.18.

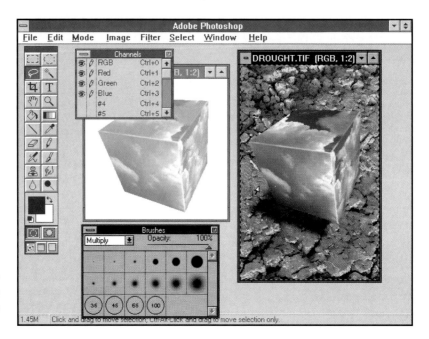

Figure 8.18

The Multiply mode removes the lighter pixels in a pasted selection area.

13. Press Ctrl+D when the drop shadow is in position, and then press Ctrl+S to save your work up to this point.

Adding Special Effects Type to the Image

An image this outstanding is worthy of some added typography that's out of the ordinary. For the final touch on this illustration, you'll create a dimensional, tonal title for the piece. ITC Kabel Extra Bold was used in the following figures for the word DROUGHT, but if you have any serious, sans serif, extra bold font, you're in business for the next steps.

1. Click on the #5 title on the Channels palette, and then double-click on the Eraser tool.

2. Click on OK to Photoshop's dialog box asking whether you want the entire channel erased. You do because you're done with the blurry shadow selection information.

3. Choose the Type tool. In channel #5, click an insertion point in the middle-bottom area of DROUGHT.TIF.

4. In the Type tool dialog box, choose your bold typeface from the available ones in the Font drop-down list. Then enter the following: Size: 40 points; Style: Bold and Anti-Aliased, and click on the Center Alignment radio button.

5. Type **DROUGHT** in the type field, and then click on OK.

6. Click and drag the floating type selection if all of it isn't completely in view. If you deselect type that's clipped off by an image window, the clipped portion is lost.

7. When you're done, you should have type in the Alpha channel that looks similar to that in figure 8.19. Press Ctrl+D to deselect the type.

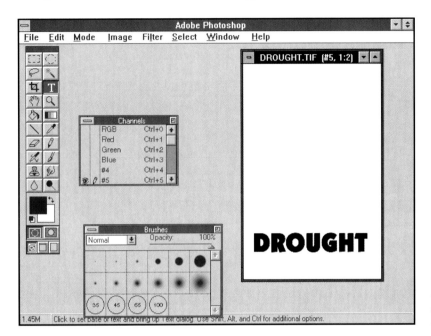

Figure 8.19
Make sure the floating type selection is within the image window.

Altering and Positioning the Type

No matter how well-positioned you believe the type presently is, you are blind to its position relative to the RGB image area's contents. Get a final position for the type selection now.

1. Click on the RGB title on the channels palette, and then choose Select, Load Selection, #5.

2. Choose the Lasso tool. Then with the Ctrl and Alt keys pressed, click and drag the marquee selection area so that it's properly centered beneath the image of the cloud box and shadow.

3. Choose Select, Save Selection, #5 to overwrite the Alpha channel's previous information about the type's location.

The Type tool cannot be used to move only the selection area in an image because pressing the Ctrl key toggles the Type tool's function to that of the Lasso tool. You always need to choose a proper selection tool—the Rectangular or Elliptical Marquee, the Lasso, or the Magic Wand tool—to move only a selection area and not its contents.

Pressing Ctrl and Alt while moving a selection area with the Type tool cursor results in duplicating the selection area's contents, which produces an interesting, if somewhat undesired, effect.

4. Press Ctrl+B to display the Brightness/Contrast command.

5. Click and drag the Brightness slider to +100%. As shown in figure 8.20, this lightens the selection of the type area, and produces light type that reads against the background, with texture of the earth inside the lettering.

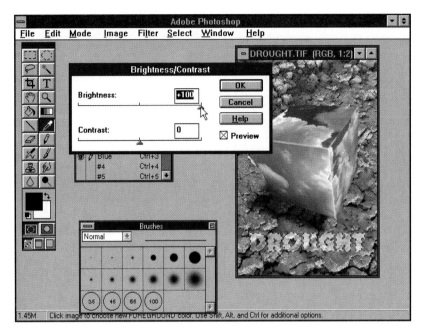

Figure 8.20

Increasing Brightness in selections changes the tonal value, but retains color values.

6. Use the same steps as you did with the shadow beneath the cloud box to create a drop-shadow effect with the DROUGHT type. Make a copy of the #5 channel, and then place it in the #4 channel (overwriting the box selection area).

7. While in the #4 channel, press Ctrl+F to apply the last Filter used (the Gaussian Blur), and then copy the entire selection to the Clipboard.

8. Click on the RGB channel on the Channels palette, choose Select, Load Selection, #5, and then choose the Edit, Paste Behind command.

9. Choose the Multiply mode on the Brushes palette, and then click and drag the pasted selection so that the blurry selection is beneath and to the left of the type.

10. Press Ctrl+D to composite the blurry selection, choose File, Save As, and name the finished image DROUGHT.TIF. You now should have a striking scene worthy of accompanying (if not dominating) a magazine article on a topic that affects the world, as shown in figure 8.21.

Figure 8.21
The finished DROUGHT image, shown in Photoshop's scroll-less display mode.

Try experimenting with other geometric shapes and other images using path segments as guides. Try out the other Image, Effects commands. The Perspective command can make an instant floor out of a 2D image, and the Skew command can turn a flat graphic into a mural on the side of a building.

PART FOUR:

Special Effects with Photoshop's Native Tools

Chapter 9

Special Effects and Type

In Photoshop, the Type tool's dialog box offers basic options as to a TrueType or Type 1 font's size and weight. But what makes a simple line of type more exciting, dynamic, and more of a design element are Photoshop's Filters and Effects commands. Because type is a graphical element in Photoshop, you can twist it, bend it, and steal the scene with a reshaped word or phrase.

Embellishing a Poster with Typography

In this chapter's assignment, you start with a graphic of chess pieces against a black background. Your job is to take the graphic and turn it into a poster advertising a chess match at Paramount's Madison Square Garden on April Fools' Day. Using some extraordinary commands and filters, you'll add color and define space so that the text enhances and integrates with the striking image of the chess pieces. The special techniques you'll see in this chapter can be applied to a wide variety of assignments in your own work.

The Images on the *Adobe Photoshop NOW! CD-ROM*

All the materials used to complete the poster can be found on the *Adobe Photoshop NOW! CD-ROM*. You'll want to load the Kibbutz and Fiefdom Type 1 fonts into Adobe Type Manager before beginning the exercises. The rest of the image and information files can be loaded from CHAP9 on the CD as they are referenced in the steps.

Creating a New Background Element

Before getting into bending and shaping type, the 3D_CHESS.TIF image you'll use as the main graphic element needs some cosmetic enhancement. The Emboss filter can be used to produce a variety of finished looks, but you'll use it as one of the steps in creating a naturalistic texture using only Photoshop's native tools. The texture will be used to spotlight the chess pieces and to add another color to the composition that will be used in the typography you add later.

1. Open the 3D_CHESS.TIF image from the *Adobe Photoshop NOW! CD-ROM*.

2. Using the Rectangular Marquee tool, select an area around the chess pieces that loosely frames them, as shown in figure 9.1. This is the background area to which you'll add texture. Creating an additional element should be done in a separate image file, to be composited into the chess image later. You'll make Photoshop automatically create exactly the right size for the new file in next steps.

Features Covered:

- Emboss command
- Channels
- Scale command
- Dissolve mode
- Displace filter
- Paths palette

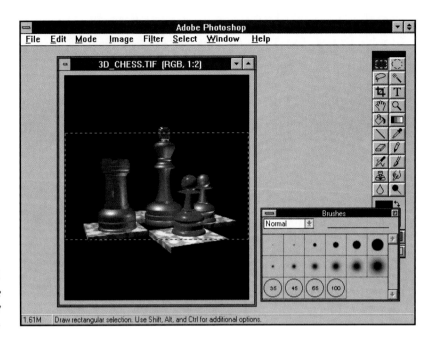

Figure 9.1

Marquee select the image area that will get a new background.

3. Press Ctrl+C, and then choose File, New (Ctrl+N).

4. By default, Photoshop prepares new image canvases to the dimension, resolution, and image type to match information on the Clipboard. In the New dialog box, you should have Width: about 4 inches, and Height, about 2.5, depending on how closely you matched your marquee selection to that in figure 9.1. Accept the New dialog options, and click on OK.

5. Marquee select a very small area in the Untitled-1 image, and then press Ctrl+C. This replaces more than one half a megabyte of image information on the Clipboard with 2 or 3 KB. This is known as "flushing" the Clipboard, and helps keep system resources at their peak.

6. Choose the Paintbrush tool. Then set the Brushes palette to Dissolve mode, Opacity to 50%, and choose the 100 pixel diameter tip.

7. Click on the Default colors icon button, and then paint a few random brushstrokes on the Untitled-1 image. You're looking for a splatter effect here, so don't concentrate on any one area, and don't cover the entire image area; you'll only be using a small portion of the area.

8. Choose the Rectangular Marquee tool, and click and drag a section within the painted area about 1 by 1/4 screen inches.

9. Choose Image, Effects, Scale.

10. While holding down the Shift key (to constrain proportions), place your cursor inside a corner handle on the Scale boundary box, and then click and drag away from the boundary box. As you can see in figure 9.2, the random pixels you stroked in Dissolve mode have become larger. They will become the basis for the texture that you create.

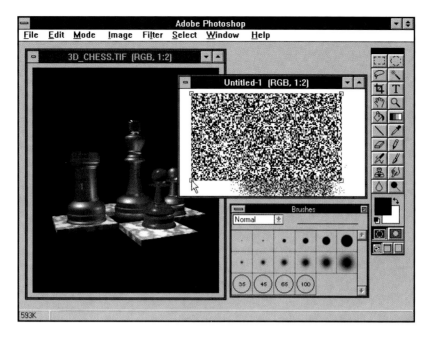

Figure 9.2
The Scale command can enlarge or shrink selection areas.

You can click and drag an Effects boundary box corner off the active image window. Don't be afraid to create an effect with a boundary box that's of epic proportions. And, if you're working with an image in the viewing mode without scroll bars (the bottom, middle button on the toolbox), you can retrieve a boundary handle that's outside of the active image. To do this, run your cursor around the gray area outside the image border. The cursor will appear as a gavel and an international "no" sign, but the moment you reach an Effect boundary handle, your cursor turns back into an arrow, and you can click and drag the boundary corner back onto the active image.

11. When the selection has been scaled to fill the whole image window, click inside the boundary box to finish the effect.

12. Press Ctrl+D to deselect the image area.

Embossing the Background Image

Photoshop's Emboss filter can be used for a number of looks, from embossed text to creating a photorealistic tin engraving. But all it's actually doing is creating a relief, and when a relief is applied to an image consisting of oversized, randomly dispersed pixels, you get texture. In the next sets of steps, you'll use the Emboss filter to create a rich backdrop for the chess pieces.

1. Choose Filter, Stylize, Emboss.

2. In the Emboss dialog box, click and drag the angle line in the circle until the Angle field reads about 114°. Enter 3 pixels in the Height: field and 100% in the Amount field, and then click on OK.

As you can see in figure 9.3, the Emboss command offsets a copy of the black image information by three pixels, identical in shape, but as white on a gray background. This is unsuitable for placing behind the richly colored chess pieces, though; it's interesting, but dull.

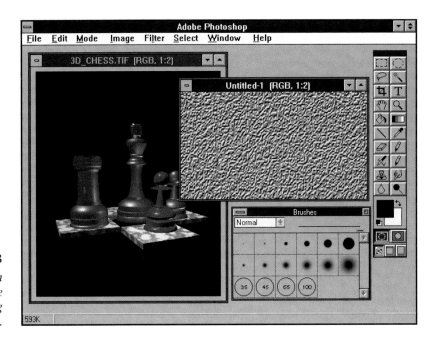

Figure 9.3

The Emboss command can be applied to monochrome or color images, producing different results.

Hand-Coloring a Monochrome Image

Whether you use the Colorize option in the Hue/Saturation command or use the Color mode with painting tools, the black in an image area doesn't change. Absolute black in an image area means that there is no color saturation, therefore, nothing to colorize. To add color across all the tonal range of Untitled-1, the black pixels have to be lightened slightly. Then a new color can be added to the image that affects all the image pixels.

1. Press Ctrl+B to display the Brightness/Contrast command.

2. Enter +4 for Brightness, -18 for Contrast, and then click OK.

3. Click on the Foreground color selection box.

4. Choose H: 41°, S: 98%, B: 93% in the HSB color model (or click and drag the circle in the color spectrum window). This an arbitrary color for the textured background; it seems to work nicely with the purples and maroons of the 3D_CHESS image. Click on OK to return to the workspace.

5. Choose the Paintbrush tool. Then set the Brushes palette to Color mode, 100% Opacity, and pick the 100 pixel diameter tip.

6. Click and drag over the Untitled-1 image area. As you can see in figure 9.4, the Color mode changes the hue and saturation of the gray textured image, but it preserves the tonal relationships created by embossing. In other words, you're tinting the image area.

7. Cover the entire Untitled-1 area with the golden foreground color. Save the image as CHESBACK.TIF when you're done.

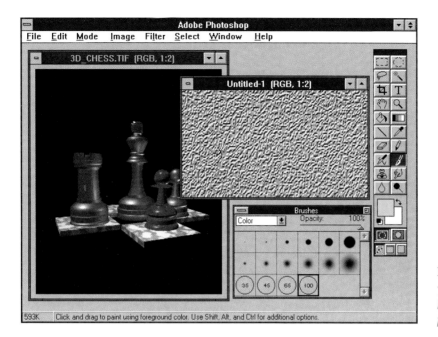

Figure 9.4
The Color mode tints image areas with foreground color.

Creating a Spotlight Effect with a Partial Mask

As mentioned in other chapters, a partial mask is created by placing grayscale information in an Alpha channel for Photoshop to use as the basis for creating a selection. To create an effect that appears as though a spotlight is being cast on the textured background, you must create a dense area in an Alpha channel toward the center, gradually falling off to white toward the edges. Then when the CHESBACK image is selected from the RGB composite view, the center of the image will be fully selected, while the other parts toward the edge are partially or not selected at all. Here's where the Gradient fill tool comes in handy.

1. Double-click on the Gradient tool.

2. Click on the **N**ormal Style radio button, and then the **R**adial type button. Enter 50 as the Midpoint Skew percentage. Click on OK.

3. Click on the Default colors icon button.

4. Press F6 to display the Channels palette.

5. Click on the Channels palette's command button, and then pick New Channel from the drop-down list.

6. Click on the Color Indicates: Selected Areas radio button, accept the default name of #4, and then click on OK.

7. With the Gradient tool cursor, click and drag from the absolute center of CHESBACK.TIF's Alpha channel to a point near but not touching the very bottom of the image window. You want the gradient fill to reach white before the edge of the image window.

8. Choose the Rectangular Marquee tool, and then select only the gradient fill, leaving just a little border of background white around it.

9. Choose **I**mage, **E**ffects, Scale.

10. Click and drag the selection area by the boundary corners disproportionately (no Shift key this time) so that you wind up with an elliptical shape similar to that in figure 9.5.

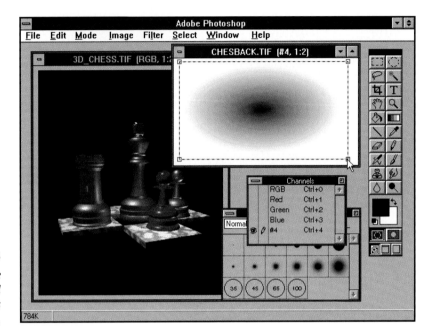

Figure 9.5

You can change the shape of a radial gradient fill with the Effects commands.

11. When the radial gradient fills the image window (with only white around the boundary edges; not one percent of grayscale), click inside the boundary box.

12. Press Ctrl+S to save your work up to this point.

Creating Partial Copies Using Partial Masks

The radial gradient is now elliptical, and a selection based on this information will have a bright, opaque center, gradually diminishing to nothingness toward the border. Now you'll copy the selection from the RGB view of the CHESBACK image and paste it behind the chess pieces. An accurate, total mask was created in the 3D_CHESS.TIF image file to help you quickly accomplish the next steps.

1. Click on the RGB title on the Channels palette.

2. Choose **S**elect, **L**oad Selection. Don't be put off by the observation that the marquee border is substantially smaller than the gray areas you created in the last steps. Marquee borders don't reflect partial masks with any degree of accuracy.

3. Press Ctrl+C and then press Ctrl+Tab to toggle to 3D_CHESS as the active image window.

4. Choose **S**elect, **L**oad Selection. The chess pieces now are selected, and the black background is masked.

5. Choose **E**dit, Paste **B**ehind, and then click and drag the copy of the background image so that it's centered behind the chess pieces, as shown in figure 9.6.

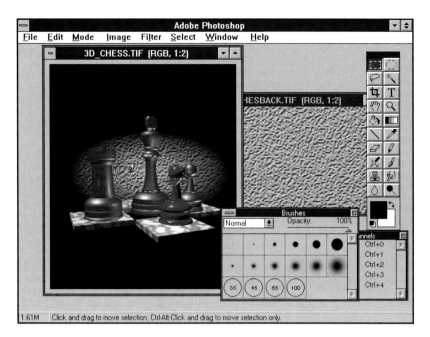

Figure 9.6
The partial mask lets the copy blend seamlessly into the 3D_CHESS black background.

6. When the background is positioned, press Ctrl+D to deselect the image. Then choose File, Save As, and save 3D_CHESS.TIF to your hard disk. Make sure that the Save Alpha channels check box is marked in the TIFF Options dialog box.

Kerning Graphics Text

The next steps cover a quick procedure to make intercharacter spacing, or *kerning*, in Photoshop as professional as if you'd used a desktop publishing program. Blocks of type should almost never be placed directly within an image. Type foundries and private font creators have widely varying standards, and sizing and letter spacing should be addressed before a word or phrase is added to a background image.

You'll be using Fiefdom, a Type 1 creation I cobbled together for your use in creating the title of the chess poster. While it's a handy font, and an appropriate one theme-wise, I gave the font poor kerning and interword spacing. Why? Because bad kerning is typical in many shareware fonts, and Fiefdom will give you hands-on experience overcoming any typeface's limitations using Photoshop.

1. Choose File, New (Ctrl+N). Enter 4 in the Width field (choose Inches from the increments drop-down list), and then enter 2.5 in the Height field (also measured in inches). Leave the rest of the fields at the defaults, and then click on OK.

2. Choose the Type tool, and then click an insertion point toward the center of the background on Untitled-2.

3. In the Type Tool dialog box, choose Fiefdom as the Font, enter 40 as the point Size, check Anti-Aliased, click on the Center Alignment radio button, and then type **Tournament** in the type field. Click on OK.

4. The T and the o in "Tournament" have too much space between them. With the Lasso tool, click and drag a tight border around the T. Include the light gray, antialiased pixels around the character, as shown in figure 9.7.

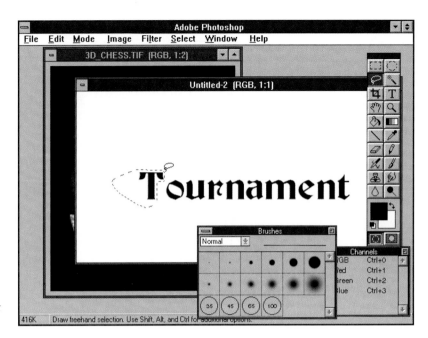

Figure 9.7

*Use the Lasso tool to select
a character to kern.*

5. Press the right arrow key three or four times. The word Tournament now has proper letter spacing.

6. Press Ctrl+D. Then choose the Type tool and click an insertion point above the word Tournament.

7. Enter 60 as the **S**ize of the next piece of type. Then type the word **Chess** in the type field, and click on OK.

8. Click and drag the floating type selection so that it's above the word Tournament.

9. Choose **I**mage, **E**ffects, Scale, and shape the word Chess so that it's squatter and looks like an extended font.

10. Click inside the Scale boundary box, press Ctrl+D, and then click another insertion point with the Type tool.

11. Enter 140 points as the **S**ize. Then type the character = in the Type field, and click on OK. This is a special character in Fiefdom, the silhouette of a pawn.

Fiefdom has a complete set of chess characters. If you'd like to use a rook or bishop in this assignment (or any of your own), refer to the READFIEF.WRI found on the Adobe Photoshop Now! CD-ROM *in the CHAP09 subdirectory. It shows which keys to press to get the chess piece of your choice in the Fiefdom font.*

12. Place your cursor inside the floating selection of the pawn. Then click and drag the cursor so that it's positioned to the left of the Chess Tournament type, and aligned to the baseline of Tournament.

13. Hold down the Alt key and click and drag to the right of the Chess Tournament lettering. A duplicate of the pawn is produced, as shown in figure 9.8. Position the duplicate to the right of Chess Tournament, on the baseline of Tournament.

Figure 9.8

Holding down the Alt key while the Type tool is active duplicates a floating selection.

14. Save your work as TOURNEY.TIF on your hard disk.

Creating a Displacement Map for the Type

Now that you have a stunning typographic creation for the chess poster, wouldn't it be nice if the type could arc over the chess pieces, not simply sit above it? The Displace command is one that you could experiment with for ages, but one of the simplest facilities it offers is to distort a selection according to a map you define. Photoshop installs several maps in the DISPMAP subdirectory beneath the PLUGINS directory, but it's more rewarding to design your own. By building a displacement map for your typography, you'll see how to create variations and understand the relationship between the map and the effect it creates. Here's how.

1. Open a new file. Make sure it's the same size and resolution as TOURNEY.TIF. The displacement map that you create will be a 1 to 1 mapping.

2. Pull on the image window on the left and right sides. You'll need to create a gradient fill next from edge to edge of Untitled-2.

3. Double-click on the Gradient tool. Click on the **L**inear Type radio button, and then click on OK.

4. Place the Gradient cursor at the very left edge of Untitled-2's window. Then click and drag a straight line, parallel to the bottom image window edge, and release at the right edge of the window, as shown in figure 9.9.

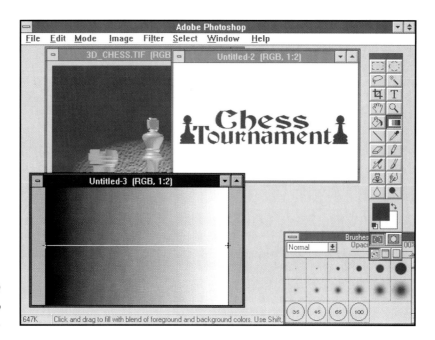

Figure 9.9

Begin a displacement map with a gradient fill.

5. Choose **I**mage, **A**djust, Curves (Ctrl+M).

6. With ultimate precision in mind, click on the far right node on the graph, and pull straight down.

7. Click a point in the center of the graph line, and drag up until the Output reads about 178.

8. You are building the shape for the arc of the typography. In figure 9.10, you can see the shape you need to redistribute the tonal range in Untitled-2 to serve as a displacement map. Click and drag points at the quarter tones to make the curve a gentle one without abrupt transitions.

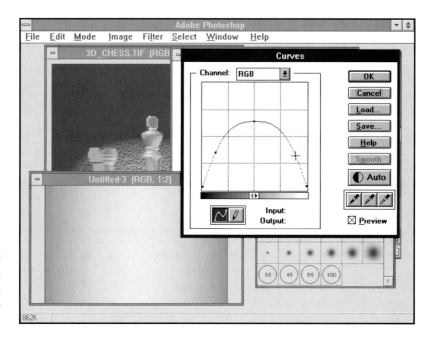

Figure 9.10

The Curves command can redistribute color pixels across a tonal range to make a displacement map.

No one achieves a perfect curves edit on their first try. In fact, I discovered many interesting variations while attempting these steps. If you want to follow these steps to the letter, DISPMAP.CRV is in the CHAP9 subdirectory on the Adobe Photoshop Now! *CD-ROM. It's a file of the exact curve used in this assignment, and you can simply use the Load option on the Curves command to access it, as well as several other predesigned curves you can load and build other maps for your own assignments.*

9. After the Curves graph is shaped in an upward slope, click on OK.

10. Save your work as DISPMAP1.PSD, the proprietary Photoshop file format, not as a TIF or other image type. Photoshop can only use a PSD file as a displacement map.

Applying the Displacement Map

In this next section, you'll see the fruits of your labor. Or if you didn't labor, at least you'll see what happens when the DISPMAP1.PSD from the *Adobe Photoshop NOW! CD-ROM* is applied to an image. You can make several adjustments in the Displace options box, but you're only looking for a setting here that'll create an arc out of the chess typography.

1. With the Rectangular Marquee tool, select the typography in the TOURNEY image, and center it within the image window. Then press Ctrl+D to deselect it.

2. Choose Filter, Distort, Displace.

3. In the Distort options box, enter 0 as the Horizontal Scale, 50 as the Vertical Scale, and click the Stretch to fit radio button, as shown in figure 9.11. The Undefined Areas setting doesn't really make any difference because Photoshop affects an entire image when there's no selection border active. Click on OK.

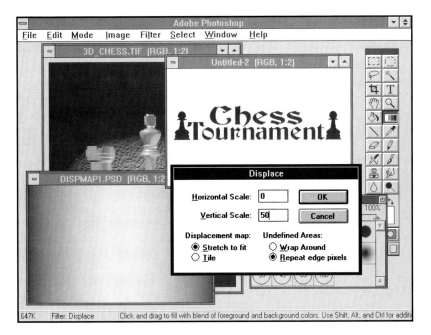

Figure 9.11

Use these settings to displace the type in a shape similar to the graph plotted earlier.

4. In the **L**oad dialog box, find the directory where you saved DISPMAP1.PSD, and choose it from the **F**ile, **N**ame field. Then click on OK.

5. *Definitely* save your work at this point. Pretty amazing, huh?

Adding the Arced Type to the Chess Image

It's time to add the finished typography to an Alpha channel in the 3D_CHESS image. As selection information, you'll be able to load it, and then color only this area with a smooth Gradient fill.

1. Press Ctrl+A, and then Ctrl+C to copy all of the arced type to the Clipboard.

2. Click on the title bar to 3D_CHESS.TIF to make it the active image. Click on the Channels palette's command button, and choose New Channel from the drop-down list. Accept the defaults, and click on OK.

3. Press Ctrl+V, and then click on the RGB title on the Channels palette.

4. Press Ctrl+D to composite the type selection into the Alpha channel.

5. Choose **S**elect, **L**oad Selection, #5.

6. Choose a selection tool, not the Type tool. Then hold Ctrl and the Alt key, and click and drag inside the marquee border until the typography is centered above the chess pieces.

7. Choose **S**elect, **S**ave Selection, #5. This overwrites the previous selection area, replacing it with information about the repositioned typography.

8. Pick a deep gold foreground color and a rich burgundy background color from the Color Picker. Click on the color selection boxes and take a spin with H: 39°, S: 96%, B: 89% as the foreground color, and H: 338°, S: 110%, and B: 44% as the background color.

9. Double-click on the Gradient tool, click on the **R**adial Type radio button, and set the Radial **O**ffset to 25%. This makes the center of a radial gradient fill a little lop-sided, hence a little more real.

10. With the selection based on the type still active, click and drag from beneath the marquee border above and to the right of it, as shown in figure 9.12.

11. Press Ctrl+D to deselect the typography, and save your work as PAWNGAME.TIF to your hard drive.

The Home-Brew Embossed Type Effect

Creating a slight highlight to the typography helps separate it from the black background. A hand-made embossed effect is easy to achieve using Photoshop's nudge feature, as follows.

1. Click on the Invert colors icon button on the toolbox. Your background color should be deep gold now.

2. Choose **S**elect, **L**oad Selection, #5.

3. Press the down arrow key on the keyboard once. Ctrl+H has been pressed to hide the marquee edges (see fig. 9.13), and at a 1:1 viewing resolution, the effect of moving the selection to reveal background gold has provided a distinctive, subtle touch to the image.

Figure 9.12

The radial type gradient fill can be used to imitate a source of light in an image.

Figure 9.13

Move a selection area by one pixel to create an embossed effect by exposing a light background.

Creating a Template for Type To Fit in

There simply aren't any of the restrictions or frustrations of getting type to fit into a limited space in Photoshop because type is a graphic; it can't be edited in place, but it can be molded like any other design element.

In the next steps, you add a date and place to the chess poster. To integrate the type as an element, imitate the steep angle that the chess squares are viewed at, and add a text block in front in the same shape. To do this, you'll want to create a template to distort the type to, and this is where the Paths palette serves as a quick aid.

1. Ignore the bad example I'm setting and clean up Photoshop's workspace a little at this point. Close the DISPMAP1 image and the TOURNEY type, but keep the Channels palette handy.

2. Press F9 to display the Paths palette if it is not already displayed.

3. Choose the Pen tool, and click four points in front of the leftmost chess square, as shown in figure 9.14. The fourth Anchor point you click should bring you back to the first point, and the path segments become an enclosed path.

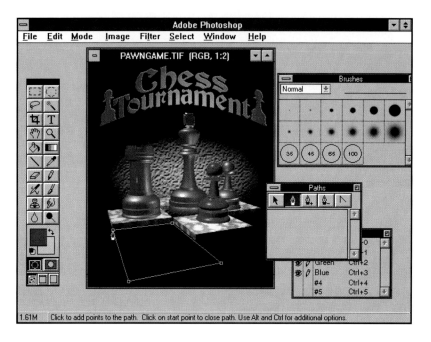

Figure 9.14

Paths are good for visual guides, that don't interfere with or affect the underlying bitmap image.

4. It took me about four or five tries to get the path angled so that it matched the wide angle perspective of the chess squares. Use the Arrow Pointer tool on the Paths palette to click and drag on the path Anchor points to get the path segments where you want them.

5. Click on the Paths palette's command button, and choose Save Path from the drop-down list. Non-saved paths are notorious for vanishing when you don't want them to.

Type that's going to be twisted and distorted should characteristically be of "strong" construction. That's why I wouldn't recommend a Fraktur or a Goudy text style for the arced type that you created earlier; the thinner strokes of ornamental and Roman fonts tend to "go away" when distorted radically, and their readability becomes illegible all too quickly.

Creating the Type To Fit the Path

Type you add to the bottom of the poster should be a Gothic face, with a bold to black weight. Kibbutz, the freeware font I created for this assignment, is a combination of Revue, Kabel, and Gill Kayo, with enough humor to take the brunt off the preposterous authority to which it pretends. Do the following steps with the Kibbutz font (or any other ultra-black sans serif you own).

1. With the Rectangular Marquee tool, click and drag an area that surrounds the path in PAWNGAME.TIF.

2. Press Ctrl+C to copy the area to the Clipboard. You don't need this image area, but you do want Photoshop to "read" the selection and offer a new file of the same dimensions.

3. Choose File, New (Ctrl+N), accept the defaults, and then click on OK.

4. Click on the Default colors icon button.

5. Choose the Type tool, and click an insertion point in the Untitled-3 image.

6. Choose Kibbutz from the Font drop-down list, set the Size at 16 points, and then type **MADISON SQUARE** in the type entry box. Click on OK.

7. Center the type in the image window, and press Ctrl+D to deselect the type. Then with the Rectangular Marquee tool, select the parts of MADISON SQUARE that need tightening, and use the nudge key to move the selection, as you did earlier with the headline typography.

8. Click an insertion point again, and set the Size to 40 points. Type **GARDEN**, click on OK, and use the Scale command to stretch and fit the selection so that it fills out the second line of type.

9. Add **APRIL 1st** and **1994** as separate lines of type to finish off the block of text. Use the Scale command so that you wind up with an image that looks like figure 9.15.

Figure 9.15

You can fit and stretch type selections with the Scale command.

10. Save the image as GARDEN.TIF to your hard disk.

Adding Perspective to a Block of Type

To make the address and date for the big chess event graphically integrate into the poster, you need to copy the type you kerned and fitted to an Alpha channel to the PAWNGAME image. Paths are visible from every view of a multi-channel image, so you can see the guidelines you designed in the RGB channel from an Alpha channel view.

1. Press Ctrl+A, and then Ctrl+C to copy the type to the Clipboard.

2. Close GARDEN.TIF. PAWNGAME.TIF becomes the active image window.

3. Click on the #4 title on the Channels palette. This is where information about the chess pieces selection area is stored, but the channel can be reused now because you're done with it.

4. Double-click on the Eraser tool. Click on OK when Photoshop's dialog box asks whether you want to erase the entire channel. Make sure you are in the #4 channel.

5. Press Ctrl+V, and then place your cursor inside the floating selection and click and drag it so that the selection is on top of the path.

6. Press Ctrl+D. Then choose Select, Load Selection, #4.

7. Choose Image, Effects, Distort.

8. Click and drag each corner of the Distort boundary box so that they fit precisely over the corners (Anchor points) of the path, as shown in figure 9.16.

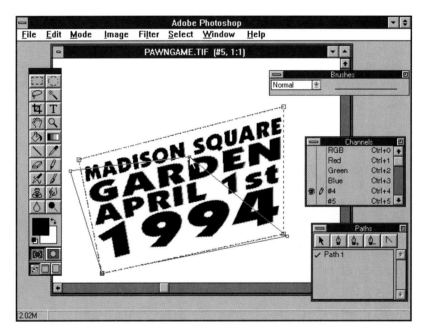

Figure 9.16

Use the path as a guideline for reshaping the distort boundary box.

9. Click inside the Distort boundary box to finish the effect when the boundary box is the same shape as the path.

10. Click on the RGB title on the Channels palette to restore your view of the color image. Choose Select, Save Selection to the #4 channel to keep this distorted type in position within the Alpha channel.

Adding Type by Deleting to Background Color

The colors used in this poster were deliberately kept to a minimum. The chess pieces and the Fiefdom type are very ornamental, and for this reason extra colors and other visual details would have stolen from the poster, rather than contributed to it.

White lettering for the address and date is the best choice of color here because the type has character and interest of its own. Here's how to quickly color the type selection.

1. Double-click on the Hand tool to get a full-frame viewing resolution of PAWNGAME.TIF.

2. Choose Select, Load Selection, #4. The loaded selection will appear as a marquee selection (see fig. 9.17).

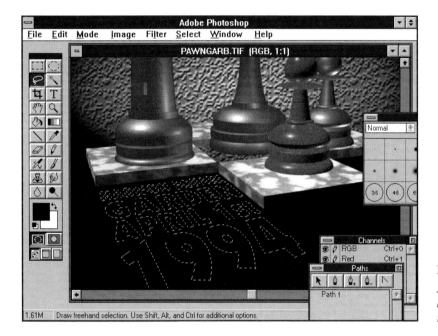

Figure 9.17

A marquee selection is based on Alpha channel information.

3. Make sure the default colors of black foreground and white background are selected on the toolbox.

4. Press the Del Key.

5. Press Ctrl+D.

6. You're done! Remove the Alpha channels from the finished image by clicking on an Alpha channel title on the Channels palette, and then choosing Delete channel from the command button drop-down list.

7. Make the saved path visible by clicking in the column to the left of its title on the Paths palette. A check mark appears, and the path becomes visible. Click on the Paths palette's command button, and choose Delete Path.

8. Save your work. Click on the menuless, scroll-less display mode button on the bottom right of the toolbox to get a better view of the piece, as shown in figure 9.18.

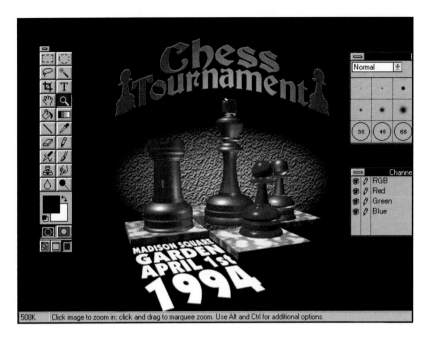

Figure 9.18

The right display button shows Photoshop's workspace in a mode without menus or scroll bars.

9. Click on the Standard display mode (left bottom toolbox button) to return things to normal.

10. Do *not* distribute this poster. Some of the patrons of the Garden's boxing, wrestling, and other matches might not understand the April Fools' connotation here and actually show up. And get a little dismayed.

Chapter 10

Producing a Floating Automobile

If you've ever spent more than 10 minutes laboring over a tight, accurate selection border around an image area that you intend to copy and paste into a different background image, set aside your past work methodology for a while. Photoshop has special features and functions that can make compositing work easier and quicker than you've ever imagined, if you know a trick or two about working with last-saved versions of an image. You actually can create a rough selection outline around a person, a tree, or whatever and wind up with a finished composite image that doesn't show a trace of halo or outline around the pasted selection. All you need to do is read on and see how to create a very special effect with a couple of ordinary backyard photos.

Features Covered:
- The Magic Eraser
- The Rubber Stamp tool
- The Lasso tool
- The Gaussian Blur filter
- The Hue/Saturation command

How Do You Make a Car Float?

In the 1960s, a lot of car manufacturers and oil companies liked to tout their product as being really special by featuring a "flying" car in their advertisements. Typically, this trick was accomplished by elevating a car on a hydraulic lift, taking the photo, and then engaging a good airbrush artist to remove the lift from the final image.

Flashing forward to the 1990s, there's still something a little magical about a lighter-than-air car, truck, boat, or even your neighbor in a captured image. But the PC world has Photoshop, and the methodology used to create this effect doesn't involve hydraulics, dye transfers, or a stellar production budget anymore. All it takes is a couple of well thought-out photographs and a working knowledge of the special properties of Photoshop's tools.

Planning Your Pictures Before Using Photoshop

In this assignment, you'll see how a suburban chariot is manipulated to appear as though it's hovering about four feet over a parking lot. As with any Photoshop endeavor, the better the images you have to work with, the better the results. So some preplanning is essential before working with raw images in Photoshop.

The finished image actually will be a composite of two separate photographs. First, I took a photo of my parking lot when it was vacant, strongly lit from the right, and at an altitude of about 4 feet. Altitude might seem like a strange consideration, but if you want to make something float off the ground, it must be at the correct viewing altitude, in addition to having the same lighting as the background image. The second picture with the station wagon was taken with the same background, but at a height of minus 4 feet—in other words, I had my chin on the ground while taking this snapshot. If you have a mismatched "viewing plane" between two images in the same photo, the viewer instinctively will notice something phony.

The Images on the *Adobe Photoshop NOW! CD-ROM*

If you'd like to get hands-on experience with car levitating as covered in the steps, the *Adobe Photoshop NOW! CD-ROM* will give you a jump start. The images used in this assignment, OUR_CAR.TIF and PARKNLOT.TIF, are located in this chapter's subdirectory. You should load them at this point. They'll be referenced by these file names throughout the steps.

Remember to have some hard disk space open on your machine; CDs are read-only, and it's tough to save your finished image to this location.

Creating a Rough Selection Border

As you can see in figure 10.1, OUR_CAR.TIF and PARKNLOT.TIF are both open in Photoshop's workspace. You only need the OUR_CAR image for a moment or two because as soon as it's been selected and copied, the image can be closed. The bulk of this assignment is done with the "host" (or background) image, PARKNLOT.TIF.

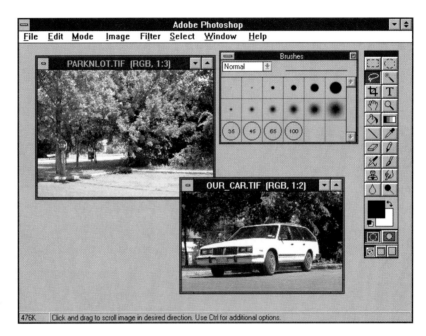

Figure 10.1

Identical lighting in two different images helps produce a more convincing composite image.

1. Double-click on the Zoom tool. This zooms the active image, OUR_CAR, to a comfortable 1:1 viewing resolution.

2. Choose the Lasso tool, and then click and drag a complete outline around the station wagon, finishing at the point where you began, as shown in figure 10.2. Accuracy is not key here because you'll be doing some special edge work with the selection later. Just don't trim any of the station wagon off; leave about 1/8th of an inch outside the outline of the car. And don't miss the antenna; I can't get FM stations without it.

3. After the marquee selection border is complete, choose **E**dit, **C**opy (Ctrl+C). Then double-click on the command button of the OUR_CAR image window to close the image.

Figure 10.2

Create a rough selection border around the car that includes a little of the background image.

Pasting the Selection into a New Background

Here's where the fun begins. Because the selection you copied in the last step included some leaves, and the background image, PARKNLOT.TIF, also features these same leaves, achieving a seamless composite of the two different images won't be as hard as if there were a symmetrical, geometric pattern of a wire fence mesh or something in the background. You'll paste the car into the host image and move it into a good position relative to the background in the next few steps.

1. Choose File, Save As, and save the PARKNLOT.TIF image with the same eight-character name to a location on your hard drive.

2. Double-click on the Hand tool. This brings your viewing resolution of the image to a full-frame view in Photoshop's workspace.

3. Choose Edit, Paste (Ctrl+V). Then select the Lasso tool and place the cursor inside the marquee border that surrounds the pasted car. Click and drag the selection to a point so that it appears to be about 4 feet above the vacant parking space in the background image, as shown in figure 10.3.

4. When you're happy with the location of the pasted selection, press Ctrl+D (Select, None), and the selection is composited on top of the background image. Don't worry that it looks a little rough around the edges. You'll fix that in the next set of steps.

   It's important that you *do not* save the image at this point. The next section explains the important Photoshop features that you can use on an *unsaved* image file.

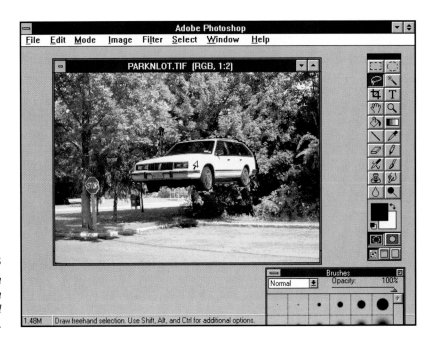

Figure 10.3

A pasted image remains a floating selection above a background image until you deselect it.

When working on a Photoshop assignment, you typically use a variety of tools. To move a floating selection into position over a background, you need to use one of Photoshop's tools that can manipulate a floating selection active as your current cursor. You used the Lasso tool to move the car in the preceding few steps, but you could have used any one of Photoshop's selection tools to do the same thing. The Lasso tool, the Elliptical Marquee tool, the Rectangular Marquee tool, the Magic Wand tool, and even the Text tool can be used to click and drag a floating selection into place.

The Value of an Unsaved Image

It might have seemed strange not to save the file in the last exercise step. Many experienced Windows users save a document or an image immediately after they have made a big-time edit to the file to avoid accidentally losing their work. Adobe has endowed two of Photoshop's tools, the Magic Eraser (aka the Eraser tool) and the Rubber Stamp tool, with some very special properties that rely on the information stored in the last-saved version of the active file. By forgoing the usually prudent step of saving PARKNLOT.TIF after having pasted a sizable area into the image, you'll be able to put these special properties to use and save yourself the doldrums of precise area selection.

By changing these tools from their default settings to last-saved version settings, you'll be able to remove the excess foliage included in the selection border around the car from the PARKNLOT image, and leave only original background area around the car. In the next steps, you'll see how to set the tools and how to carefully trim around the outline of the car. But let's not set any speed records on this one because the car image also can be erased with the PARKNLOT image in its unsaved state.

1. Press Ctrl++ twice to get a 2:1 viewing resolution of the PARKNLOT image. The retouching work will start where most car work is required, under the chassis, so give yourself a clear view of this area. Click on the Hand tool, and click and drag the active image up or down to position it better.

2. Double-click on the Rubber Stamp tool. This calls the Rubber Stamp Options dialog box to the screen, as shown in figure 10.4. Click on the down arrow next to the Option: field. Then choose From Saved and click on OK. The Rubber Stamp tool now is set to brush away any image area not included in the last-saved version of an image, which means the entire pasted copy of the area from OUR_CAR.

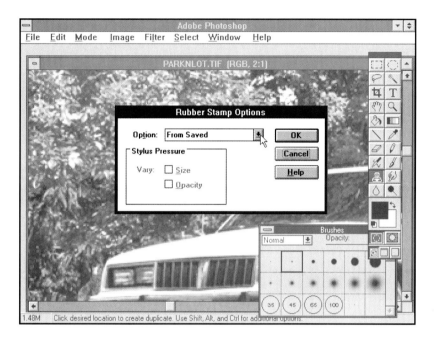

Figure 10.4
Choose from various cloning options in the Rubber Stamp Options box.

3. Select the second smallest tip from the top row of the Brushes palette, set Opacity to 100%, and choose Normal painting/editing mode.

Sometimes design programs can be ornamental to a fault when it comes to fancy cursor design, and Photoshop's no exception; some cursors can obscure your view, making it difficult to determine the "hot spot" of the cursor. Fortunately, Photoshop gives you the choice of working with the default ornamental cursor, or a leaner, more Spartan, more precise crosshair cursor.

4. Press the Caps Lock key. When the Rubber Stamp cursor is placed over an active image window, you'll get a crosshair cursor instead of Adobe's little cartoon of a rubber stamp. You need to perform precise editing next, and the crosshair cursor gives you a much clearer view of the image area.

5. Click and drag the Rubber Stamp tool's cursor in a short stroke across the bottom of the car (see fig. 10.5). Photoshop pauses your activity for a second while it reads the last-saved version into RAM—a message about this appears on the status bar. The bottom part of the car is the trickiest area you'll be working on. The car casts a shadow on the pavement in the OUR_CAR image, and the undercarriage and the shaded pavement are very close in color value.

If you're ever in a quandary about what size Brushes palette tip to assign to a painting or editing tool, consider first the viewing resolution of the image you're retouching. At a 2:1 resolution (as with this assignment), the pixels that make up the image are obvious. To perform precise edge work where detail counts, a small, two- or three-pixel diameter tip like the one used in this assignment is a good choice.

continues

Brushes tips always match the relative viewing resolution of the active image, so there's never a need to resize a tip in Photoshop when you zoom in or out of a picture. The only tool that has a fixed-size cursor is the Eraser tool.

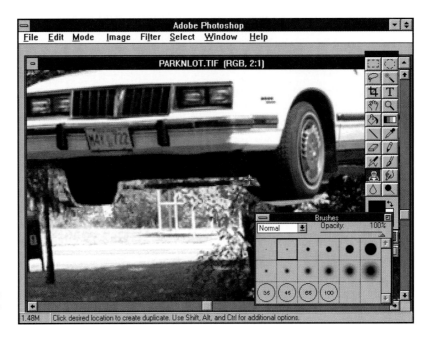

Figure 10.5

The Rubber Stamp tool can restore image areas with its From Saved setting.

This is about as hard as it gets for eliminating unwanted, pasted selection areas in an image that hasn't been saved after pasting. When compared to using Quick Mask mode, or sweating it out with the Lasso tool alone to refine a selection border, restoring image areas back to a From Saved version is a breeze. Obviously, there will be occasions where you need an accurate selection border around an image area, and this method will be untenable. Also, if you're working on an unsaved version of a 5 or 6 MB image, you might be inviting trouble, unless you have plenty of RAM installed in your computer. Photoshop works best and operates faster if it has room to load at least three separate copies of the image file into your system RAM.

But working with a smaller image file, such as PARKNLOT.TIF, is neither a threat nor a strain on most systems, and this technique accomplishes a lot in lightning time.

The Eraser Tool Has Its Magic, Too

The Rubber Stamp tool, using the From Saved option, works great for the edge work around the car. It's unnecessarily laborious, however, to continue using the Rubber Stamp (at *any* Brushes tip diameter) to clean away the image area between the edge work you do with the Rubber Stamp and where the selection edge from the paste ends in this image.

This larger area that you continue to separate from the car image using the Rubber Stamp tool can easily be removed with the Eraser tool in its Magic Eraser setting.

1. Change your viewing resolution of the image to 2:1. The Eraser tool's fixed size is a good one to use at this view.

2. Choose the Eraser tool.

3. While holding down the Alt key, click and drag over the areas beneath the car that you didn't catch with the Rubber Stamp tool.

Don't go into the car area because it, too, is removable in this last-saved version of the image file. Figure 10.6 shows the results of the Magic Eraser. A good quick visual clue that it's the Magic Eraser, and not the standard Eraser tool, is that the cursor has little stripes inside of it when operating in magic mode.

Figure 10.6

The Eraser tool, when used in combination with the Alt key, removes image areas that haven't been saved.

Alternating Tools/Working around the Periphery

Between the Rubber Stamp tool's From Saved setting and the Magic Eraser you have all the necessary tools for removing the unwanted leaves from the PARKNLOT image. But knowledge of these tools alone won't help your work along unless you develop a technique for accomplishing an assignment. For this particular exercise, it's very useful to alternate between the two tools—first separating a short piece of leaf area from the car using the Rubber Stamp, and then switching to the Magic Eraser tool to remove the area between the selection's edge and the edge you created with the Rubber Stamp.

It's also particularly helpful for an artist to have "direction," and in this example, counterclockwise was chosen. It's easier to work systematically with both tools all the way around the car, policing the immediate image area you're working in for any stray shards of unwanted foreground areas. Figure 10.7 shows a 4:1 zoomed-in view of the area beneath the car's front panel being retouched. It really helps to zoom in and out of an image to check your progress. I almost removed the tire's mud flap during this assignment because it wasn't distinct at a 2:1 viewing resolution.

Figure 10.7

Zooming in and out of an image provides different perspectives on the image's graphical content.

You'll see an easy way to recover from a particular imaging mistake in the next section, but there might be times in this assignment when the trick won't apply. That's why you should remember the Ctrl+Z (Undo/Redo) shortcut key whenever you work in Photoshop. Ctrl+Z is quicker than mousing your way to the Edit menu, and pressing these two keys will revoke the last action performed.

Unfortunately, Photoshop's "gimme back" is limited to your last action, not your last two or three, as with some programs such as Word for Windows and AutoCAD. That's why you also should develop a style in Photoshop where you make one continuous stroke with tools. Click, hold, and drag the cursor for an extended period of time until a sizable portion of your task has been completed. Photoshop counts one mouse click as one action, and by continuous motion after clicking, you can undo an extended amount of error should it occur.

Accidents Will Happen

Unlike vector-design programs where discrete objects are constructed independent of other objects, a bitmap image is a weave of pixels—a continuous fabric from which you can select areas to isolate. And many a time a bitmap image has been completely ruined because one area was accidentally altered.

An example of "bitmap recovery" is covered in the next few steps, in case you've forgotten to hold down the Alt key while using the Eraser tool. These steps have nothing to do with making the car float, and you can skip over them if you've got the rhythm of pressing the Alt key when switching back to the Eraser from the Rubber Stamp tool.

Oops! In figure 10.8, I forgot to hold down the Alt key while using the Eraser tool, and instead of erasing the image area back to the last-saved version, the ordinary Eraser tool has removed all the photo detail to expose Photoshop's default white background color.

Figure 10.8

In its normal mode, the Eraser tool removes foreground areas to expose background color.

This is not a big disaster because you're not working in a saved image, and the information about the last-saved version is still held in system RAM for Photoshop to tap into. Simply release the mouse button, and then hold down the Alt key, and click and drag over the image area that was destroyed. The Magic Eraser now erases the erasure, and restores the area to its last-saved version, as shown in figure 10.9.

Figure 10.9

Regardless of any changes, the Magic Eraser will restore the area to the last-saved version.

In figure 10.10, the whole outline of the car has been given the Rubber Stamp/Magic Eraser treatment, and I've zoomed out to a 1:1 viewing resolution (by pressing Ctrl+ – once or twice), to see how the image is shaping up.

Figure 10.10

By removing everything except the car from the pasted-in copy, the car now appears to be floating.

By virtue of the leafy background being almost identical in the OUR_CAR and the PARKNLOT images, you might find during the course of these retouching steps that you're not certain whether a specific area is from the car selection area you pasted, or part of the original background. This is where you can give your artist's eye a little creative leeway.

Random patterns of organic material—piles of rocks, leaves, sand, and seeds—tend to blend together naturally, both to the viewer and as captured in a photograph. Let this reality work for you in this chapter's exercise and in your own work. If an area looks good to your eye at a 1:1 viewing resolution, leave it alone; perfect retouching is a relative concept more dependent upon what your own eye tells you.

Partially Removing an Image Area

Now that the outline of the car integrates pretty seamlessly into the background image, it's time for a little embellishment to enhance the overall image. The windows on the car display its surrounding from its original background. The leaves suggest a certain continuity in the car's present background, allowing some of the leaves in the PARKNLOT image to show through. The car windows, however, are duller than they should appear in the finished image because the car was photographed at a low angle, causing more sunlight to reflect off the windshield than to pass through it.

The way to make the windows more transparent is to use the Rubber Stamp tool once more, with the same From Saved option, to partially reveal the new background leaves. It's a subtle effect, but one that nonetheless helps carry off the illusion that the car is floating.

1. Zoom into the car's front windshield, and click while diagonally dragging across this image area. A 2:1 viewing resolution will reveal the transparent areas of the original car selection as well as the door frames and seat belts, which are areas you won't want to touch.

2. Click on the Rubber Stamp tool, and then click and drag on the Opacity slider on the Brushes palette until the number value displayed at the right of the slider reads about 30%. Leave the painting/editing mode at Normal, and choose the top, second from the left Brushes tip for the Rubber Stamp tool.

3. Click and drag over only the leafy areas in the car windshield. Be careful to avoid internal car areas, such as the door frame (see fig. 10.11).

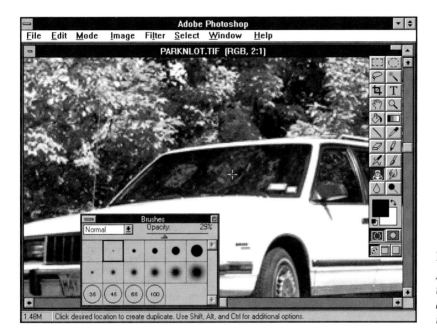

Figure 10.11

A low Opacity setting on the Brushes palette creates a partial effect over the image area.

4. Click on the Hand tool and move your view within the image window so that you can get a clear view of the car's side windows.

5. Repeat the process with the car's side windows. You'll notice no difference after using the semi-opaque Rubber Stamp setting in certain areas, while other areas will reveal a sort of highlight as brilliantly lit background leaf areas are partially restored.

6. Double-click on the Hand tool as your work progresses to get a view of the overall image and some perspective on how the image is turning out.

For a less subtle effect (and for really clean car windows), you might want to try zooming in again to the window areas and increasing the Opacity on the Brushes palette. Then click and drag across the car window areas again. This will expose more of PARKNLOT.TIF's original background leaf areas in the composite image. Be careful not to set the Opacity too high, however, or it will look like the windows are missing, not clean.

*The Brushes palette's Opacity slider can be adjusted without dragging and clicking on the slider arrow in case you quickly need to change Opacity while you're editing an image. When a painting or editing tool is active, you can either use a 101 keyboard's numerical pad, or the keyboard numbers to alter the Opacity in increments of 10. Typing **4**, for example, while painting or editing will drop the Opacity slider's value down to 40%. Typing **7** will result in a 70% opacity, and so on. Unfortunately, you can't set a more specific value, 78% for example, by keystroking the Opacity. But you can get 100% by typing **0** from the keyboard.*

Additionally, when you want to perform a semitransparent composite paste into a background image, the keyboard numbers can be used to set the degree of opacity. A selection must be the active tool (instead of a painting/editing tool) when composite pasting.

Creating and Editing a Shadow

The station wagon image is a striking one now that its original background is no longer apparent in its new setting, and the car's windows reveal some of the present environment. Having completed all the retouching work on the car border, now is a good time to save the image to your hard disk. When you choose File, Save As, you're updating the PARKNLOT.TIF image file, and the From Saved option for the Rubber Stamp tool will no longer work in removing any more of the pasted car's border area.

There's still something lacking from this image (besides gravity). Everything in the world that has light bounced off it and has a solid surface behind it casts a shadow on the surface. This is what a lot of designers miss when they retouch pictures, and objects look suspended in mid-air, whether this is their intention.

In the next series of steps, you'll see how to give this floating car a shadow in its new background environment. This calls for a little artistic flair because there's nothing on which to base the shape of the car's shadow except for the rectangular feel of the car. You'll use the Lasso tool to define the shape and location of where the shadow should appear, and then you'll refine the selection in the Alpha channel that will hold the lassoed selection area.

1. Double-click on the Hand tool to give a full-frame view of the PARKNLOT image.

2. Choose the Lasso tool, and click and drag a shape over the pavement that suggests the general outline of a shadow that would exist if the car were actually floating in this picture. Use figure 10.12 as a guide for the location of the future shadow. As you can see, the shadow isn't directly under the car—it needs to go to the left beneath the car because the sun is at a steep angle to the picture's right. Other, real shadows in the image confirm this observation, and you might want to design the outline so that it actually encroaches on part of the curb to the left of the car.

3. Choose Select, Save Selection when you're done designing the shadow with the Lasso tool.

Using the Lasso tool to create a selection area usually results in an outline that's a little too geometrically harsh to serve as a natural shape, such as a shadow. You might have sharp corners existing in the defined selection area, or a side to the selection that's not to your liking. That's okay, though. A saved selection can be modified with selection or painting tools from your view of it in an Alpha channel. Check out the shadow shape you defined in the next steps.

Figure 10.12

Lasso tool selection areas can be saved and edited as grayscale images in an Alpha channel.

4. Press F6 (**W**indow, Show C**h**annels) to call the Channels palette to Photoshop's workspace.

5. Click on the #4 channel title (Ctrl+4) to get a view of the selection area you created with the Lasso tool and saved a moment ago.

6. If you have a black background and white selection area in your view of channel #4, click on the Channels palette's command button now. If you have a black selection area and a white background, you can skip the next two steps.

Alpha channel selection areas are generally easier to edit if the selection area is portrayed as black, and the masked areas are white. This is determined by which Color Indicates radio button is chosen in Channels Options at the time you saved the selection.

7. From the command button's drop-down list, choose Channel Options.

8. Click on the Color Indicates: Selected Areas radio button, and then click on OK. You'll see Alpha channel #4 invert its color scheme. You're in business now.

9. If you have any unappealing sharp edges in your shadow design, choose the Paintbrush tool. Then click on the Default colors icon button to the bottom left of the color selection boxes, and stick with the same Brushes palette tip and settings you used with the Rubber Stamp tool in the previous steps.

10. Click and drag around areas of the black selection border you want to add to and soften. Editing a selection in a channel is just like painting in Photoshop, except the result is editing a selection, not actually painting an image area.

An innate feature of the Paintbrush tool is to create strokes with soft edges. Unlike the Pencil tool, no matter what size tip you select to apply strokes, the Paintbrush always leaves a pixel or two around the periphery of your stroke. The top row of the default Brushes tips have a hardness setting that confines the spread of a brush stroke to one or two pixels. The rest of the Brushes palette's tips are designed to offer more spread, as is indicated by the tip icons you select. To alter the amount of spread, double-click on a tip icon, and the Brush Options dialog box will appear. You then can adjust the hardness of the tip by moving the slider or typing a percentage value in the text box. The smaller the percentage of hardness, the more spread (the more semitransparent pixels on the edge of a brush stroke) you'll get with that particular tip.

11. If you want to subtract from the black selection area in places that are sticking out too much, click on the Invert colors icon button. This reverses the default foreground/background colors so that you're editing with white instead of black. Applying a white color to the black selection in an Alpha channel removes an area that Photoshop uses as information in creating a selection border.

Softening a Shadow with a Gaussian Blur

As you might have guessed by now, you're not going to paint a car shadow directly into the PARKNLOT image. There's too much left to chance when you freehand paint a sizable visual element, and Photoshop's Channels give you wonderful freedom to edit and refine an image selection area you can later adjust (with the submenu commands located under the **I**mage menu) to produce professional retouching work.

What you will do is darken the shadow selection area using one of Photoshop's commands to create a realistic shadow from the #4 channel selection. But first, you should apply a slight Gaussian Blur to the selection to gently fade the selection edge into nothingness. Shadows in real life usually don't have distinct edges, and our goal here is to imitate real life. The more reality you infuse this image with, the more striking the surreal visual content will become.

1. Choose Fi**l**ter, Blur, Gaussian Blur. The Gaussian Blur produces the most sophisticated and realistic of Photoshop's Blur features. This effect is used frequently on magazine covers to produce drop-shadowed text.

2. Select a small **R**adius value for the Gaussian Blur. Enter a 4 pixel value in the text box (see fig. 10.13). Gaussian Blur is a very concentrated effect, and a little goes a long way.

3. Click on OK to confirm your entry and apply the effect. You are returned to the Alpha channel view of PARKNLOT.TIF where the Gaussian Blur filter has created a soft edge to the black selection area (see fig. 10.14).

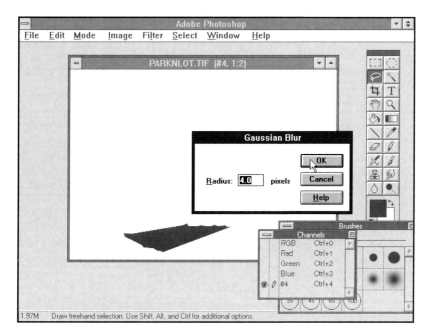

Figure 10.13

A value between .1 and 100 pixels can be entered in the Gaussian Blur dialog box.

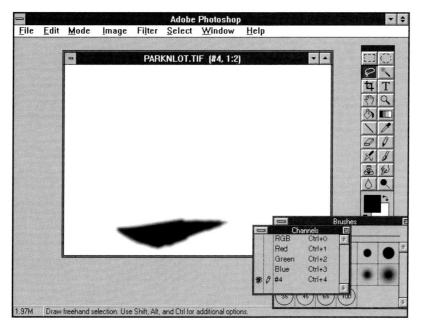

Figure 10.14

Photoshop bases a selection area on brightness values it finds in an Alpha channel.

The Gaussian Blur filter creates shades of gray around the outline of the selection area you originally created using the Lasso tool. In an Alpha channel, with the option of Color Indicates: Selected areas chosen, black represents an area that's completely selected, while the shades of gray produced by the Gaussian Blur represent partially masked areas. When Photoshop builds a section border based on information in an Alpha channel, it evaluates how light or dark each pixel in the Alpha channel is. It uses this information to determine which pixels are included in a selection, and to what degree their counterparts in the RGB composite image are capable of being affected by filters and other adjustments. This is yet another way Photoshop can create soft edges in a bitmap format, which by its definition assigns square blocks (with harsh corners) color information in an imaginary grid we call a canvas, or background image area.

Producing the Shadow by Adjusting Pixel Values

Now that a realistic shadow has been created, it's time to apply the shadow to the RGB composite view of PARKNLOT.TIF. There are a number of Adjust commands in Photoshop to change the color and tonal value of a selection area you've created, but the best one for this particular assignment's grand finale is the Hue/Saturation command. The Hue/Saturation dialog box features individual controls for fine-tuning each of the three components of the HSB color model.

A brief moment of color theory before proceeding will help you see the correlation between the actions in the next steps and the artistic reason why you need to perform them. You don't want to change the value of the hue in the selection beneath the car image to create the shadow. *Hue* represents the wavelength of light an image area reflects into your eye. It's the principle component of a color, and the quality that distinguishes, say, purple from blue. The area beneath the car would not change hue were an actual object to cast a shadow upon it.

You also don't want to change the saturation of the selection area to create a shadow. *Saturation* is how much color is in an area. When you desaturate an image area, you leave only the grayscale, tonal information, as you'd find in a black-and-white photo. On the other hand, super-saturating an image area increases the amount of pure color within it, decreasing any neutral density (gray) in the area. This produces neon-like, fluorescent-appearing pixels, which wouldn't realistically represent a shadow in an image, either.

The brightness (or lightness) that pixels exhibit makes an image area shaded or brightly lit. *Brightness* is the measurement of how much or how little light is bounced off an object in real life. So to create the shadow for this image, you need to create the appearance that very little light is being reflected off the pavement beneath the car. To do so, follow these steps:

1. Click on the RGB title on the Channels palette. This returns you to a normal, color composite view of the PARKNLOT image.

2. Position PARKNLOT.TIF in the upper left corner of Photoshop's workspace. The next step calls the Hue/Saturation dialog box to the screen. It will obscure your view of the image unless you move the image out of the way before calling the dialog box.

3. Choose **S**elect, Load **S**election, and then press Ctrl+H (or choose **S**elect, Hide **E**dges). You now have the Alpha channel selection area active, and the marquee edges are hidden so that you can see the changes you'll be making without the distraction of the border. The area beneath the car will be the only area in the image you'll be changing—it's the only area selected.

4. Choose **I**mage, **A**djust, Hue/Saturation (Ctrl+U).

5. Check the Preview box on the Hue/Saturation dialog box so that you get an active view of how the changes you'll make will affect the active PARKNLOT image.

6. Click and drag the Lightness slider to the left, decreasing the apparent amount of light being cast in your selection area. This creates a virtual shadow. Figure 10.15 shows the process in action. A value of –76 works very well for the negative Lightness value, but you might want to experiment with a little higher or lower value to suit your own taste.

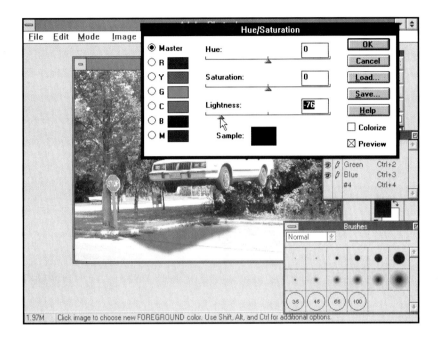

Figure 10.15

Decreasing the Lightness in a selected area effectively creates a shadow.

7. Click on OK, press Ctrl+D to deselect the invisible active selection area, and you have your finished floating car (see fig. 10.16).

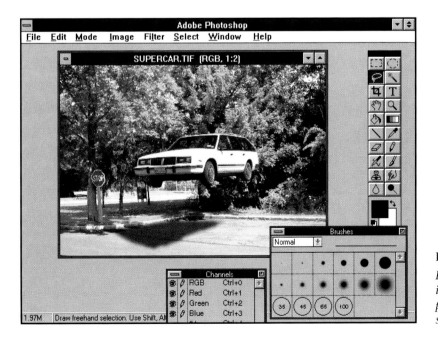

Figure 10.16

Decreasing the Lightness in the selected area preserves some of the selection's visual content.

Clean-Up Time

Before you save your work to hard disk, there's an Alpha channel you no longer need. It's a good idea to delete these extra information channels when you're certain you've finished retouching an image.

1. Click on the #4 title on the Channels palette, to return to the view of the blurry shadow selection.

2. Click on the command button on the Channels palette's upper left corner.

3. Choose Delete Channel. As you can see in the lower left corner of Photoshop's status bar, deleting the Alpha channel shrunk the active image's file size by a third.

4. Choose Save As from the File menu, and name this completed piece something other than PARKNLOT.TIF so that you can find it easily later.

After you've put a fair amount of effort into retouching an image in Photoshop, you can use a feature Photoshop has that offers some immediate artistic gratification. In figure 10.17, the right display mode was clicked on the toolbox. This is the last of three buttons at the very bottom of the toolbox that toggles off the menu, the scroll bars, and the image window from an active image. Pressing the Tab key causes all the open palettes and the toolbox to disappear and provides you with a beautifully uncluttered view of your work. Pressing the Tab key a second time toggles you back to a view of Photoshop's toolbox so that you can once more gain control of the workspace.

Figure 10.17

If this image were real, the author would have to buy new tires less often.

There are several ways to create both shadows and highlights in image areas, and you've seen only one technique in this chapter. Check out the additional methods used in other exercise assignments throughout this book. We'll be bending a little "virtual neon" in the next chapter, and I need to take a break for a moment to find a step ladder. I think I left a quart of milk in the front seat of my station wagon...

Chapter 11

Creating Sources of Light

Making objects appear to have a glow using Photoshop is easy. What's hard is deciding what type of glow looks best. You can make something look like a smoldering cinder, or add a highlight edge that imitates neon. This chapter shows you three different techniques for adding a source of light to a digital image to make your work look absolutely brilliant.

The Images on the *Adobe Photoshop NOW! CD-ROM*

If you want to "see the light" on your own monitor, you can follow along with the steps in this chapter using the images on the *Adobe Photoshop NOW! CD-ROM*. The image files you need are referenced in the steps, and everything's located in the CHAP11 subdirectory of the CD.

Adding Drama to a Lava Lamp

I photographed a table top scene of a lava lamp, and spent quite a while adjusting the lighting to convey a sense of awe and drama not typically ascribed to this 1960s toy. But I thought the scene would be much more effective if the lava lamp were perched upon some glowing rocks to suggest actual lava.

Creating Volcanic Rocks from Garden Variety Ones

My homeowner's policy specifically excludes damage caused by bringing molten rocks indoors, so the second best approach was to photograph ordinary ones. You'll see now how Photoshop's features and tools can help turn up the heat.

1. Open the LAVALAMP.TIF image, and then open the ROX107.TIF image from the *Adobe Photoshop NOW! CD-ROM*.

As you can see in figure 11.1, the rocks already have been masked, and a white border surrounds them. This is to provide a clear view of the image as you retouch it. The #4 channel in the ROX107 image contains the Alpha channel you'll use to select the rocks and copy them to the LAVALAMP image.

2. Double-click on the Zoom tool to get a 1:1 viewing resolution of the ROX107 image.

3. Double-click on the Quick Mask mode button. Click on the Color Indicates: Selected Areas radio button, and then click on the Color selection box.

Figure 11.1

The rocks need more verve to compositionally support the lava lamp.

4. Choose a chartreuse color for the quick mask. You'll be changing some of the rock to a reddish-orange, and you need a contrasting color for the quick mask. Click on OK in the Color Picker, and then click on OK in the Quick Mask Options box.

5. Choose the Paintbrush tool. Then pick the second-largest, middle row tip on the Brushes palette, and set the Opacity on the palette to about 40%.

6. Click and drag over the areas of the rocks that the light hit when they were photographed, as shown in figure 11.2. You're creating a partial mask here, so don't try to cover areas completely with Quick Mask.

Figure 11.2

A less-than-100% opacity creates a partial mask when in Quick Mask mode.

7. Choose a higher Opacity (such as 80%) and make one or two more strokes in the areas you've previously masked. These areas will display a more pronounced effect when you edit the selection because you are covering them more completely with Quick Mask.

8. Click on the Standard mode button, and then press Ctrl+H to hide the marquee edges of the selection that you just created.

9. Press Ctrl+U to display the Hue/Saturation command's dialog box.

10. Click on the Colorize check box, and then enter the following values (or click and drag the sliders): Hue: +22, and Saturation: +77. Leave the Lightness value. As you can see in figure 11.3, the rocks appear to be taking on a glow

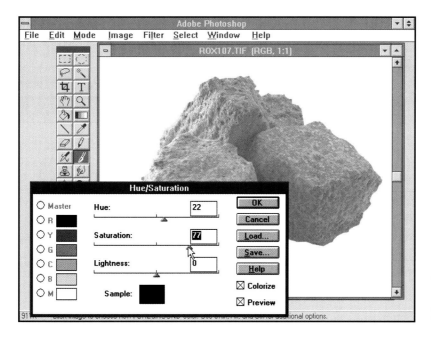

Figure 11.3

Photoshop replaces color values but leaves the grayscale information when you colorize.

11. Click on OK, and you're finished with phase 1 of creating glowing rocks. Don't deselect the selection border you created. Press Ctrl+H to toggle the marquee lines back on as a visual reminder.

Intensifying the Glowing Effect

The ROX107 image definitely displays a heightened degree of temperature now. But the original image was not tonally balanced and therefore lacks contrast. You should begin with images that are a little dull when creating this type of glowing effect, though, because the Hue/Saturation's Colorize function will over-saturate, or *clip*, image areas that already have a concentration of dense color pixels in them.

The Levels command is used next to increase the contrast in only the areas that haven't been colorized. See what a difference it makes.

1. Choose Select, Inverse to select the rock and background areas instead of the colorized rock areas.

2. Press Ctrl+L to display the Levels command.

3. Click and drag the Black point slider to 21, then click and drag the Midpoint slider to 1.07 (or enter their values manually in the Input Values boxes on top).

4. As you can see in figure 11.4, tweaking the black and midpoints adds some contrast to the darker selected areas, while leaving some detail in the midranges and upper tones.

Figure 11.4

The Levels command redistributes tonal values of image pixels in three ranges.

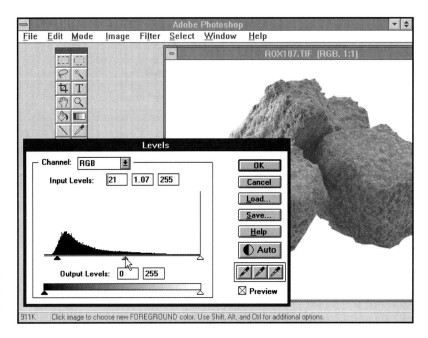

5. Click on OK, and then press Ctrl+D. The selection border you created with Quick Mask goes away forever. Save the ROX107 image to your hard disk now. Make sure the <u>S</u>ave Alpha Channels check box is checked in the TIFF Options box.

Adding Some Sizzle to the Rocks

This next trick puts the finishing touches on the ROX107 image. The Dissolve mode in Photoshop places randomly distributed pixels across a stroke or a fill, and it's ideal when used in combination with the Quick Mask to create random selection areas in an image. Next, you'll create some very naturalistic highlights on the rocks.

1. Click on the Quick Mask mode button.

2. Choose the Paintbrush tool, and select Dissolve mode from the drop-down list on the Brushes palette.

3. Choose the 100 pixel diameter tip on the Brushes palette, and choose a 45% Opacity.

4. Click and drag one or two strokes across the colorized areas of the rocks, as shown in figure 11.5.

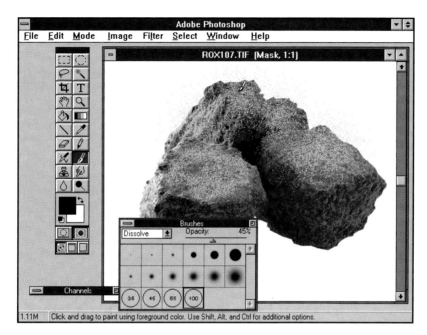

Figure 11.5

Dissolve mode splatters pixels of foreground color. It's great for fireworks and weathering areas, too!

5. Click on the Standard mode button, press Ctrl+H to hide the marquee edges, and then press Ctrl+U to display the Hue/Saturation command.

6. Enter the following values: Hue: +9, Saturation: +20, and Lightness: +8. You aren't colorizing here. Instead, you're progressively modifying the selection area to enhance the molten look of these rocks, as shown in figure 11.6.

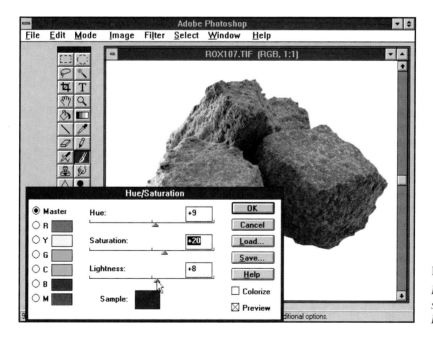

Figure 11.6

Progressively modify selected areas with the Hue/Saturation command.

Unlike vector-type drawing programs where you can specify a fill color for an object and then change your mind later, bitmaps work on the "delta" theory. Each successive change you apply to a selection area moves it along, progressively farther from the original image.

*For this reason, plan your bitmap image editing carefully, and always keep a spare original image tucked away safely on disk. Photoshop has a **R**evert command in case you get into trouble with an image, but if you use it, you will lose all edits, including the ones you really liked.*

7. Click on OK. Then press Ctrl+D, and save the ROX107 image to your hard disk.

Masking the Base of the Lava Lamp

You'll be adding the ROX107 image and others to the base of the lava lamp. This means it's time to mask the lamp so that you have the option to paste rocks in front of or behind the lamp.

The best tool for creating a selection border with as many hard lines and angled curves as this lamp is the Paths palette. You'll be using the Paths palette's tools to accurately define the shape of the lava lamp base so that you can make a selection area of the same shape.

1. Press F9 to display the Paths palette.

2. Choose the Pen tool. Then, starting at the upper right corner of the black lava lamp base, click, hold, and drag a starting point. This produces an Anchor point and a path segment between your cursor and the first Anchor point.

3. Click a second point, hold, and drag. The path segments are controlled by the direction your cursor moves while you click and hold. Don't expect perfection with the path segments. You'll need to modify them later with the Corner tool. Look at figure 11.7 to compare your progress.

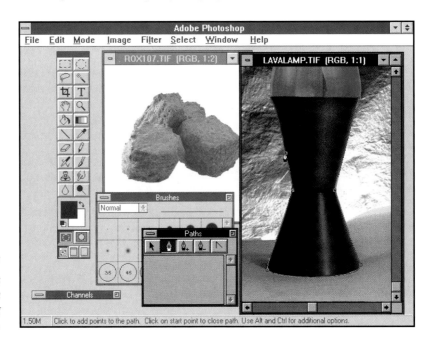

Figure 11.7

The Pen tool operates similar to Bézier design tools in drawing applications.

4. When you reach the starting Anchor point, the Pen tool displays a little circle in the bottom corner of the cursor. This means you're completing a path, and you should make one final click.

5. Choose the Corner tool. This tool toggles an Anchor point as symmetrical direction lines and asymmetrical ones. Click, hold, and drag away from an Anchor point to access the direction points (at the end of the direction lines) with the Corner tool.

6. Shape the path to conform to the base of the lava lamp. Use the Arrow Pointer tool to move Anchor points and turn direction points (which shape the path segments).

The Paths palette does not have the easiest tools to master. It's a different way of working, and a background with a design program like Adobe Illustrator, Micrografx Designer, or CorelDRAW! definitely wouldn't hurt your understanding of Photoshop paths.

Chapter 6, "Combining Images," devotes more attention to using the Paths palette tools. You have to play with this one for a few hours, and then you'll become proficient and actually like using paths.

7. When you have an accurate path designed, click on the command button on the Paths palette, and choose Make Selection.

8. In the Make Selection dialog box, enter 0 pixels for the Feather Radius, check the Anti-Aliased box, and then click OK.

9. As soon as the marquee selection appears, choose Select, Save Selection.

10. You now should have both a marquee selection border and a path displayed in the LAVALAMP image, as shown in figure 11.8. Press Ctrl+D to deselect the saved area.

11. Press the Backspace key twice to get rid of the unwanted path. Then save LAVALAMP.TIF to your hard drive, making sure the Save Alpha channels option is checked in the TIFF Options dialog box.

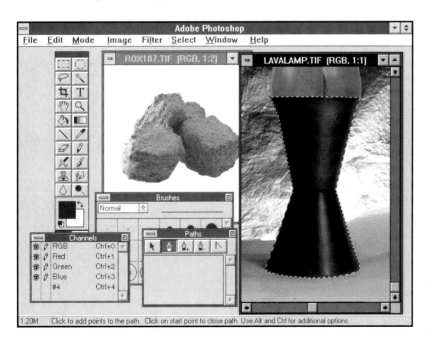

Figure 11.8

Photoshop doesn't convert a path to a selection. It bases a selection area on a path.

Unless you have the cool nerves of a gunslinger, never press the Backspace key to obliterate a path when a selection marquee is active. Pressing the Backspace key once removes the last Anchor point you created, and pressing twice removes all the path segments. If you press Backspace a third time with a selection area active, the image area is removed, and the background color in the area is exposed.

Adding Rocks to the Background Image

You have the option now to place the ROX107 image selection in front of or behind the lava lamp's base. You'll place it in front of the base in the next steps. You'll also discover how easily the selection area you defined last can be modified to include the selection area of the rocks. By adding the information about the rocks to the same Alpha channel you saved the Lava Lamp base's selection in, you'll be able to paste more rock behind both the lamp and the ROX107 image.

1. Click on the title bar of ROX107.TIF to make it the active image window.

2. Choose **S**elect, **L**oad Selection, and then press Ctrl+C.

3. Press Ctrl+Tab to toggle to LAVALAMP.TIF as the active image.

4. Click on the Invert colors icon button. Your background color should be black.

5. Press Ctrl+V, and choose a selection tool, such as the Lasso tool.

6. Click and drag the pasted rocks toward the bottom right of the LAVALAMP image. There's no right position for them, and half of the selection area might go outside of the image window because these are large rocks. Get the selection of the rocks in a position you feel will be their final one.

7. Press F6 to display the Channels palette if you don't already have it displayed on the workspace.

8. Click on the #4 title on the Channels palette.

9. Press the Del key. The rocks selection area now has been added to the information about the base of the lava lamp's selection, as shown in figure 11.9.

10. Press Ctrl+D, click on the RGB title on the Channels palette, and then press Ctrl+S to save your work.

More Colorizing, More Compositing, More Rocks

To complete the foreground coverage of the LAVALAMP image, you'll want to open the ROX109 image next. I used only three rocks for all the image files used here because the wonderful thing about rocks is that you get a different one every time you roll one over on its side.

Use the same Quick Mask techniques on the ROX109 image to define the highlight areas. Use Colorize, the Levels adjustment on an inverted selection area, and finally apply Hue/Saturation to a Quick Mask selection area created in Dissolve mode.

You can see in figure 11.10, the ROX109 image is then copied and pasted into the left, bottom side of the LAVALAMP image. Again, the foreground area in Alpha channel #4 is deleted while the marquee selection area around ROX109 is still active.

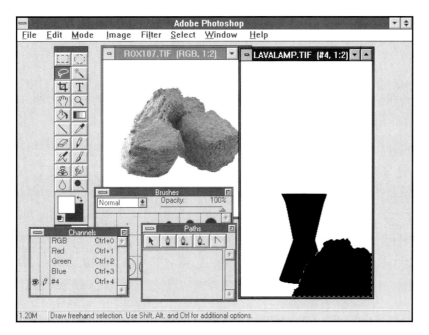

Figure 11.9

Removing the foreground to expose black background adds information to the Alpha channel.

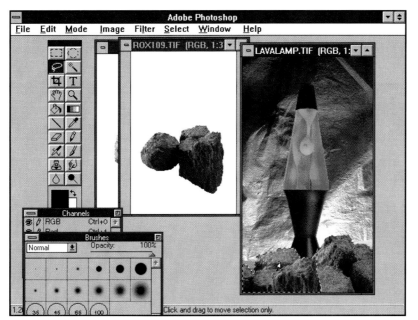

Figure 11.10

Use the same techniques for enhancing, copying, and pasting ROX109 as you did with ROX107.

Resizing Rocks and Finishing the Foreground

Now it's time to finish the bottom of the image with a few more lava rocks and Photoshop's Paste Behind command. The ROX108 image was digitized at the same dimensions and resolution as the two other ROX images, which means that the image has to be resized to create perspective in the LAVALAMP image.

Open the ROX108 image, and then apply the same glowing effect you did to the other two rocks image files. When you're done, these are the steps you need to follow to complete the effect.

1. Choose Image, Image Size.

2. Make sure the Proportion check box is marked, but leave the File Size check box unmarked.

3. In the New Size field, click on the increments drop-down list for Width, and choose percent.

4. Enter 50 in the Width field box. The Height adjusts automatically, and you need not set the increments to percent either. Click on OK.

The ROX108 image shrinks to 50 percent of its original size, and now is suitable to include as a background element at the bottom of LAVALAMP.TIF.

5. Press Ctrl+C, and then Ctrl+Tab to toggle LAVALAMP.TIF to the active image window.

6. Choose Select, Load Selection.

7. Choose Edit, Paste Behind.

8. Click and drag the image until it sits to the left of the lava lamp, and above the ROX109 pasted copy, as shown in figure 11.11.

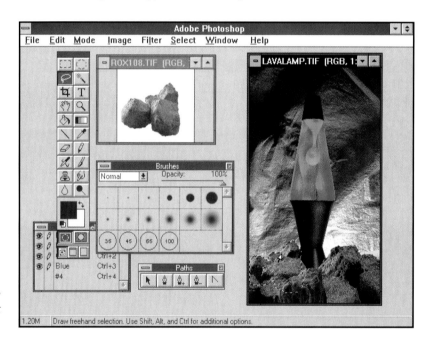

Figure 11.11

Paste Behind places a copied area in front of the background image but behind an active selection.

9. Press Ctrl+D. You don't need to add this selection area to the Alpha channel.

10. Choose Select, Load Selection, and then press Ctrl+V.

11. Choose Image, Flip, Horizontal.

12. The pasted copy mirrors, and you have a different set of rock images. Click and drag the selection to the right of the Lava Lamp, above the ROX107 copy. It's okay if the ROX108 copy is partially obscured by the ROX107 image. In fact, it's good because this helps create more of a random rock effect.

13. Press Ctrl+D, and then Ctrl+S to save your work.

Enhancing the Glow of the Lava Lamp

It was pretty simple to add some warmth to the rocks because it was artistically permissible to define the area and edit it to add the glow. You lost some visual information about the rocks, but this was the concept, and glowing lava rocks in real life would indeed have visual information missing where they glow.

But the hero of the image, the lava lamp, needs to have a glow applied to it next, and none of the visual information about the glass container part of the lamp should be altered. You want the lamp to glow, but still see all the lava blobs. The first step is to define the glass area, and again the Paths palette is the quickest way to accomplish this.

1. Double-click on the Zoom tool to get a 1:1 viewing resolution of the LAVALAMP image. Scroll up the image so that the glass portion of the lamp is in full view. Resize the image window if necessary.

2. Choose the Pen tool, and define an outline of Anchor points and path segments around the glass area, as shown in figure 11.12. Click, hold, and drag on Anchor points with the Corner tool to make the path segments on either side meet at a slope, or a sharp angle.

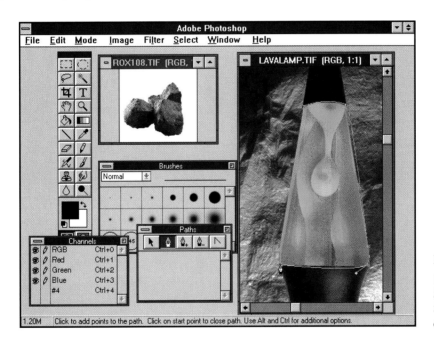

Figure 11.12

Use the Paths palette tools in concert to shape a path to fit the lamp's outline exactly.

Clicking and dragging with the Pen tool produces curved path segments, but if Bézier drawing is frustrating, try clicking on each extreme of an image area that you want to shape a path around. Then click and drag on each Anchor point to curve the path segments. Click and drag on a direction point (the little handles on the direction lines that come out of an Anchor point) with the Corner tool to break the symmetrical property of an Anchor's direction lines. Finally, use the Pointer tool to click and drag on a direction point to shape the path segment it belongs to.

3. After the path is defined around the glass area, click on the command button on the Paths palette, and choose Save Path from the drop-down list. Accept the default name of Path 1, and click on OK.

4. The Make Selection dialog box will have your last entries saved. Accept these values, and click on OK.

5. Choose Select, Inverse. As you can see in figure 11.13, everything except the glass part of the lava lamp is now selected, and the glass is masked. This is good because you'll be doing some potent image editing shortly.

6. Choose Select, Save Selection. Choose the #4 channel to overwrite the saved selection of the base of the lamp and rocks that you no longer need.

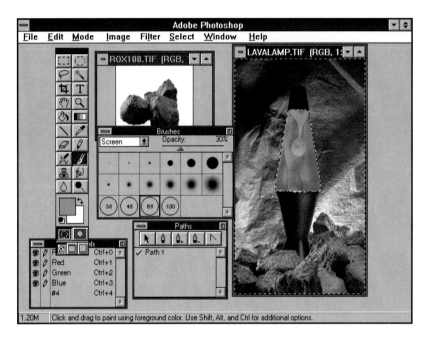

Figure 11.13

The Select, Inverse command makes a mask out of the selection area that you last defined.

Stroking a Path To Produce a Neon Glow

One of the biggest problems professional photographers encounter is capturing the light emanating from a source in a strongly lit scene. Lava lamps really do emit a natural glow seen under subtle room light, but the haze around this one was wiped out when I added a light directly behind it to illuminate the backdrop.

To restore, and actually do better than the lava lamp's native glow, you'll use the Stroke Path command in the following steps. With the selection you defined earlier loaded, the neon produced will only be visible around the lamp, and the detail work of the lava lamp blobs will be masked.

1. Choose the Paintbrush tool. Then while holding down the Alt key, sample a foreground color for the neon from the blue lava areas in the glass part of the lamp.

2. Choose Select, Load Selection, and then press Ctrl+H to hide the marquee edges.

3. Choose the 100 pixel Brushes palette tip, pick Screen mode from the drop-down list on the palette, and set Opacity to about 20%.

4. Click on the column to the left of the Path 1 title on the Paths palette. This makes the path active and visible, and is signified by a check mark.

5. Choose Stroke Path from the Paths palette's command button drop-down list. This is the beginning of the neon glow, as shown in figure 11.14.

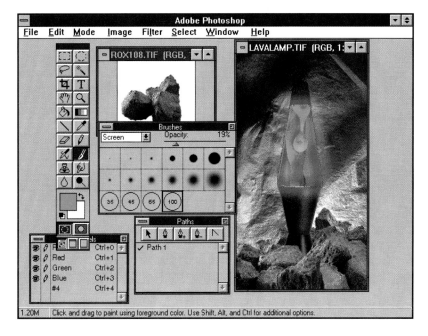

Figure 11.14

Stroking a path in Screen mode bleaches the selection area to the foreground color.

6. Choose a smaller Brushes tip (35 pixels is good), and increase the Opacity to 50%.

7. Click on the command button on the Paths palette again, and choose Stroke Path. This is the way you build a neon glow.

8. Choose a medium sized tip from the second row on the Brushes palette, increase the Opacity to 80%, and stroke the path a final time.

9. Click on the check mark next to the Path 1 title on the Paths palette to get a better look at your neon work.

10. Do *not* save the image yet.

Cleaning Up the Neon Effect

While handsomely executed, the neon glow around the glass of the lava lamp is a little too intense on the top and bottom, and makes our hero look more like an atomic melt-down than an "execu-toy." By not saving in the last step, you can use the Rubber Stamp tool and a special option to reduce some glare in the image. The From Saved Rubber Stamp Option is used next to restore the lava lamp top and bottom to its pre-glow state.

1. Double-click on the Rubber stamp tool.

2. From the Options drop-down list, choose From Saved, and then click on OK.

3. Choose Normal mode, and 100% Opacity on the Brushes palette. Keep the same tip that you used last.

4. Scroll up to the very top of the lamp to the cap.

5. Click and drag where the cap meets the glass, as shown in figure 11.15. The Rubber Stamp gently removes the neon stroke. You only need to do this once or twice, and you might want to diminish the Opacity to let the neon gently fall off instead of abruptly ending.

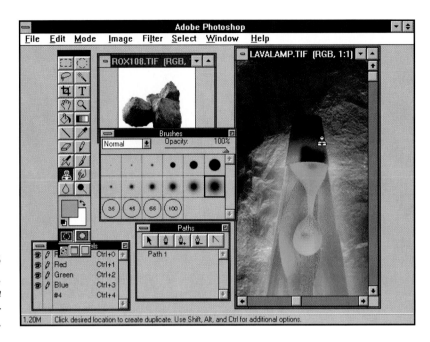

Figure 11.15

The Rubber Stamp tool, like the Magic Eraser, can restore image areas to last-saved versions.

6. When you're done, scroll down to where the glass of the Lava Lamp meets the base. Repeat the Rubber Stamp steps with this area.

7. When you're done, you're done. Delete the superfluous Path in this image file, delete the extra Alpha channels, and save the piece. As shown in figure 11.16, I added a little type to the top of the image, and saved it as ETERNAL.TIF. Lava lamps come with a tag that has this slogan, and I thought is was appropriate. At the very least, it's survived the last three decades.

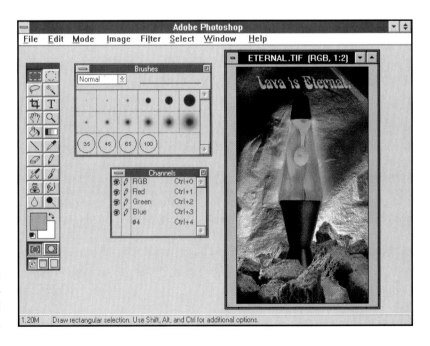

Figure 11.16

Two techniques for creating glows around images.

The "Down and Dirty" Glow

You now know two different ways to make something appear to glow, and you'll find variations on these techniques as an assignment calls for one and you grow more comfortable using the Paths palette. But there's still another, easier way to achieve a neon-glow effect around an image. You get less precision with this method, but it's a really good one when you have 30 or 40 presentation slides to crank out, and they all need an element or two highlighted.

Begin with the WATCH.TIF image on the *Adobe Photoshop NOW! CD-ROM*. WATCH.TIF has an Alpha channel in it that has information that describes the outline of the watch. The watch image is to be placed on the PASSAGE.TIF background, and you want the watch to radiate a glow. With the selection area defined, here's how to perform some "60 second" neon.

Silhouetting a Watch into a Vista View

1. Open the WATCH.TIF and the PASSAGE.TIF images from the *Adobe Photoshop NOW! CD-ROM*. Click on the WATCH.TIF title bar to make it the active image.

2. Choose **S**elect, **L**oad Selection, and then press Ctrl+C to copy the watch.

3. Press Ctrl+Tab to toggle to the PASSAGE.TIF image.

4. Press Ctrl+V, then with a selection tool, click and drag the watch image so that it's positioned as in figure 11.17.

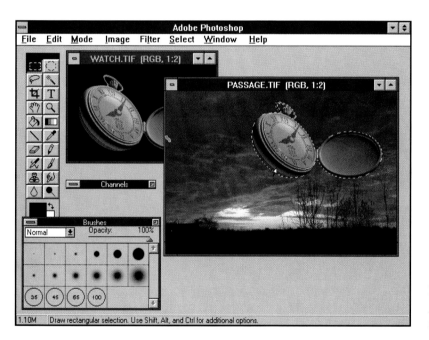

Figure 11.17
Position the watch image using any selection tool.

5. Choose **S**elect, **S**ave Selection. Then choose **S**elect, **S**ave Selection again, but choose New, not #4. You'll now have two identical selections in different Alpha channels.

6. Click on the #5 title on the Channels palette, and then choose **S**elect, **B**order.

7. Enter 4 pixels in the **W**idth field, and then click on OK.

8. Click on the Default colors icon button, and then on the Invert colors icon button to make sure your background color is black.

9. Press the Del key. As you can see in figure 11.18, deleting the Border makes the silhouette of the watch thicker.

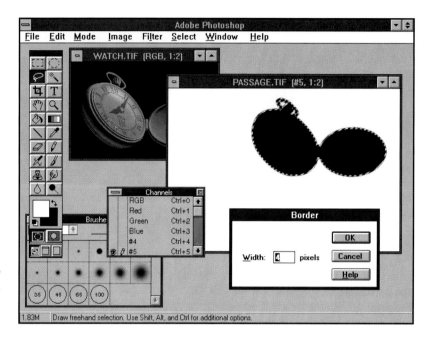

Figure 11.18

Deleting the border around the selection area in the Alpha channel increases the selection information.

10. Press Ctrl+D to deselect the border.

11. Choose Filter, Blur, and then Gaussian Blur. Enter 8 pixels as the Radius, and then click on OK.

12. Press Ctrl+I to invert all of the selection information in the #5 channel, as shown in figure 11.19.

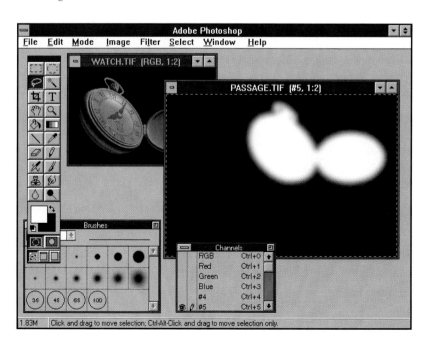

Figure 11.19

The Image, Map, Invert command creates a negative of a selected image area.

Don't confuse the Image, Map, Invert command with the Select, Inverse command, as it could easily ruin your day, if not your imaging work. Select, Inverse only changes a selection area into a masked area, leaving the rest of an image selected. Image, Map, Invert actually inverts the chroma of image pixels, producing something resembling a photographic negative. An easy way to tell them apart is that the less volatile command, Select, Inverse, has no shortcut key.

Merging and Fine Tuning the Watch with the Vista

1. Press Ctrl+A, and then Ctrl+C to copy all of Alpha channel #4 to the Clipboard.

2. Click on the RGB title on the Channels palette, and then choose Select, Load Selection, #4.

3. Choose Edit, Paste Behind. Don't deselect anything yet. Still got a selection tool active?

4. Choose Screen mode (the converse of Multiply) on the Brushes palette. The PASSAGE scene reappears.

5. Press Ctrl+U to display the Hue/Saturation command.

6. Check the Colorize check box, then Enter Hue: –101, and Lightness: –49. Leave the Saturation at 100%. As you can see in figure 11.20, a purple neon glow now surrounds the watch image.

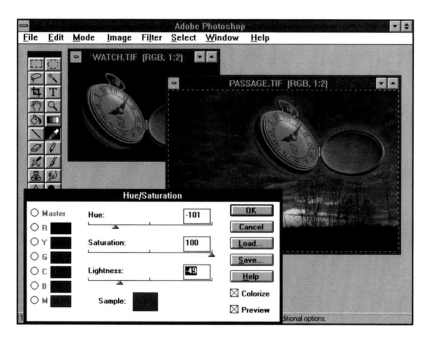

Figure 11.20

The Colorize option only affects the white area pasted behind the watch image.

You can create any color of neon your heart desires with the last steps, but with a selection area that's been composited in Screen mode, don't ever set the Lightness above zero with a colorized selection. Why? For the same reason the black areas of the pasted selection vanished. The Screen mode will only drop out 100% black image areas, and leave the white and lighter ones as they are. By increasing the Lightness after colorizing a Screen mode composite, the black areas would turn gray, adopt some white color, become subject to the same colorizing as the white area you just colorized, and the entire image would take on a purple tint.

7. Click on OK to return to your image. Press Ctrl+D, and then delete the Alpha channels you added, as you no longer need them. Save the image as PASTIME.TIF to your hard disk.

8. Click on the maximize button in the upper right corner of the image window, and then press the Tab key to get a view of your finished image without the toolbox or palettes. As you can see in figure 11.21, it's 5 past 8, and we really should get going now.

Figure 11.21

The finished image, complete with lightning-fast neon.

Chapter 12

Adding Dimension to a 2D Graphic

There might be several instances where you have a beautiful illustration that lacks a background. You might be handed a traditional camera-ready industrial photograph whose subject has been stripped out of a background of a factory. Or you might have spent hours on an illustrated portrait and simply didn't consider what you now need to "throw behind" the picture.

In any case, a lot of wonderful imaging suffers from lack of dimension and substance because the background of the image doesn't support it. In this chapter's assignment, you have an image of a piggy bank that will be the center attraction of a financial institution poster. It's a good image, but you're going to make it a *great* one by setting it into a scene you create that adds both dimension and a point of reference for the viewer.

Features Covered:

- Channels
- Patterns
- Gaussian Blur
- Crop tool
- Effects commands

Adding a Logo to a Curved Surface

To begin, the PIG.TIF image in figure 12.1 was created in a modeling program, similar to that described in Chapter 5, "The EPS Image." An Alpha channel matte was created within this image in anticipation that PIG.TIF was not to be a completed image, but rather that the virtual piggy bank would be copied into a background at a future point. Although this particular image was entirely computer generated, the following steps are the same for a scanned photograph of a piggy bank.

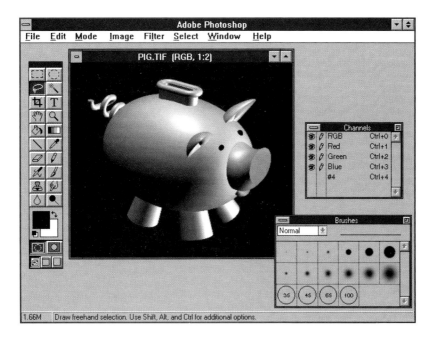

Figure 12.1

A realistic computer image sorely in need of a background.

As you can see, the side of the piggy bank in this assignment is mercilessly unadorned and cries out for a hypothetical bank's logo. The logo can't be flat, however; it must match the curvature of the piggy bank if it is to look as though it belongs on the side of the piggy bank.

The best graphics tool for creating a dimensional logotype is a drawing, vector-type program, such as Adobe Illustrator or CorelDRAW!. In figure 12.2, a low-resolution copy of PIG.TIF was imported into CorelDRAW!, and an outline was drawn on top of the imported TIFF image that had the general feel of the piggy bank's curvature. A simple logo is designed in black and white, and an outline is applied to it that matches the shape of the area outlined on the piggy bank. CorelDRAW!'s Enveloping feature distorts the logo so that it conforms to the area within the outline. In Chapter 5, a path drawn in Photoshop was exported to a draw-type program to use as the basis for the envelope's shape. But importing an image and then using the program's native tools to design an envelope for a vector design, like you do here, is just a different route to the same goal.

Figure 12.2

Vector-based design programs usually offer an enveloping function.

The modified logo is exported as an Encapsulated PostScript (EPS) file that Photoshop can import, rasterize, and use as a selection to be added to the original PIG.TIF image.

The Images on the *Adobe Photoshop NOW! CD-ROM*

I realize that not everyone owns a vector-based design program, and for that reason, 2NDBANK.EPS, the design created in CorelDRAW! in the last figure, is on the *Adobe Photoshop NOW! CD-ROM*, in the CHAP12 subdirectory, along with all the other images necessary for following along with this bank poster design.

Coloring the Imported EPS Image Logo

As long as an EPS file has been rasterized and is held in your system RAM, Photoshop doesn't care what *type* of image it is. For this reason, you can assign an Alpha channel to the EPS image, and then use a copy of the rasterized image to serve as a mask that you can paint on top. EPS files exported from drawing programs typically don't support color, only grayscale information. In this next set of steps, you'll color the EPS image so that it makes a more striking logo on the side of the piggy bank.

1. Choose **F**ile, **O**pen. Then choose 2NDBANK.EPS from the *Adobe Photoshop NOW! CD-ROM*.

2. Accept the defaults of **W**idth: 1.292 and H**e**ight: 1.375 in the EPS Rasterizer dialog box. These are the dimensions the CorelDRAW! EPS exported file was designed to use, and they fit the dimensions and resolution of PIG.TIF.

3. Make certain the **R**esolution is 150 pixels/inch (the resolution that you'll consistently use in this assignment), and that the mode for the rasterized EPS is RGB Color. Then click on OK.

4. Press Ctrl+A and then Ctrl+C to select the entire RGB composite image of 2NDBANK.EPS and copy it to the Clipboard.

5. Press F6 to display the Channels palette. Click on the control button on the Channels palette, and choose New Channel from the drop-down list.

6. Accept the default name of #4 for the New Channel, click on the Color Indicates: Selected Areas radio button, and then click on OK.

7. Press Ctrl+V (**E**dit, **P**aste), and the copy of the 2NDBANK image will plop into the #4 channel view of the image.

8. Click on the RGB title on the Channels palette.

9. Click on the Default colors icon button, and then double-click on the Eraser tool.

10. Click on OK in the Photoshop dialog box that asks you if you want to erase the entire image. You have a selection based on the original image all set to load in the #4 channel, and it's by using the selection, not the black-and-white image, that you'll be able to color the bank logo.

11. Press F7 to display the Colors palette. You can use the HSB color model on the Colors palette by clicking on the command button and selecting HSB Color from the drop-down list.

12. Click and drag the sliders to H: 48°, S: 100%, and B: 98% to specify a gold color. Choose the Paintbrush tool and spread a little foreground color on the scratch pad area on the Colors palette. Then select a rich red from the default swatches, and do the same thing. Finally, choose an electric blue. You should have three distinctly different primary color samples on the scratch pad area, to sample and switch between as you color the bank logo.

13. Choose **S**elect, **L**oad Selection. Using the Eyedropper tool, click on the gold color on the scratch pad area to select it as the color that you apply to the SECOND UNION area of the 2NDBANK image.

14. Choose the Paintbrush tool, pick a small tip from the second row of the Brushes palette, and then color the SECOND UNION area of the EPS image, as shown in figure 12.3.

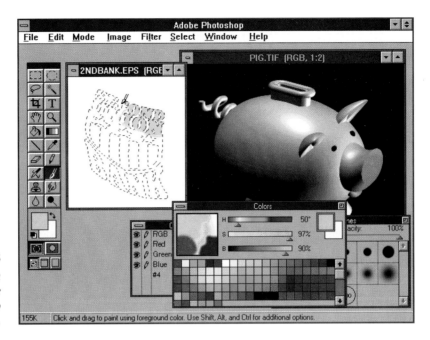

Figure 12.3

The active selection area defines the border of the image area you want to colorize.

There are a lot of special effects covered in this chapter, and for this reason, coloring the entire 2NDBANK.EPS image is not necessary to continue building this bank poster. The completed image, 2NDBANK.TIF, also is on the Adobe Photoshop NOW! *CD-ROM.*

But here's a good trick or two for the diligent individual who wants hands-on experience with creating a color TIFF image out of a black-and-white EPS. Hold down the Alt key while using the Paintbrush tool, and the Paintbrush's function switches to an eyedropper. Then resample your foreground color, release the Alt key, and continue painting.

When you're done painting the logo, switch to the #4 channel view of the image, choose black as your foreground color image, and paint the stripes and stars areas. Then when you load the selection from the RGB view of 2NDBANK, the gold, blue, red, and white areas will be perfectly selected.

Adding the Logo to the Piggy Bank

If you followed the preceding tip, you should save your newly colored logo to your hard disk as 2NDBANK.TIF now and mark the **S**ave Alpha Channels check box in Photoshop's Save As dialog box. If you didn't color the EPS as yet, load the 2NDBANK.TIF image from the *Adobe Photoshop NOW! CD-ROM* and wrap up this part of the assignment next.

1. Open the PIG.TIF image from the *Adobe Photoshop NOW! CD-ROM* if you don't already have it open.

2. Click on the title bar of 2NDBANK.TIF to make it the active image window.

3. Choose **S**elect, **L**oad Selection, and then press Ctrl+C (see fig. 12.4).

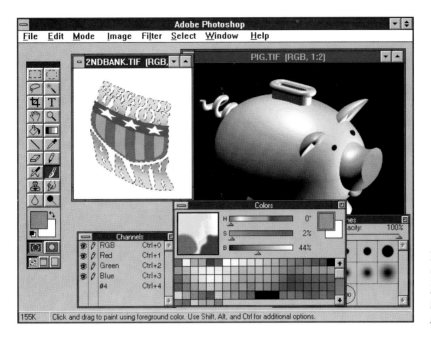

Figure 12.4

The selection border for the logo is defined by copying the entire image to an Alpha channel.

4. Double-click on the 2NDBANK.TIF's command button to close it. You're done with it, and you have a copy on the Clipboard.

5. Double-click on the Zoom tool. The PIG.TIF image fills your workspace. Click on the Hand tool, and then click and drag within the active image window so that the side of the piggy bank is in clear view.

6. Press Ctrl+V. Make sure a selection tool is active (such as the Lasso tool), place your cursor inside the selection of the logo, and click and drag it so that it's positioned like the selection in figure 12.5.

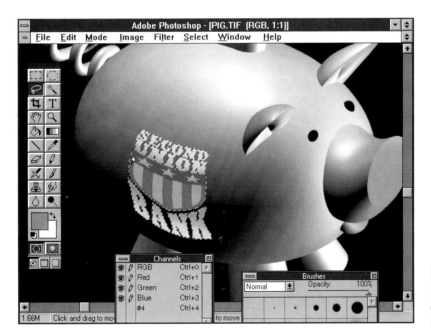

Figure 12.5

The copied logo adds dimension to the image of the piggy bank.

7. When you're happy with the logo's position, click outside the marquee border to deselect it. Choose File, Save As and save PIG.TIF to your hard disk. Make sure that Save Alpha Channels is checked in the TIFF Options dialog box.

8. Double-click on PIG.TIF's window command button to close it. You'll be creating a large background for the piggy bank image, and you need to conserve your system resources.

The 2NDBANK.TIF image on the Adobe Photoshop NOW! CD-ROM *contains a minor enhancement that was added to it before copying it to the PIG.TIF image. I stroked a wide, 40 percent opacity shade of gray across the center of the selection, and then used the Dodge/Burn tool to brighten the top and bottom of the bank logo selection. This produced an effect that imitates the lighting on the piggy bank—a light-colored top descending into shadow, and a bit of a kick light (a small photographer's light usually pointing in the opposite direction as the main light) toward the bottom. Flat color in an image area suggests flat lighting, which is something you want to avoid in your work, especially with digital, virtual images like this piggy bank.*

Creating a 3D Background

Simple type can be transformed into an entire dimensional background with the aid of a few of Photoshop's adjustments and effects. The APENNY.EPS image on the *Adobe Photoshop NOW! CD-ROM* was created using Benguiat Bold and a Zapf Dingbat. See first how the Define Pattern command can turn a short sentence into an entire backdrop for the piggy bank.

1. Open the APENNY.EPS image from the *Adobe Photoshop NOW! CD-ROM*. Accept the defaults in Photoshop's EPS Rasterizer dialog box, and click on OK.

2. Press Ctrl+A. Then choose Edit, Define Pattern.

3. Choose File, New, and specify Width: 5 inches, Height: 5 inches, Resolution: 150 pixels/inch, and RGB Color Mode. Then click on OK. This file will be the canvas for the bank poster. You've created it a little larger than its final size to leave room for the bleed for the effect you'll produce shortly.

4. Press Ctrl+A, and then choose Edit, Fill.

5. Click on the Pattern radio button in the contents field, leave Mode set at Normal and Opacity at 100%, and then click on OK.

6. You now should have a pattern fill of the typeset phrase filling Untitled-1's image window, as shown in figure 12.6.

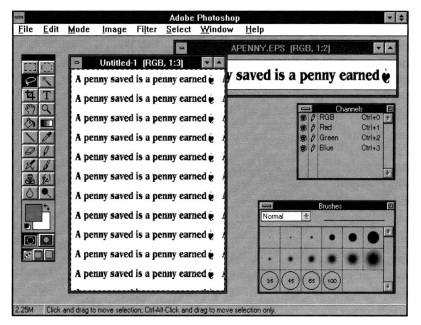

If you're unhappy with the leading between lines of type in the Untitled-1 image, you can always redefine the pattern created from the APENNY.EPS image. Patterns can only be defined by the **S**elect, **A**ll *command or with the Rectangular Marquee tool. To tighten the leading you need to decrease the white space bordering the type. Choose the Rectangular Marquee tool, and then marquee select the type in the APENNY image, leaving only a fraction of white space as the boundary to your selection. Then use the* **E**dit, Define **P**attern *command again, and repeat the last few steps.*

Manually Offsetting a Pattern

Unfortunately, Photoshop version 2.5 for Windows has no provision for offset tiling of a pattern fill. But you can modify the design that now fills Untitled-1's window to create a tiled offset pattern of the type. Staggering the lines of type forms a more aesthetic design.

1. Choose the Rectangular Marquee tool, and select the second line of type in the Untitled-1 image.

2. Hold down the Shift key, and marquee select the fourth line of type.

3. Continue to select every other line of type until you've reached the bottom of the image.

4. Press Ctrl+C to copy the alternating lines of text to the Clipboard.

5. Place the cursor inside any of the marquee borders and click and drag to the right until half of the text is outside of the image window frame, as seen in figure 12.7.

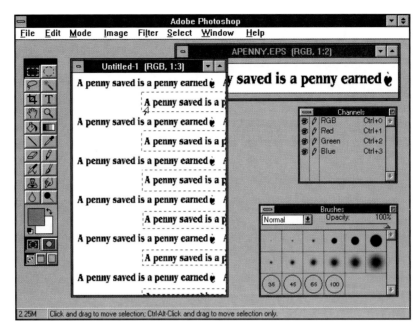

Figure 12.7

Selection areas outside an image window are deleted when the image is composited.

6. Press Ctrl+V, and then click and drag the copied selections so that their right sides fill the white space left when you moved the left sides of the type to the right, as shown in figure 12.8. Use the arrow keys to nudge the selections until they share a baseline with the type on the right.

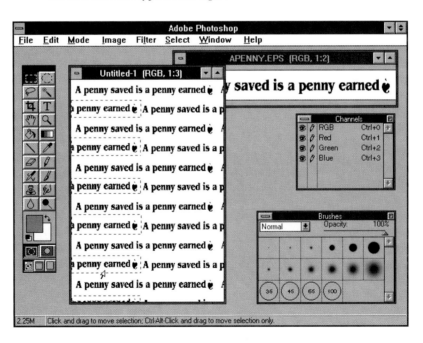

Figure 12.8

The copied selection areas are pasted and fitted to create a tiled pattern.

Embossing and Colorizing To Add Dimension

The tiled pattern of the type is only the first step in the creation of a background that isn't merely placed behind the piggy bank, but surrounds the bank dimensionally. The background needs a color and a texture that can visually support the image of the piggy bank and contrast with the pig's simplistic shape. Here's how to liven up the tiled pattern.

With UNTITLED-1 as the active image, follow these steps:

1. Choose Select, All. Then choose Edit, Copy.

2. Click in the command button on the Channels palette, and then choose New Channel. Accept the defaults and click on OK.

3. Press Ctrl+V to copy the tiled pattern into the new channel. Photoshop can use this graphical information to create a selection border for the type.

4. Click on the RGB title on the Channels palette to restore your view to the original image.

5. Choose Filter, Stylize, Emboss.

6. Click and drag the line in the circle of the Emboss dialog box until Angle reads about 114 (degrees). Then type **3** in the Height box, set the amount to 100%, and click on OK.

7. Choose Image, Adjust, Hue/Saturation (Ctrl+U).

8. Click on the Preview check box and click on the Colorize check box.

9. Choose Hue: 121°, Saturation: 65%, and Lightness: –37%, either by entering these numbers, or by clicking and dragging in the sliders, as shown in figure 12.9. Click on OK.

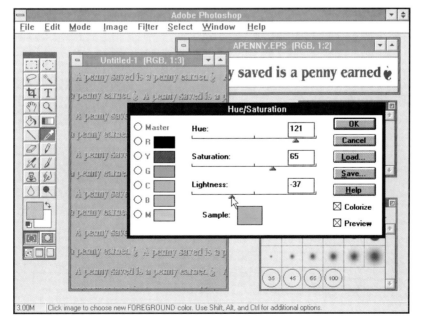

Figure 12.9

The deeper an image density area, the darker the color.

10. Choose **S**elect, **L**oad Selection, and then press Ctrl+H to hide the marquee lines, giving you a clearer view of this next edit.

11. Choose **I**mage, **A**djust, Hue/Saturation again. Only the selected type in the embossed, colorized image will be affected now.

12. Choose Hue: 21°, Saturation: 28%, and leave the Lightness as it is. Click on OK.

Making a Wall and a Floor from a Flat Graphic

The tiled pattern should be designed to suggest that there is space between the background and the piggy bank, when, in actuality, the piggy bank is placed on top of the background. This is where the Effects submenu comes into play. You'll use the Distort command (which operates similarly to the Scale, Perspective, and Skew commands) to create the feeling of space. All of the Effects commands treat a selection area as if it were plastic. You can stretch and bend an area and still maintain smooth pixel transitions because Photoshop interpolates "in-between" pixels to place between neighboring pixels that have been moved within the bitmap.

Wallpapering the Background Digitally

These next few steps are processor-intensive. Even with a fast machine, don't expect to view the results of the Distort command immediately.

1. Open the PIG.TIF image from your hard disk and look at its perspective. Looking at PIG.TIF, use what you see as a visual guide for creating a matching perspective in the Untitled-1 image.

2. Choose the Rectangular Marquee tool, and select the top three-quarters of the Untitled-1 image area.

3. Choose the Eyedropper tool, and Alt+click over the green background to choose that green as your background color.

4. Choose **S**elect, Fea**t**her. Then type **6** in the **R**adius box, and click on OK. The area inside the selection border now will make a smooth transition to the bottom of the image when the Distort command is applied to the selection area.

5. Choose **I**mage, **E**ffects, Distort. A boundary box appears around the selection area. The four squares around the box serve as handles.

6. Click and drag the image window edges to reveal the gray background within the window that borders the image.

7. Click and drag the upper left corner of the Distort boundary box clear outside of the image window, by a distance of about 1 1/2 screen inches.

8. After the result of this action is displayed, click and drag the upper right corner of the Distort box straight down by about 1/2 a screen inch.

9. When the effect is displayed, the type should be running downhill at about a 15-degree angle from left to right. If so, click inside the Distort boundary box to confirm your actions and finalize the Distort effect. If not, reposition the corners as necessary.

If you had a white background selected in the color selection boxes before performing the last set of steps, a white seam would appear along the bottom edge of the selection border. This is because the Feather command was used. The Feather command actually destroys visual detail by averaging a transition between a selected area and, in this instance, an image background. It's great for smoothing an edit, but you must always remember when you reshape a selection area, as you did with the Distort command, that you have a harmonious background color specified, and that the feathering feature can be used to fill in the right color for the transition along the selection edge.

Making a Dimensional Floor

The "wall" to this background tiled pattern definitely benefited from the slight angle you added to it in the last steps. But the really important task comes next: to create a "floor" for the piggy bank to rest on. This is done the same way as the upper portion of the Untitled-1 image. Make sure you use the PIG.TIF image as a reference as you use the Distort command. Use your artist's eye to evaluate how much the bottom quarter of Untitled-1 should appear to come toward the viewer so that the piggy bank will appear to be sitting on a surface. Here's the final step to creating a dimensional background for the bank poster.

1. Choose Select, Inverse to make the bottom quarter of Untitled-1 the active image area.

2. Choose Image, Effects, Distort.

3. Click and drag the bottom left corner of the boundary box down and to the left by about 1 1/2 screen inches.

4. Click and drag the bottom right boundary handle to the right and down, outside of the image window.

5. When the selection area appears to have the same angle as the viewing point of the piggy bank, click inside the boundary box to finish the effect, as shown in figure 12.10.

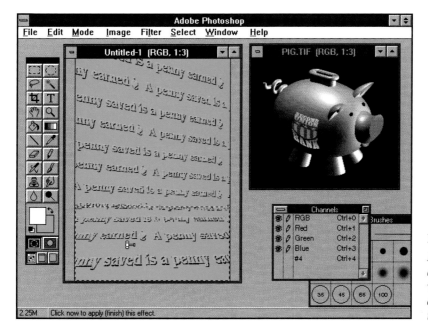

Figure 12.10

Flat surfaces take on dimensional qualities when the Distort command is applied to them.

6. Double-click on the Crop tool, and enter 4 inches for **W**idth, and 6 inches for H**e**ight. Then click on OK.

7. Marquee select the center of the Untitled-1 image area. Avoid selecting the areas without embossed type toward the top of the image.

8. Click inside the cropping border to execute the crop.

9. Choose **S**elect, **N**one (Ctrl+D), and save this image as PIGYBACK.TIF to your hard disk. Save the Alpha channel, too. You'll reuse the channel, but not the contents of the channel. It's faster to overwrite the contents of the channel than it is to create a new one.

Resizing the Piggy Bank for Its New Background

I had a rough idea of how large the bank poster should be when I modeled the piggy bank, but I didn't build the model to a specific predetermined size. With the Crop tool you can, however, scale the image while you crop the image area. The Crop tool has an options box where dimensions and resolutions can be set. The task you have at this point is to measure the area of the PIGYBACK image to determine what a good size for the piggy bank would be.

1. Press F8 to display the Info palette in the workspace.

2. Choose the Rectangular Marquee tool, and then click and drag a good width within the PIGYBACK image where you think the piggy bank should go.

3. Look at the bottom of the Info palette. As you can see in figure 12.11, the X (the width) coordinate for the rectangular selection area is 3.307 inches. The height doesn't really matter because you'll be cropping only the width of the piggy bank.

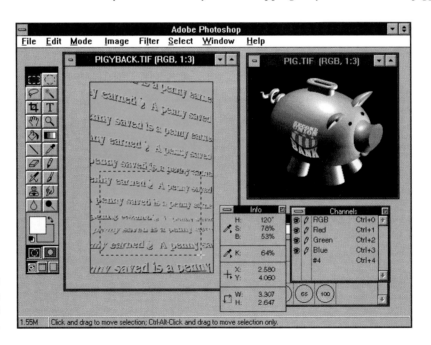

Figure 12.11

The Info palette provides valuable information about active image dimensions.

4. Double-click on the Crop tool. This calls up the Crop tool Options dialog box.

5. Type **3.5** in the Width field, and choose Inches in the drop-down box to the right of the field. Make certain there is nothing (but not a zero) in the Height field, and set the Resolution to 150 pixels/inch. Then click on OK.

6. Click and drag a tight cropping area around the piggy bank in the PIG.TIF image, and then click inside the cropping boundary border. The PIG.TIF image becomes 3.5 inches wide, a height that's proportionately smaller, and adopts a resolution of 150 ppi, the same as the PIGYBACK image.

7. Choose Select, Load Selection. PIG.TIF was modeled with a program that generated an Alpha channel that serves as an accurate selection border around the piggy bank.

8. Press Ctrl+C to copy the piggy bank image. Then click on the title bar of PIGYBACK.TIF.

9. Press Ctrl+V to paste the piggy bank copy into the PIGYBACK image.

10. Place your cursor inside the piggy bank image. Then click and drag the selection to a position toward the bottom of the background image, as shown in figure 12.12.

Figure 12.12

The resized piggy bank now fits perfectly into the PIGYBACK image.

11. When you're happy with the positioning, choose Select, Save Selection, #4, not New. This overwrites the information in the Alpha channel about the tiled type pattern.

12. Press Ctrl+D to deselect (composite) the piggy bank into the background. Then choose File, Save.

13. Double-click on PIG.TIF's command button to close it. You're finished with it now. You can save the changes if you like, but it's not necessary. If you elect not to save, you'll have a larger piggy bank on your hard disk.

Defining a Shadow Area beneath the Piggy Bank

If the piggy bank appears to be lighter than air, it's because the PIGYBACK image lacks an important visual element. Any object in real life that has a highlight on it, as the piggy bank does, would have a corresponding shadow beneath it.

Now that the piggy bank selection area is saved to an Alpha channel, you'll hand paint a shadow beneath the piggy bank and then remove the selection area from the shadow selection to make the shadow cast only on the PIGYBACK image's "floor." What you'll do next is a quicker, less confusing way than having to subtract one selection area from another and struggling with Photoshop's Image, Calculate, Subtract command.

1. Double-click on the Quick Mask mode button.

2. In the Mask Options dialog box, click on the Color selection box, choose a brilliant red in the Color Picker, and then click on OK. Quick mask color can be set to any color and opacity, and by choosing red, the quick mask you paint to define the pig's shadow will be visible and contrast sharply against the green.

3. Make sure the Color Indicates: Selected areas radio button is chosen, and then click on OK.

4. Press Ctrl++ to zoom your field of view to a 1:2 resolution of the PIGYBACK image.

5. Choose the Paintbrush tool and paint a silhouette of the piggy bank beneath it in the image. Don't worry about painting Quick Mask over the piggy bank's legs and bottom—you'll remove any overlapping selection areas automatically in step 14. You can get a general "feel" for how this piggy bank shadow should be by taking a look at figure 12.13.

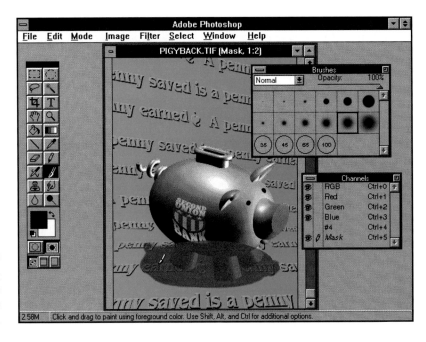

Figure 12.13

The red Quick Mask overlay defines an active selection when you switch back to Standard mode.

6. When you're done painting, click on the Standard mode button to the left of the Quick Mask mode button. The quick mask becomes an active selection area with a marquee border around it.

7. Choose **S**elect, **S**ave Selection, New.

8. Click on the #5 channel title on the Channels palette.

9. Press Ctrl+D to deselect the area.

10. Choose Fi**l**ter, Blur, Gaussian Blur.

11. Type **8** in the **R**adius field, and then click on OK.

12. Choose **S**elect, **L**oad Selection, #4. A marquee border of the piggy bank appears over your view of the blurry shadow.

13. Click on the Default colors icon button.

14. Press the Backspace key. This removes the selected areas of the piggy bank and creates a sharp selection edge in the otherwise fuzzy shadow area, as shown in figure 12.14.

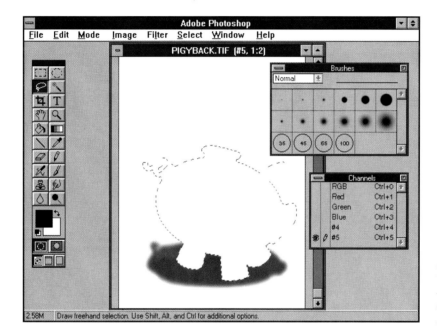

Figure 12.14

Load a selection, and then delete it to expose background color.

Using the Paint Bucket To Create a Shadow

The Multiply mode will be used to create a realistic shadow into the selection area created by the information in Alpha channel 5. Multiply mode adds color to a selection area in progressive steps; repeated application of color to an area results in an area becoming more and more saturated with the foreground color. This helps the shadow effect, as you'll see next.

1. Click on the RGB title on the Channels palette. You'll see the color view of the piggy bank and background.

2. Choose **S**elect, **L**oad Selection, #5.

3. Double-click on the Paint Bucket tool and set the **T**olerance to a fairly high number, such as 200. Check the **A**nti-aliased check box, click the Foreground color radio button in the Contents field, and then click on OK.

4. Choose Multiply as the current mode on the Brushes palette's drop-down box, and click and drag the Opacity slider to about 40%.

5. Place the Paint Bucket cursor inside the selection area and click. You'll get a partially covered area with soft borders, as shown in figure 12.15. It's important not to overdo the shadow effect; illustrated shadows should let visual detail through, as they do in real life. Setting the Opacity to less than full strength allows the detail to show through.

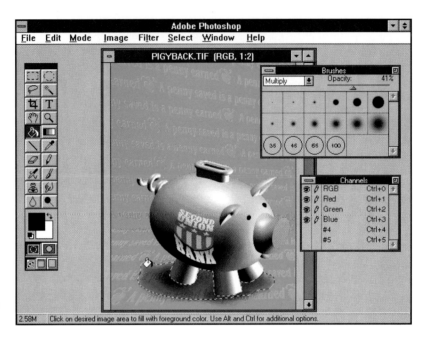

Figure 12.15

The blurred selection allows color in the center and trails off at the edges.

6. Click a second time inside the selection area. Notice that the areas in the selection area are becoming darker and more opaque, but in a disproportionate way. This is the function of the Multiply mode. It's similar to repeatedly stroking over the same area of a piece of paper with a felt-tip marker.

7. Press Ctrl+D, and then choose File, Save to save PIGYBACK.TIF to your hard disk.

Enhancing the Dimensionality of the Bank Poster

The next and final elements that need to be added to the bank poster are some coins. After all, what's a piggy bank without a few pennies? The images of pennies you'll use have different dimensions and resolutions. In the next few steps, you'll scale them so that they appear to cascade into the piggy bank from afar. The Crop tool and the Info palette will be your gauge and guide to how large the different penny images should be.

1. Open the PENNY1.TIF image from the *Adobe Photoshop NOW! CD-ROM*.

2. Click on the title bar of the PIGYBACK.TIF image.

3. Choose the Elliptical Marquee tool, and click and drag a large ellipse, as shown in figure 12.16. To create the appearance that pennies are being flipped from the viewer into the bank, PENNY1 will be the largest penny image, positioned at the top of the PIGYBACK image, with the following pennies decreasing in size.

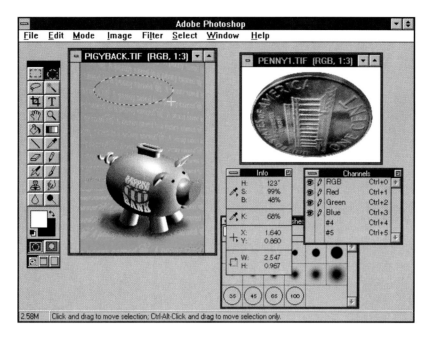

Figure 12.16

Design an ideal size for a penny image with the Elliptical Marquee tool.

4. Notice that the Info palette displays a width of the elliptical selection. Mine reads about 2 1/2 inches, so the Crop tool should be reset for 2.7 inches to give a little border to the cropped penny image.

5. Double-click on the Crop tool, and set the **W**idth in the options field to 2.7 inches. Click on OK.

6. Click and drag a tight cropping border around the penny image in PENNY1.TIF, and then click inside the border to crop it.

7. Choose **S**elect, **L**oad Selection, and a selection border defined in this image appears around the penny.

8. Press Ctrl+C to copy the resized penny, and then press Ctrl+Tab to switch to PIGYBACK as the active image window.

9. Press Ctrl+V to paste the penny copy into the PIGYBACK image.

10. Place your cursor inside the floating penny selection, and then click and drag it until it's positioned similarly to figure 12.17. When you deselect it, the penny area outside the image window disappears forever.

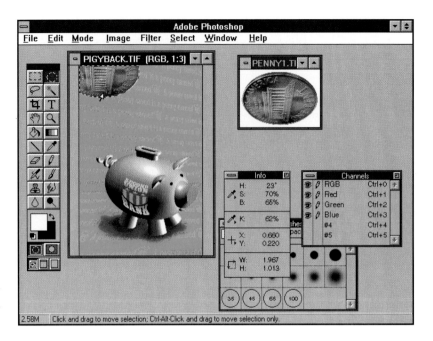

Figure 12.17

The PENNY1 copy will appear to be the closest to the viewer.

11. When you're happy with the penny's positioning, choose **S**elect, **D**efringe, type **1** in the field for pixel amount, and then click on OK. The selection border created for this and the other pennies have soft edges, and defringing the copy removes semiwhite background edge pixels copied along with the penny from the original file.

12. Choose **S**elect, **S**ave Selection, #5. This overwrites the Alpha channel information about the blurry piggy bank shadow—you don't need it any more.

13. Press Ctrl+D to composite the penny into the PIGYBACK background image.

Scaling and Positioning More Pennies

Now that the first, closest penny has a selection border defined for it in an Alpha channel, you have the option to paste a second penny either in front of or in back of it. By pasting the PENNY2.TIF image found on the *Adobe Photoshop NOW! CD-ROM* behind the first penny, you'll create a diminishing perspective in this bank poster assignment.

1. Open the PENNY2.TIF image from the *Adobe Photoshop NOW! CD-ROM*.

2. Double-click on the Crop tool and choose 1.5 inches as the desired **W**idth. This figure was arrived at by using the same methods with the Info palette and the marquee tool that were used to determine the size of PENNY1 in the previous steps.

3. Click and drag a tight marquee area around the PENNY2 image, and then click inside the border.

4. Choose **S**elect, **L**oad Selection, and then press Ctrl+C to copy only the penny to the Clipboard.

5. Press Ctrl+Tab to switch back to PIGYBACK.TIF as the active image window.

6. Choose **S**elect, **L**oad Selection. This activates the large penny in the PIGYBACK image as a selection area.

7. Choose **E**dit, Paste **B**ehind.

8. Click and drag inside the marquee border of this second penny until it's positioned like the one seen in figure 12.18.

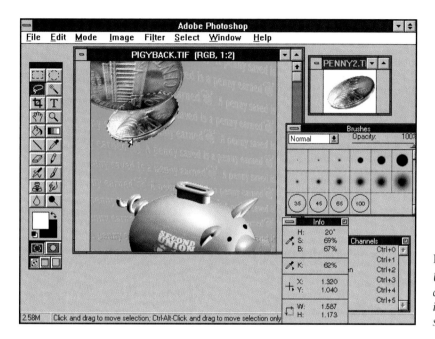

Figure 12.18

*Use the Paste **B**ehind command to place an image behind an active selection area.*

9. Choose **S**elect, **D**efringe, and then click on OK to accept the present setting of 1 pixel.

10. Press Ctrl+D to deselect everything, and then Ctrl+S to save your work up to this point.

Adding Creative Lighting to the Pennies

From a realistic standpoint, the PENNY2 image is apparently farther away and slightly behind the first penny. This means that a slight shadow might be cast on the second penny by the first. Here's how to further enhance the realism of this scene.

1. Choose **S**elect, **L**oad Selection, #5. This loads the selection area you saved earlier of the PENNY1 image.

2. Choose **S**elect, **I**nverse. The PENNY 1 image is now masked, and the rest of PIGYBACK.TIF is selected and can be edited.

3. Choose the Paintbrush tool. Choose the 35 pixel diameter Brushes palette tip. The mode should still be set to Multiply, and the Opacity set at 40%.

4. Click and drag across the top of the second penny. Don't worry about stroking over the PENNY1 image because it is masked, impervious to any editing.

5. Stroke a second time, and maybe a third, according to your personal artistic judgment. As you can see in figure 12.19, an interaction is achieved between the two pennies because one now appears to be casting a shadow on the other.

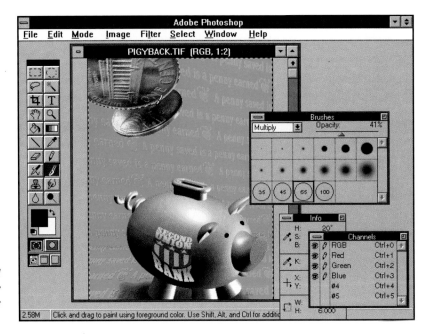

Figure 12.19

A simple, soft-edged shadow can be rendered by using the Multiply mode and a partial opacity.

How To Put a Penny in the Piggy Bank

We'll skip ahead a step now to come to the grand finale of our savings bank adventure. Briefly, the PENNY34.TIF image on the *Adobe Photoshop NOW! CD-ROM* is an image with two pennies positioned so that one overlaps the other. You'll want to add these the same way you did the first penny, specifying about 1.3 inches as the Crop tool option to crop the PENNY34 image. Then, just as before, load the selection, copy the pennies to the Clipboard, and place the selection beneath the PENNY2 image in PIGYBACK.TIF. Defringe the selection by 1 pixel before deselecting it, and make sure these penny images don't obscure the coin slot on the piggy bank.

Now, you'll perform a little direct deposit and make the final image, PENNY5.TIF, appear to be landing within the coin slot of the piggy bank.

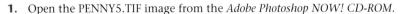

1. Open the PENNY5.TIF image from the *Adobe Photoshop NOW! CD-ROM.*

2. Double-click on Crop tool and enter .480 inches in the **W**idth field. I calculated this to be the width of the opening on the piggy bank coin slot using the same Info palette technique described earlier.

3. Click and drag a tight border around the PENNY5 image, and then click inside of the border.

4. Choose Fi**l**ter, Sharpen, Sharpen.

The PENNY5 image originally had rather large dimensions. By reducing it as radically as you did in the last step, some heavy-duty averaging had to be performed by Photoshop to reduce the number of pixels that make up this image. This ruined the sharp focus of the penny. Because the PENNY5 image constitutes an area of little visual detail (but a lot of visual importance), the plain-vanilla Sharpen filter, of which there are no customizable settings, does the trick by accentuating the color similarities of neighboring images' pixel values.

5. Choose Select, Load Selection, and then press Ctrl+C.

6. Press Ctrl+Tab to switch back to PIGYBACK.TIF as the active image window.

7. Click on the Quick Mask mode button.

8. Choose the Hand tool, and position your view of the active image window so that you have a good view of the piggy bank coin slot. A 1:1 viewing resolution should suffice.

9. Choose the Lasso tool, and while holding down the Alt key, click two points on the front edge of the lip of the coin slot.

10. Continue clicking points beneath the coin slot so that the neck of the coin slot is completely selected. Release the Alt key and mouse button, and let Photoshop complete the marquee border.

11. Click on the Invert colors icon button. Your background color should be black. In Quick Mask mode, anything deleted within a selection area becomes filled with quick mask.

12. Press the Del key. As you can see in figure 12.20, you've now defined a selection area that'll become active when you switch back to Standard mode.

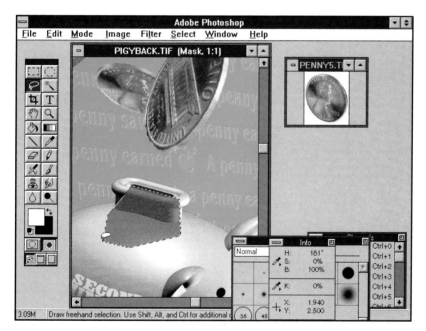

Figure 12.20

Select black as the background color, and then create a Quick Mask overlay by deleting a selection.

13. Click on the Standard mode button. Your quick mask area now becomes an active selection area.

14. Choose Edit, Paste Behind. Then place your cursor inside the penny selection area, and click and drag it so that it's about halfway into the coin slot, as shown in figure 12.21.

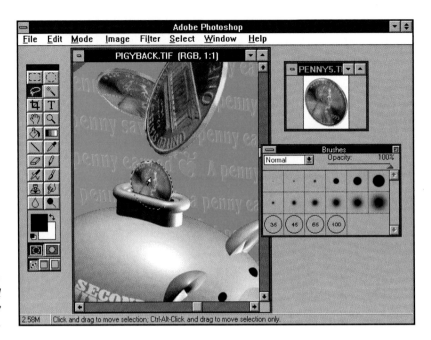

Figure 12.21

Use the Paste Behind command to put the penny into the coin slot.

15. Choose Select, Defringe, and then click on OK to accept the defaults.

16. Press Ctrl+D to deselect the floating penny.

17. Delete the superfluous Alpha channels in the PIGYBACK image by clicking on the channel title on the Channels palette, and then choosing Delete Channel from the command button drop-down list on the palette. This action reduces the image file size substantially, and allows other "Alpha channel unaware" software programs to import the image.

18. Choose File, Save As, and name your finished piece PIGGYBNK.TIF.

Double-click on the Hand tool now to get a scope on the finished image from a full-frame perspective. As you can see in figure 12.22, you've taken a simple graphic of a piggy bank and given it dimension, realism, and some implied movement and action. You can create a wall and a floor for a 2D graphic using these steps any time you feel a design needs more depth.

The penny images on the Adobe Photoshop NOW! CD-ROM *aren't exactly real; they were scanned on a UMAX flatbed scanner, and then mapped to a wireframe CAD model of a penny using Visual Software's Renderize Live for Windows. This might seem like a lot of work and an expensive hardware/software solution to capture something as simple as a penny, but necessity is sometimes the mother of invention.*

I spent a week trying to capture a photo of pennies "in flight" (suspended before a backdrop with a coat hanger). The resulting images were unacceptable to use in this chapter because the design of my camera's macro lens simply wasn't sharp enough. So I modeled and bump-mapped scanned two-dimensional images of pennies to produce exactly the angles and lighting I needed. For more information about using modeling and rendering programs with Photoshop, see NRP's Inside Adobe Photoshop for Windows.

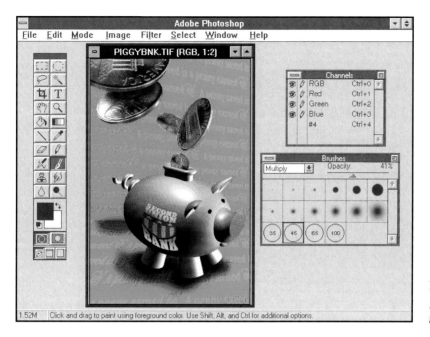

Figure 12.22

...and the dollars will mind themselves!

PART FIVE:

Back o' the Book

Bonus Appendix: Fractals, Plug-Ins, and Photoshop

More and more Windows design programs are adopting the plug-in standard first conceived by Adobe. Plug-ins are filters manufactured by third-party vendors that add capabilities to Photoshop and to any other software program that was written to the standard. Usually, these plug-in filters are designed to accomplish an effect, such as watercolor, fractal patterns, or custom gradient blends, with only a mouse click or two.

You'll take a look in this appendix at how two programs, HSC's Kai's Power Tools and Fractal Design's Painter, can assist in the creation of photorealistic stained glass artwork, with Photoshop playing the host program to integrate and choreograph the selections created.

Features Covered:

- The Magic Eraser
- Channels
- Paths palette
- Stroke Paths option
- Fractal Design Painter
- Kai's Power Tools

The Images on the *Adobe Photoshop NOW! CD-ROM*

Unlike the assignments in other chapters, the *caming* (the leading between stained glass) in the stained glass piece cannot be exactly reproduced without owning Kai's Power Tools. There is no equivalent Photoshop filter to Kai's Gradients on Paths extension. But you'll see an example of how to fake the caming using Photoshop's native tools. The pieces of virtual glass that were created in Fractal Design's Painter are located on the *Adobe Photoshop NOW! CD-ROM* in the APPENDIX subdirectory, and you can follow the steps used to design this part of the image.

Sizing Image Areas for the Stained Glass

You'll see how astonishingly close to real life the procedure is for creating virtual stained glass in this appendix. As in real life, a cartoon is created first and is used to fit the pieces of stained glass into the composition.

The cartoon, MARINA.EPS, was created in a vector art design program, and then imported into Photoshop's workspace. As you can see in figure A.1, Ctrl+R was pressed to display rulers around the MARINA image. This was a vital first consideration before creating the virtual stained glass elements in Painter—you need to see what the maximum size of each partition in the stained glass cartoon is, and then build a piece that fits.

> *A vector design program, such as Adobe Illustrator, can be an invaluable assistant in creating complex designs that you edit in Photoshop. For all its powerful tools, Photoshop doesn't have the guidelines or grids that computer graphics designers need to scale and precisely position vector objects.*

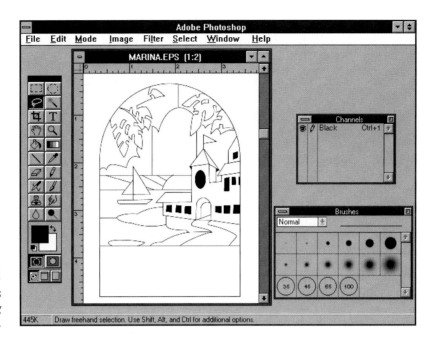

Figure A.1

The design is exported as an EPS from a drawing program into Photoshop.

Twenty-one pieces of virtual stained glass were used in the creation of the image, each piece averaging more than 100 KB. The MARINA image was not designed with large image dimensions because during the creation of the piece, several stained glass documents were open simultaneously, and Photoshop kept multiple copies of the MARINA image in RAM as the piece was edited.

All the images held in memory inevitably place a stress on system memory. I don't recommend recreating this piece if you have less than 8 MB of RAM in your system.

Creating Virtual Stained Glass

Because the scene depicted in the stained glass cartoon is tropical, you have to keep with the spirit of the theme when choosing colors in Fractal Design Painter. For instance, the stained glass piece used for the ocean part of the image began in Painter as a turquoise canvas. Painter's Glass Distortion filter creates wonderful distortions in an image, complete with reflective highlights, as the filter gathers information from sharp tonal shifts in image areas. So a texture was applied to the turquoise background, and then I added complementary colors with a virtual 500 lb. Pencil, one of Painter's many lifelike color application tools (see fig. A.2).

The Glass Distortion then is applied to the piece, as shown in figure A.3. Painter has a preview box for the effect, with options for the Amount and Variance of the effect.

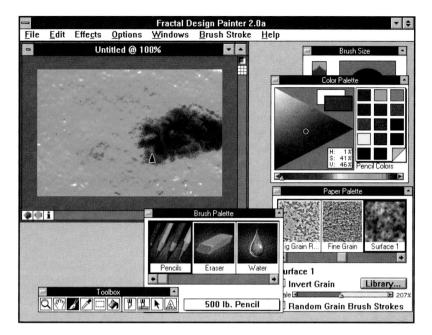

Figure A.2

Fractal Design Painter has many digital equivalents to real life artist's tools.

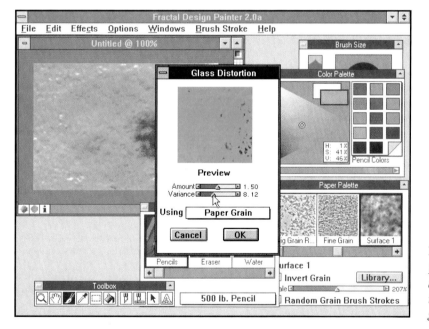

Figure A.3

Painter's Glass Distortion offers many permutations to create different pieces of glass.

About 90 percent of the stained glass pieces used in this assignment were created in Painter by applying different colors and textures to images, and then applying slight variations with the Glass Distortion command. As you can see in figure A.4, it's an odd assortment of sizes and colors, and Painter rendered the pieces with a very realistic quality. All the stained glass pieces then are saved as TIF images, a very common file format that retains all the visual and color fidelity of RGB image types.

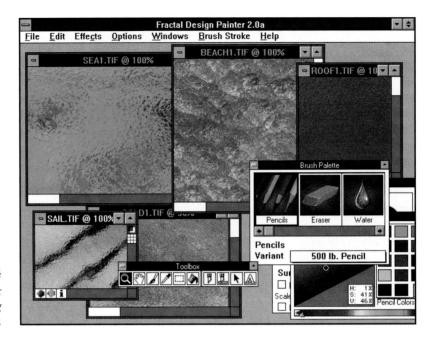

Figure A.4

Fractals are the electronic basis for generating textures found in nature.

Some of the stained glass image files on the Adobe Photoshop NOW! CD-ROM *are not products of Fractal Design Painter, but are scans of actual stone and a fractal pattern or two. Painter is an excellent source for natural paint and textures, but it's not the only way to acquire material for an assignment like this.*

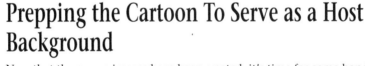

Prepping the Cartoon To Serve as a Host Background

Now that the source images have been created, it's time for some hands-on experience with the latest twist on stained glass sculpting. You'll be using the MARINA.EPS image on the *Adobe Photoshop NOW! CD-ROM* as the background that "holds" the stained glass together. EPS images must be rasterized to become material bitmaps that can be edited, but unlike an original TIFF or Targa file format, EPS images cannot contain channels. An Alpha channel is key to creating the stained glass image because the EPS design can only be effectively used as a guide, and not something used to create a selection. Additionally, the black-and-white EPS image ultimately will be replaced by the leading that holds stained glass in position. You need something a little more permanent, and creating an Alpha channel selection of the MARINA image, before you add the stained glass images, is a smart first move.

1. Open the MARINA.EPS image from the *Adobe Photoshop NOW! CD-ROM*.

2. Photoshop's EPS Rasterizer appears. **W**idth 3.792, and H**e**ight: 5.333 should be the defaults for the image. Choose **R**esolution: 150 pixels/inch, and Mode: RGB Color. Make sure the **A**nti-Aliased box is checked, and click on OK.

3. Press Ctrl+A, and then Ctrl+C to copy the MARINA design to the Clipboard.

4. Press F6 to display the Channels palette. Then click on the command button and choose New Channel from the drop-down list.

5. Accept the default name for the Alpha channel, and click on the Color indicates: Selected Areas radio button. The color is unimportant in this exercise as you won't be using the Quick Mask mode. Click on OK.

6. Press Ctrl+V to paste the copied image, and then Ctrl+D to deselect the copy in the Alpha channel. You now have a selection area that defines the stained glass spaces, which can't be obscured or destroyed by future editing work.

7. Save the image as MARINA.TIF to your hard disk. Check the Save Alpha Channels box in the TIFF Options dialog.

Adding a Piece of Stained Glass to the MARINA

The steps in the remainder of this appendix require you to save the image frequently. The Magic Eraser will be used to eliminate areas of overlapping stained glass. Photoshop's Magic Eraser needs a previously saved version of the image to accomplish its magical restorative function.

1. Open the SEA1.TIF image from the *Adobe Photoshop NOW! CD-ROM.*

2. With the Rectangular Marquee tool, select about one half the height of the SEA1 image. It was created in Painter larger than necessary to allow for some "play" when selecting it. Choose an area you find eye-catching.

3. Press Ctrl+C, and then minimize the SEA1 image to an icon on the workspace.

4. With MARINA.TIF as the active image window, choose Select, Load Selection.

5. Choose Edit, Paste Behind. The SEA1 copy will appear on top of the white MARINA areas, but behind the black selection lines.

6. Click and drag the SEA1 copy so that it's positioned as shown in figure A.5.

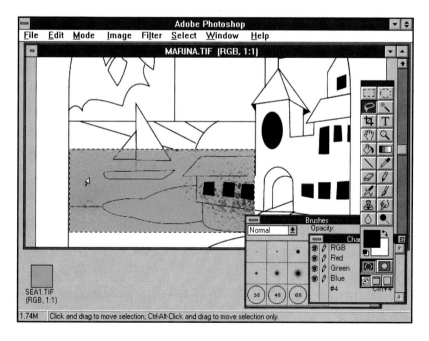

Figure A.5

The Paste Behind command covers the masked MARINA areas, but places SEA1 behind the black lines.

7. When the SEA1 selection is positioned so that it covers the outlined area, press Ctrl+D, but *do not* save the selection!

Trimming the Virtual Stained Glass To Fit into Place

The glass is in place, but as you can see, it covers several areas that need different stained glass pieces. The area you want to fill with this piece of stained glass is the section of ocean directly below the sun where the sailboat is floating. This is not a problem as long as you haven't saved the MARINA.TIF image. A pristine copy is tucked away by Photoshop in a temporary area on your hard disk and can be accessed by the Eraser tool. In Magic Eraser mode, you'll restore areas outside the black boundary that contain the SEA1 copy. Eliminating superfluous areas is a far quicker and easier approach to refining an image area than is creating an elegant selection border in this assignment.

1. Press Ctrl++ to zoom into a 2:1 viewing resolution of MARINA.TIF. Use the Hand tool to include all of the SEA1 copy in your view. You'll need to remove all of the parts of SEA1 that fall outside of the upper section of ocean in MARINA that you are filling with this piece of glass.

2. Choose the Eraser tool, and then, while holding down the Alt key, click on an area outside of the black boundary surrounding the upper section of ocean in MARINA that you pasted SEA1 behind. Photoshop will load a last-saved copy of MARINA.TIF into memory to use as source material, and the action may take a moment or two.

3. When you regain control of the cursor, hold down on the Alt key, and click and drag over an area outside of the black boundary surrounding the section of ocean in MARINA behind which you pasted SEA1. The area is restored to white, and you apparently have a SEA1 selection that was shaped to fit the border.

4. Continue holding the Alt key, and click and drag over the rest of the areas outside the black boundary surrounding the upper section of the ocean. As you can see in figure A.6, the bottom of the SEA1 copy looks refined.

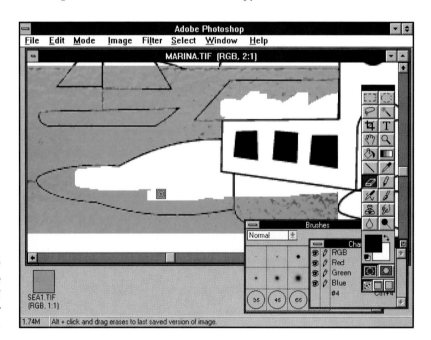

Figure A.6

While holding down the Alt key, the Eraser tool becomes the Magic Eraser tool.

5. Scroll around to other border areas where the SEA1 copy is encroaching on them, and remove them by using the Magic Eraser tool. Don't forget to remove SEA1 from the area occupied by the sailboat.

6. Zoom in to a higher resolution of the MARINA image to get into the sharp corners of the border shape with the Magic Eraser.

7. Double-click on the Zoom tool to return to a 1:1 viewing resolution to get some perspective on the image. Only when you're certain no more artifacts are outside the black border surrounding the upper section of ocean, press Ctrl+S to save MARINA.TIF in its present state.

Adding a Different Piece of Stained Glass

If you own Fractal Design Painter and Kai's Power Tools, you'll find that the hardest part of creating a unique virtual stained glass image is deciding on the colors for the stained glass pieces. This is where I was very selective in terms of color scheme and texture for the Painter images.

The rest of the stained glass images are added to the MARINA image the same way as shown before, but now it's time to see how the stained glass piece for the mansion in the image is added. The piece is adjacent to the SEA1 area, and the Magic Eraser is used again to refine the border of the glass and restore areas of the SEA1 area that are obliterated when the second piece of glass is pasted.

1. Open the WHITE1.TIF image from the *Adobe Photoshop NOW! CD-ROM*.

2. Try copying the entire image to the Clipboard (Ctrl+A, and then Ctrl+C) so that you have the leeway to position it to your liking. WHITE1 has some nice image details that you'll want to include in the final MARINA image.

3. Minimize WHITE1 to an icon on Photoshop's workspace. MARINA again becomes the active image window.

4. Choose Select, Load Selection, and then choose Edit, Paste Behind. Click on a selection tool (such as the Lasso) to make it active.

Although it doesn't contribute to good working practice with Photoshop, other toolbox tools can be used to move a floating selection by holding down the Ctrl key. The Ctrl key switches paint and editing tools to the arrow pointer tool, and you can click and drag inside a floating selection to reposition it. I can't, however, recommend this alternative method of repositioning selections when you have more than two or three other design concerns in the forefront of your mind.

5. Place your cursor inside the floating WHITE1 selection, and then click and drag it so that it covers the mansion outline in the MARINA image, as shown in figure A.7. Don't worry about obscuring the SEA1 area—Photoshop has a last-saved version of it on your hard disk.

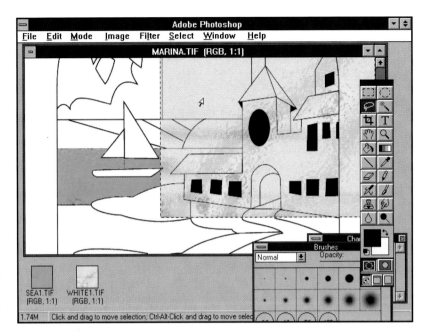

Figure A.7

Position the WHITE1 area so that some of the fractal detail work is within the mansion's black boundary.

6. Press Ctrl+D when the WHITE1 copy is positioned, and then choose the Eraser tool.

7. While holding down on the Alt key, click and drag the Magic Eraser across areas outside the black boundary of the mansion. You should include areas of WHITE1 that are presently on top of the SEA1 area, too. The Magic Eraser restores the image to your last-saved version, which includes the refined SEA1 area, as shown in figure A.8.

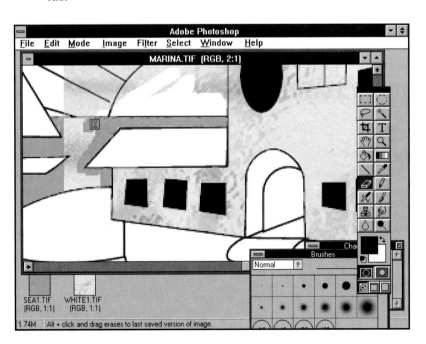

Figure A.8

The Magic Eraser restores white backgrounds and the SEA1 areas from the last-saved version.

8. Choose File, Save (Ctrl+S) when you've removed all the WHITE1 areas outside of the black boundary of the mansion.

Selecting Only the Size of Stained Glass You Need

As you progress with the MARINA image, you'll see the piece come together. All the different textured glass areas contrast with one another, and the techniques you've used so far will become fairly effortless to execute.

You'll also want to begin selecting only the image areas in the stained glass files that you really need—it's not always necessary to copy an entire stained glass image area, and it's sort of tedious to have to Magic Erase ponderously large, superfluous areas. Try eyeballing an area of the GOLD4.TIF image to use as the piece for the sun in MARINA.TIF.

1. Open the GOLD4.TIF image from the *Adobe Photoshop NOW! CD-ROM*.

2. Make it the same viewing resolution as the MARINA.TIF image, that is, if MARINA.TIF is now at 2:1, press Ctrl++ or – to make GOLD4 the same viewing resolution.

3. With the Lasso tool, click and drag a selection area in the GOLD4 image that will fit comfortably over the corresponding sun area in the MARINA image.

4. Press Ctrl+C, and then minimize the GOLD4 image, making MARINA.TIF the active image window.

5. Press Ctrl+V, and then place the cursor inside the floating selection and click and drag it into the sun border, as shown in figure A.9.

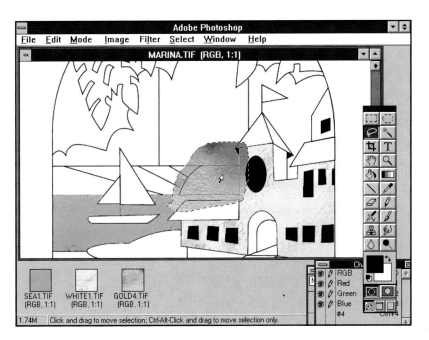

Figure A.9

Estimate how large a selection of stained glass you need to fill an area.

6. Press Ctrl+D. Then choose the Eraser tool, and Alt+click and drag around the outline of the sun, restoring the last-saved versions of areas outside of the black border of the sun.

7. When done, press Ctrl+S to save your work up to this point.

As you can see in figure A.10, I skipped ahead to complete phase 1 of the virtual stained glass piece. The techniques described earlier were used to fit all of the Painter images into their respective areas, and it's time to add the virtual caming to the image.

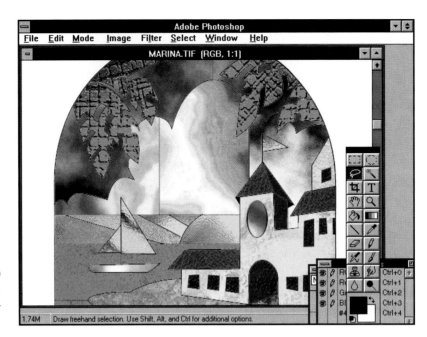

Figure A.10

The virtual stained glass image needs leading between pieces.

The stained glass image files on the Adobe Photoshop NOW! CD-ROM *are named for easy reference to their position in the MARINA image. The brown window areas to the mansion, for example, were copied from the BROWN1.TIF image, and the SKY TIFFs are intended as pieces to be placed in the sky areas of MARINA.TIF. Look at figure A.10 when designing this piece to see what color or image area is used.*

Using Kai's Extensions To Imitate Caming

You can do a million and one things with Kai's Power Tools for Windows. It's a suite of exploration tools for graphics artists that offers a wealth of fractal textures and automatic, user-defined gradient fills that would take a frustratingly long time to build manually. Kai's Power Tools operate within Photoshop (or other imaging programs) as a group under the Filters menu, and after they are installed, Photoshop recognizes them like any other native filter, such as the Spherize command.

Kai's Gradient Designer Extension is particularly useful in this assignment. With it, you can design a gradient fill composed of a number of different transitional colors. This complex gradient then can be applied to the border of an active selection area that's been feathered. The Extension's *Gradients on Path* name is a misnomer with respect to how it functions in Photoshop; a path segment cannot be assigned a complex gradient.

Kai's Power Tools is a great addition to your imaging tools, but if you don't own it, you'll see a way to imitate the Gradient Path effect shortly. Here's how to create virtual caming.

1. Start with a tricky area of the stained glass image, and zoom and scroll to the upper left area of the clouds.

2. Press F6 to display the Paths palette. Selecting an area with smooth curves like these using the Lasso tool or the Quick Mask is difficult at best.

3. Using the Pen tool, click Anchor points on each area of the clouds where a sharp change in direction occurs. Close the path you've created by clicking your first Anchor point.

4. Choose the Corner tool on the Paths palette, and then click and drag an Anchor point to curve the adjacent path segments and to produce direction points at the end of direction lines. Release the direction point, and then click and drag on it to break the symmetrical quality of the direction lines belonging to the Anchor point.

5. Choose the Arrow Pointer tool (or press the Ctrl key to switch the Corner tool to a pointer), and click and drag the direction points on the end of the direction lines so that the path segments fit the curve of the cloud area (see fig. A.11).

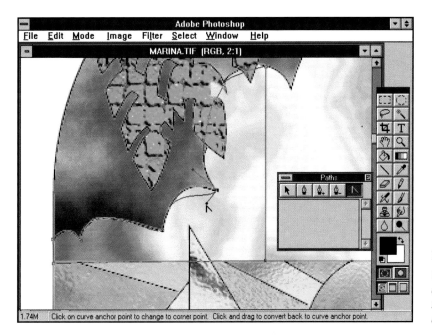

Figure A.11

Use the Paths palette to define an area composed of smooth geometric curves and straight lines.

6. Click on the command button on the Paths palette and choose Make Selection from the drop-down list.

7. In the Rendering field, enter 1 for the Feather Radius, check the Anti-Aliased box, and then click on OK.

Owners of Kai's Power Tools should follow the next series of steps carefully. If you don't own Kai's Power Tools, watch the magic, and you might want to get them!

8. Choose Filter, KPT Extensions, Gradients on Paths.

9. Pick a Color Gradient either from Kai's pre-set gradients or one you might have created. As you can see in figure A.12, I've chosen a home-made Brass with Highlights gradient to run along the selection marquee. Click on OK after a gradient pattern has been selected.

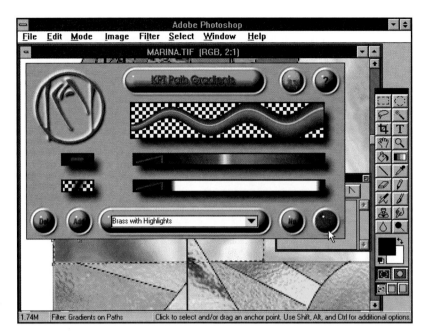

Figure A.12

Kai's Power Tools Extensions and "pre-sets" behave like any other native Photoshop Filter.

10. Press Ctrl+D, and then press the Backspace key twice to remove the unsaved path from the image area.

Figure A.13 shows what the KPT Gradient along Path created. It's a stunning visual simulation of brass caming. It's also running through the top of the sailboat and parts of the palm fronds.

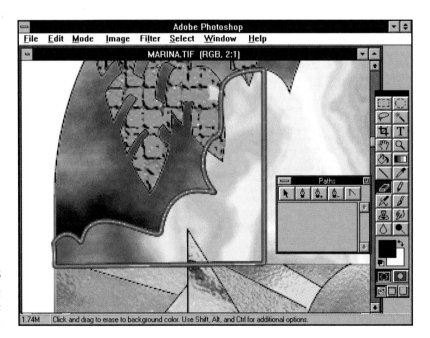

Figure A.13

A complex gradient is applied to a selection area that has been feathered.

Refining the Virtual Caming in the MARINA Image

Kai's Gradients on Paths Extension is limited to producing this neon tube/leading effect with an enclosed selection area. This results in covering areas of the image with virtual caming where caming should not be. Therefore, you need an approach to using KPT Gradients with a design like MARINA.TIF. Create a small selection area, feather it, apply the KPT gradient to it, and then use the Magic Eraser to restore areas where you don't want the gradient caming.

1. Zoom in to an area that needs restoring. In the last example, the KPT gradient breezed through the sail on the sailboat.

2. Click on the Eraser tool, and then, with the Alt key depressed, click and drag over the sailboat area. As you can see in figure A.14, saving frequently bears its rewards, and the Magic Eraser restores the sailboat top to its original condition.

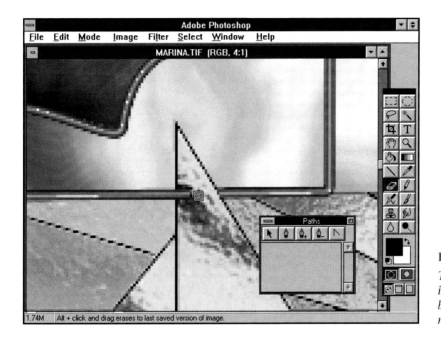

Figure A.14

The Magic Eraser restores image areas to a state before you edited or modified them.

How To Polish Virtual Brass

Kai's Power Tools are an "independent study" collection of utilities, and for this reason, their designers didn't really anticipate my personal need for brass caming. And while the effect is pretty good-looking, Photoshop's Dodge/Burn tool is definitely welcome here to enhance the brass a little. To make the KPT brass (or any other area) truly gleam, you want to accentuate some highlights.

1. Choose the Dodge/Burn tool. Photoshop's installation program makes Dodge the default position for the tool. If it's not this way, double-click on the tool, choose Dodge from the option box, and click on OK.

2. The width of the KPT gradient is only 3 to 4 pixels, determined by the feather radius you defined. So choose the 3 pixel diameter tip on the Brushes palette (the second, top row one), and choose Highlights from the modes drop-down list on the palette.

3. Click and drag in areas of the brass caming. As you can see in figure A.15, only the lighter portions of the KPT gradient are lightened to accentuate the gold color.

4. Press Ctrl+S to save your work up to this point.

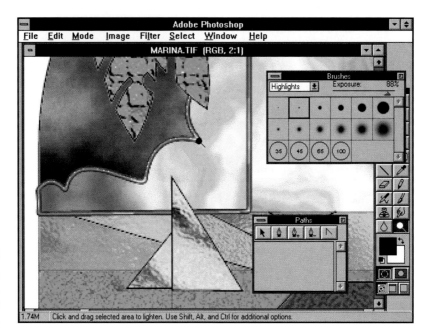

Figure A.15

The Dodge/Burn tool can be set to lighten shadows, midtones, or only highlights.

Adding Pieces of Brass Caming

As you add the KPT gradients to the in-between areas of the stained glass, the areas where real-life brass would be welded together is problematic. The solution is a digital equivalent to welding—the Smudge tool. Take a look at how two pieces are visually linked in a realistic way after creating an adjacent piece of brass in the image.

1. For stained glass areas made up of only straight edges, the Lasso tool can serve to quickly define the area. Choose the Lasso tool to define the sailboat sail.

2. Hold the Alt key, and click the points on the sail where the edges meet. The Alt key enhances the functionality of the Lasso tool to create straight marquee lines between the points you click.

3. Choose Select, Feather. Then enter 2 in the Radius field, and click on OK.

4. Press Ctrl+F to apply the last filter (KPT's Gradients on Paths). As you can see in figure A.16, the virtual brass caming appears along the selection marquee.

5. Zoom to a 4:1 viewing resolution of the area where the brass of the sailboat top meets the brass around the clouds.

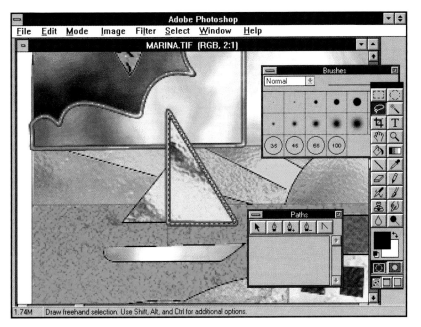

Figure A.16

To repeat the last Photoshop filter used, press Ctrl+F.

6. Choose the Smudge tool, and then pick Lighten from the modes drop-down list on the Brushes palette. Keep the same 3 pixel diameter Brushes tip for the Smudge tool.

7. Click and drag with your cursor, starting in a light area where the two brass pieces meet and ending your stroke in a darker area. As you can see in figure A.17, the Smudge tool treats pixels like wet paint, and the areas where the two gradients meet now look welded together. Double-click on the Zoom tool to get a 1:1 perspective on how this piece is evolving.

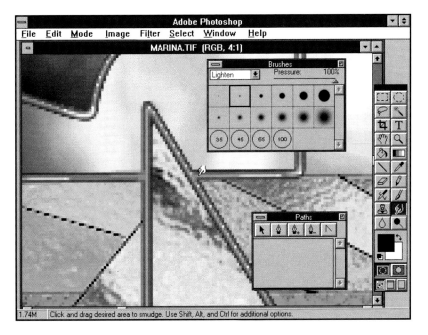

Figure A.17

The Smudge tool is handy for getting rid of sharp edges in an image.

Inventing Your Own Power Tools

Short of earning a degree in programming, there really isn't another way to create brass caming as realistically in Photoshop without getting Kai's Power Tools. But if you think about it, you can achieve a narrow, metallic-looking line with a highlight by stroking a Photoshop path using the same techniques covered in Chapter 11, "Creating Sources of Light," with the neon Lava Lamp. Will you get the same effect? No. But everyone who uses Photoshop without additional plug-ins can create an interesting effect by following the next steps.

1. Choose H: 13°, S: 38%, and B: 19% as your foreground color from Photoshop's Color Picker.

2. Use the Pen tool on the Paths palette to click two Anchor points in a horizontal line anywhere on the MARINA image where there's a straight, horizontal line.

3. Choose the Paintbrush tool, and then pick the third, top row Brushes palette tip, choose Normal mode, and set the Opacity slider at 100%

4. Click on the Paths palette's command button, and choose Stroke Path from the drop-down list.

5. Choose H: 31°, S: 88%, B: 97% as your foreground color, and pick the smallest, top row tip from the Brushes palette.

6. Choose Stroke Path from the command button drop-down list on the Paths palette once again. As you can see in figure A.18, this technique produces a soft-edge, highlighted line. It's serviceable in this instance, but it's easier to plunk down the money for Kai's.

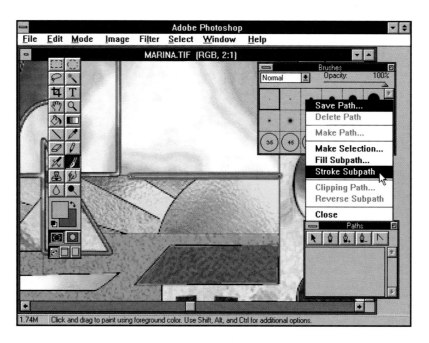

Figure A.18

Repeatedly stroking a path with different colors and brushes produces a soft line with a highlight.

7. Press the Backspace key twice to remove the unsaved path, and then save your work up to this point.

Adopting a System To Speed Up Your Technique

The value of shortcut keys shouldn't be underestimated in Photoshop, and certainly not with building a complex piece like the MARINA image. I found a certain "rhythm" to designing the brass caming around the image areas, and if you intend to use Kai's Power Tools to make a similar piece, here are the steps you'll want to remember to quickly bring the piece to completion.

1. Press Ctrl+S to save the previous version of your edited piece.

2. Define curve areas using the Paths palette tools and straight-line borders using the Lasso tool in combination with the Alt key.

3. For Paths, create selection areas from them and feather them from the same dialog box. For Lasso selections, choose Select, Feather, enter 1 pixel Radius for thin brass caming and 2 pixels for wider brass.

4. Press Ctrl+F to execute the last filter used, Kai's Gradients on Paths.

5. Press Ctrl+D to deselect the active marquee selection, and if you build a path to create the selection area, press the Backspace key twice to delete the unsaved path.

6. Choose the Eraser tool, and while holding down the Alt key, restore areas that Kai's Power Tools rendered a gradient over that you don't want in the final design.

7. Choose the Smudge tool, and click and drag over areas where the virtual brass caming should be "welded" together.

8. Use the Dodge/Burn tool to polish the brass at irregular intervals to add a naturalistic touch.

9. Save your work, and repeat the last steps. In figure A.19, the finished piece looks dimensional and photo-realistic.

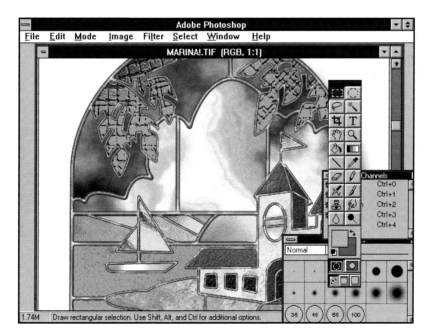

Figure A.19

The completed image, created in Painter, and edited with Kai's Power Tools in Photoshop.

Commercial Possibilities for Stained Glass

I deliberately left the bottom portion of the MARINA.EPS image with an empty space in it, hoping, as many designers do, to modify the image later after finding a corporate foster parent for the fine art piece.

As luck would have it, my mother-in-law owns real estate in Florida and wanted an advertisement for her condominiums there. When you create a visually striking image, never ignore the commercial potential. Here's how to add a logotype to the MARINA image.

Positioning the Text for the Advertisement

1. Open the WILMA.EPS file from the *Adobe Photoshop NOW! CD-ROM*. The design was created in a vector design application, but you could just as easily scan someone's logo.

2. Press Ctrl+A, and then Ctrl+C to copy the entire design image to the Clipboard.

3. Press Ctrl+Tab to switch to MARINA.TIF as the active image window.

4. The selection information about the MARINA image has outlived its usefulness, so it might be overwritten. Click on the Default colors icon button, and then click on the #4 title on the Channels palette.

5. Double-click on the Eraser tool, and click on OK to Photoshop's dialog box asking whether you want to erase the entire Alpha channel.

6. Press Ctrl+V to paste the WILMA copy into the #4 channel.

7. Press Ctrl+D (deselect), and then click on the RGB title of the Channels palette.

8. Choose Select, Load Selection, and then choose a selection tool.

9. While holding down the Ctrl and Alt keys, place your cursor inside the selection area, and click and drag it so that it's located in the bottom, white portion of the stained glass piece.

10. When the WILMA copy is centered, choose Select, Save Selection, #4. This overwrites the original WILMA selection information, and you now have a properly positioned selection area of the logotype.

Fine Tuning the Text's Appearance

1. Choose Select, Load Selection. Then with the Lasso tool, press Ctrl and drag and click around the Marina del Wilma type. This deselects the name of the condo and leaves the logo and message at the bottom selected.

2. Pick up a warm background color with the Eyedropper tool from the MARINA image by pressing on the Alt key while you sample. The mansion roof area is good.

3. Press the Del key. Photoshop removes the foreground white in the selection area, replacing it with background color.

When adding type or logotype to an image, use the Eyedropper tool to sample colors from the image to use as type colors. This is the easy, foolproof way to avoid adding a visually dissonant color to an illustration.

4. Choose **S**elect, **L**oad Selection again, and, with the Lasso tool and Ctrl key depressed, click and drag around the logotype and condo information area you previously filled in. Now only the Marina del Wilma name should be selected.

5. Pick a new background color by pressing Alt and clicking with the Eyedropper tool over a palm frond.

6. Press the Del key, and the Marina del Wilma image area will be filled with a cool background green.

7. Press Ctrl+D, and save this image as CONDO.TIF to your hard drive. You're done, and now have a fine art version of the stained glass piece, as well as a commercial copy, as seen in figure A.20.

Figure A.20

Add colored type to an image by deleting a selection area to reveal the background color.

8. Seek a client of your own to add to the bottom of the MARINA.TIF image. Florida real estate changes hands almost daily...

The Adobe Photoshop NOW! CD-ROM

You may have noticed something special about this book when you first picked it up. Besides being the first complete task-oriented, project-based book for Adobe Photoshop for Windows, it's also a workbook; the chapters are divided into practical exercises that teach you Photoshop techniques for use in your own work. Hey, you have to start someplace with any new application!

What's on the *Adobe Photoshop NOW! CD-ROM*

To give you hands-on experience with the techniques described throughout this book, a companion CD is tucked into an envelope in the back of this book. This CD contains all the images that you work with in the chapter exercises, in addition to a lot of shareware/freeware utilities and fonts, freeware image backgrounds and textures, stock images and the *Adobe Photoshop NOW!* Online Glossary. Stock images in digital computer format can be a lifesaver for the budding imaging-type person, and these samplers are meant to give you a taste of what's available from these computers.

Please do not use the images contained in the sampler directories for any commercial purposes per our agreement with the manufacturers who allowed us to use them. For further information, restrictions, and special requirements pertaining to the stock images, read the accompanying text on the Adobe Photoshop NOW! CD-ROM *from your Windows text editor (use Windows Write, Word for Windows, and so on).*

How Do You Use the Sucker

For following along with the exercises in each chapter, we've made it really easy to open the files from the *Adobe Photoshop NOW! CD-ROM*. All you need to know is the following:

- You must have a CD disk drive properly hooked to your system. You must have a CD-ROM drive—external, internal, or over a network—linked to your PC to take advantage of the CD enclosed in the back of the book.

- You must know how to "navigate" the directory structure of the *Adobe Photoshop NOW! CD-ROM*. If you're familiar with directory structures in Windows File Manager, the *Adobe Photoshop NOW! CD-ROM* is set up exactly the same way. If not, we have a "mock" exercise coming up that you can use for a guide.

- The directory tree on the *Adobe Photoshop NOW! CD-ROM* branches from the root into different file categories. The subdirectory you'll be working from to do all the chapter exercises is called EXERCISE. The subdirectories beneath EXERCISE are labeled "CHAP01," for images used in Chapter 1, and so on. The other *Adobe Photoshop NOW! CD-ROM* subdirectories relate to shareware/freeware fonts, utilities, and images, and to other software vendors and their products. There are some rules you need to follow, legality-wise, if you decide to access these other CD subdirectories. Check the README.TXTs in each of these subdirectories before wandering too far!

An Exercise Before You Do the Exercises

Adobe Photoshop NOW! is a visual book as well as a hands-on one, so in keeping with this format, the following exercise will show you how to open an exercise file from the *Adobe Photoshop NOW! CD-ROM*. Whenever you come to a chapter exercise, the first step usually is to open a file from the *Adobe Photoshop NOW! CD-ROM*. When we refer to a file on the CD, there will be a disk icon positioned next to the text like the one accompanying this paragraph. We also have the step in an exercise marked:

Open the XXXXXXX.TIF image from the Adobe Photoshop NOW! CD-ROM.

The Xs represent the file name for the particular image you need. Do this now.

1. Take the *Adobe Photoshop NOW! CD-ROM* out of its envelope, located in the back of this book.

2. Place the CD face up, into the CD-ROM drive's caddy or in your CD-ROM drive.

3. Double-click on the Photoshop icon in its Windows Program Manager group or in File Manager, select **F**ile, **R**un to launch Photoshop.

4. When Photoshop's workspace is open on your screen, choose **F**ile, **O**pen (Ctrl+O).

5. Click on the EXERCISE subdirectory in the **D**irectories box.

6. Click on the chapter directory (CHAP#) holding the image you want to open.

7. Click on the image file in the File **N**ame list box, and then click on OK.

If you followed along, you see how easy it is to get the materials you need to actually follow the steps to doing great imaging work found in this book.

Oops! I Can't Save Files to the CD

Be aware that this CD, like all CD disks, is Compact Disc Read-Only Memory; you cannot *write* to the *Adobe Photoshop NOW! CD-ROM*, and all your work must be saved to a writeable type of media, like your hard or floppy disk. This gets confusing sometimes because Photoshop and a lot of other programs give you the option to save to the CD, but then pop up a strange warning.

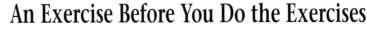

If you're the ambitious type, you'll accumulate several megabytes of finished exercise images through the course of following along with Adobe Photoshop NOW!. *You may want to keep these images organized on your hard disk by creating a subdirectory called MYWORK (or any other inspired eight character or less name). After you use* **F**ile, **S**ave, *or* **F**ile, Sa**v**e As, *you'll be able to retrieve these images, as called for at various points in the exercises, as easily as you can find them on the* Adobe Photoshop NOW! CD-ROM.

If you're new to the Windows environment and aren't a "Directory Tree Guru" yet, you may want to learn more about directory structures, copying files, and good hard disk "housekeeping." New Riders Publishing offers Windows for Non-Nerds *and* Inside Windows 3.1, *which describe in detail how to organize your Windows applications and files. These books are perfect companions for you PC imaging adventures.*

The *Adobe Photoshop NOW!* OnLine Glossary

Just what you've been waiting for—an online help system that provides the added information you're always looking for to help you master a program. The *Adobe Photoshop NOW!* OnLine Glossary is not a substitute for Photoshop's Windows Help Line, but rather a collection of terms, definitions, and cross-references that come in handy when you explore new techniques along with the book. For instance, you want to save an RGB masterpiece, and want to know if the TIF format is cool. Most documentation will tell you that a TIFF image is the Tagged Image File Format, and that's about it. NRP's OnLine Glossary, however, will tell you the color-capability of the TIFF format, your alternatives, and whether or not you can save Alpha channels with it. You haven't even used the OnLine Glossary, and see how useful it is already?

To install the Glossary, copy the PS_NOW!.HLP file from the *Adobe Photoshop NOW! CD-ROM* to your hard drive. The OnLine Glossary may be added to any Program Manager group, and it has a special icon for quick identification.

Installing the Demo/Shareware Applications

Be sure to read the README files before loading any of the demos, shareware fonts, shareware utilities, or before viewing sampler images. The demo/shareware software can be loaded by copying to your hard disk and double-clicking on the EXE files. The fonts are loaded like all fonts: Program Manager, Control Panel, Fonts/<u>A</u>dd.

What's In Store

We hope you'll find working with images in exercises to be an exciting medium. Most folks find "how to" books rather dry, and New Riders Publishing is happy to provide users interested in manipulating digital images this CD alternative. *Adobe Photoshop NOW!* brings education to a more intimate, real-life level, and you'll find very practical uses in your own imaging work for the techniques, tricks, and tips that it brings to you.

Have fun! That's what imaging is all about!

For other great imaging books set up with the same ease of use, check out New Riders Publishing's Inside Adobe Photoshop for Windows, Inside CorelDRAW!, Inside Adobe Illustrator for Windows, *and* CorelDRAW! NOW!.

INDEX

INDEX

INDEX

Photoshop Now!
REGISTRATION CARD

Fill out this card to receive information about future Photoshop books and other New Riders titles!

Name _____ **Title** _____

Company _____

Address _____

City/State/ZIP _____

I bought this book because: _____
_____

I purchased this book from:
☐ A bookstore (Name _____)
☐ A software or electronics store (Name _____)
☐ A mail order (Name of Catalog _____)

I purchase this many computer books each year:
☐ 1–5   ☐ 6 or more

I currently use these applications: _____
_____
_____
_____

I found these chapters to be the most informative: _____
_____

I found these chapters to be the least informative: _____
_____

Additional comments: _____
_____

☐ I would like to see my name in print! You may use my name and quote me in future New Riders products and promotions. My daytime phone number is: _____

New Riders Publishing 201 West 103rd Street • Indianapolis, Indiana 46290 USA

Fold Here

PLACE
STAMP
HERE

New Riders Publishing
201 West 103rd Street
Indianapolis, Indiana 46290
USA

WANT MORE INFORMATION?

CHECK OUT THESE RELATED TITLES:

	QTY	PRICE	TOTAL
Inside CorelDRAW! 4.0 Special Edition. This updated version of the #1 selling tutorial on CorelDRAW! features easy-to-follow lessons that quickly help readers master this powerful graphics program. Complete with expert tips and techniques—plus a bonus disk loaded with shareware—this book is everything CorelDRAW! users need. ISBN: 1-56205-164-4	____	$37.95	_____
Inside CorelDRAW!, Fourth Edition. (covers version 3.0) Tap into the graphics power of CorelDRAW! 3.0 with this #1 best-seller. This book goes beyond providing just tips and tricks for boosting productivity. Readers will also receive expanded coverage on how to use CorelDRAW! with other Windows programs! ISBN: 1-56205-106-7.	____	$39.95	_____
CorelDRAW! Special Effects. Learn award-winning techniques from professional CorelDRAW! designers with this comprehensive collection of the hottest tips and techniques! This full-color book provides step-by-step instructions for creating over 30 stunning special effects. An excellent book for those who want to take their CorelDRAW! documents a couple of notches higher. ISBN: 1-56205-123-7.	____	$39.95	_____
CorelDRAW! NOW!. Users who want fast access to thorough information, people upgrading to CorelDRAW! 4.0 from a previous edition, new CorelDRAW! users—all of these groups will want to tap into this guide to great graphics—now! Developed by CorelDRAW! experts, this book provides answers on everything from common questions to advanced inquiries. ISBN: 1-56205-131-8.	____	$42.95	_____

Name _____

Company _____

Address _____

City _____ State ____ ZIP _____

Phone _____ Fax _____

☐ Check Enclosed ☐ VISA ☐ MasterCard

Card # _____Exp. Date _____

Signature _____

*Prices are subject to change. Call for availability and pricing
information on latest editions.*

Subtotal _____

Shipping _____

*$4.00 for the first book
and $1.75 for each
additional book.*

Total _____
*Indiana residents add
5% sales tax.*

New Riders Publishing 201 West 103rd Street • Indianapolis, Indiana 46290 USA

Orders/Customer Service: 1-800-428-5331
Fax: 1-800-448-3804

- Fold Here -

PLACE
STAMP
HERE

New Riders Publishing
201 West 103rd Street
Indianapolis, Indiana 46290
USA

GO AHEAD. PLUG YOURSELF INTO
PRENTICE HALL COMPUTER PUBLISHING.

Introducing the PHCP Forum on CompuServe®

Yes, it's true. Now, you can have CompuServe access to the same professional, friendly folks who have made computers easier for years. On the PHCP Forum, you'll find additional information on the topics covered by every PHCP imprint—including Que, Sams Publishing, New Riders Publishing, Alpha Books, Brady Books, Hayden Books, and Adobe Press. In addition, you'll be able to receive technical support and disk updates for the software produced by Que Software and Paramount Interactive, a division of the Paramount Technology Group. It's a great way to supplement the best information in the business.

WHAT CAN YOU DO ON THE PHCP FORUM?

Play an important role in the publishing process—and make our books better while you make your work easier:

- Leave messages and ask questions about PHCP books and software—you're guaranteed a response within 24 hours

- Download helpful tips and software to help you get the most out of your computer

- Contact authors of your favorite PHCP books through electronic mail

- Present your own book ideas

- Keep up to date on all the latest books available from each of PHCP's exciting imprints

JOIN NOW AND GET A FREE COMPUSERVE STARTER KIT!

To receive your free CompuServe Introductory Membership, call toll-free, **1-800-848-8199** and ask for representative **#597**. The Starter Kit Includes:

- Personal ID number and password

- $15 credit on the system

- Subscription to CompuServe Magazine

HERE'S HOW TO PLUG INTO PHCP:

Once on the CompuServe System, type any of these phrases to access the PHCP Forum:

GO PHCP   **GO BRADY**
GO QUEBOOKS   **GO HAYDEN**
GO SAMS   **GO QUESOFT**
GO NEWRIDERS   **GO PARAMOUNTINTER**
GO ALPHA

Once you're on the CompuServe Information Service, be sure to take advantage of all of CompuServe's resources. CompuServe is home to more than 1,700 products and services—plus it has over 1.5 million members worldwide. You'll find valuable online reference materials, travel and investor services, electronic mail, weather updates, leisure-time games and hassle-free shopping (no jam-packed parking lots or crowded stores).

Seek out the hundreds of other forums that populate CompuServe. Covering diverse topics such as pet care, rock music, cooking, and political issues, you're sure to find others with the sames concerns as you—and expand your knowledge at the same time.

GRAPHICS TITLES

INSIDE CORELDRAW! 4.0, SPECIAL EDITION

DANIEL GRAY

An updated version of the #1 best-selling tutorial on CorelDRAW!

CorelDRAW! 4.0
ISBN: 1-56205-164-4
$34.95 USA

CORELDRAW! SPECIAL EFFECTS

NEW RIDERS PUBLISHING

An inside look at award-winning techniques from professional CorelDRAW! designers!

CorelDRAW! 4.0
ISBN: 1-56205-123-7
$39.95 USA

CORELDRAW! NOW!

RICHARD FELDMAN

The hands-on tutorial for users who want practical information now!

CorelDRAW! 4.0
ISBN: 1-56205-131-8
$21.95 USA

INSIDE CORELDRAW! FOURTH EDITION

DANIEL GRAY

The popular tutorial approach to learning CorelDRAW!…with complete coverage of version 3.0!

CorelDRAW! 3.0
ISBN: 1-56205-106-7
$24.95 USA

NETWORKING TITLES

#1 Bestseller!

INSIDE NOVELL NETWARE, THIRD EDITION

DEBRA NIEDERMILLER-CHAFFINS & DREW HEYWOOD

This best-selling tutorial and reference has been updated and made even better!

NetWare 2.2, 3.11 & 3.12
ISBN: 1-56205-257-8
$34.95 USA

MAXIMIZING NOVELL NETWARE

JOHN JERNEY & ELNA TYMES

Complete coverage of Novell's flagship product...for NetWare system administrators!

NetWare 3.11
ISBN: 1-56205-095-8
$39.95 USA

NETWARE: THE PROFESSIONAL REFERENCE, SECOND EDITION

KARANJIT SIYAN

This updated version for professional NetWare administrators and technicians provides the most comprehensive reference available for this phenomenal network system.

NetWare 2.x & 3.x
ISBN: 1-56205-158-X
$42.95 USA

NETWARE 4: PLANNING AND IMPLEMENTATION

SUNIL PADIYAR

A guide to planning, installing, and managing a NetWare 4.0 network that best serves your company's objectives.

NetWare 4.0
ISBN: 1-56205-159-8
$27.95 USA

To Order, Call 1-800-428-5331